Adobe® Premiere® Pro 2.0

CLASSROOM
IN A BOOK®

www.adobepress.com

Adobe

From the Author

Welcome to Adobe® Premiere Pro® 2.0 Classroom in a Book. Whether you are new to video editing on a PC or have some experience with entry-level editing software, this book is for you.

Adobe Premiere Pro 2 is a professional product that gives you a full complement of powerful and efficient tools that enable you to create high-quality videos: from single-camera digital video productions to multiple-camera high definition projects.

With Premiere Pro you get a wide range of highly customizable video effects and transitions, high performance titling, robust audio editing, and tight integration with other Adobe applications. Premiere Pro's superior performance lets you work faster and more creatively.

Learning how to use all that power and functionality takes some effort. The goal of this Adobe Premiere Pro 2.0 Classroom in a Book is to make that process intuitive, logical and enjoyable.

Lesson Assets, Introductory Videos and Expert Sidebars

I created 18 hands-on lessons, designed to follow a standard, video editing workflow: from shooting excellent raw footage and building a basic sequence of video clips to adding transitions, special effects, text, graphics and finally exporting your finished project to a videotape, the Internet, or a DVD. You will use assets—videos, audio files, still images and graphics—provided on this book's companion DVD to complete those lessons.

I introduce all of those lessons with brief video demonstrations of the topics you'll tackle. Those videos ease the learning process and can serve as a helpful reminder if you need to brush up on things later.

I also include several sidebars from experts in this field: from story production tips from NBC-TV correspondent Bob Dotson to editing and shooting tips from former TV news colleagues of mine.

This book is several hundred pages long. There's lots to do. So let's get cracking.

Jeff Sengstack

Lesson files . . . and so much more

The *Adobe Premiere Pro 2.0 Classroom in a Book* DVD includes the lesson files that you'll need to complete the exercises in this book, as well as other content to help you learn more about Adobe Premiere Pro 2.0 and use it with greater efficiency and ease. The diagram below represents the contents of the DVD, which should help you locate the files you need.

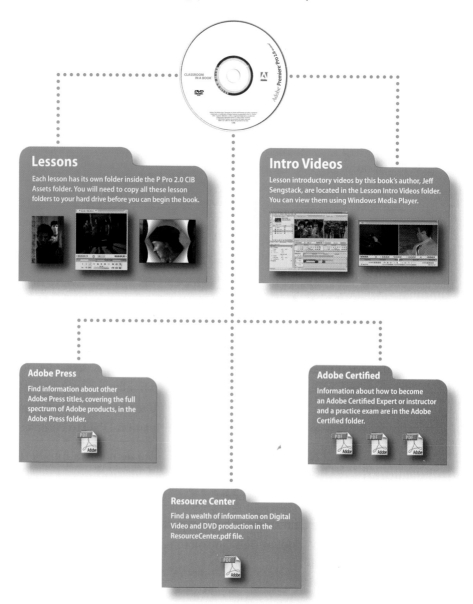

Lessons

Each lesson has its own folder inside the P Pro 2.0 CIB Assets folder. You will need to copy all these lesson folders to your hard drive before you can begin the book.

Intro Videos

Lesson introductory videos by this book's author, Jeff Sengstack, are located in the Lesson Intro Videos folder. You can view them using Windows Media Player.

Adobe Press

Find information about other Adobe Press titles, covering the full spectrum of Adobe products, in the Adobe Press folder.

Adobe Certified

Information about how to become an Adobe Certified Expert or instructor and a practice exam are in the Adobe Certified folder.

Resource Center

Find a wealth of information on Digital Video and DVD production in the ResourceCenter.pdf file.

Contents

Getting Started

1 Touring Premiere Pro 2.0

2 Taking a Quick Run-through of Premiere Pro 2.0

3 Shooting and Capturing Great Video Assets

4 Selecting Settings, Adjusting Preferences and Managing Assets

5 Creating Cuts-only Videos

6   **Adding Video Transitions**

7   **Creating Dynamic Titles**

8   **Applying Specialized Editing Tools**

9   Adding Video Effects

10   Putting Clips in Motion

11   Acquiring and Editing Audio

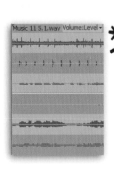

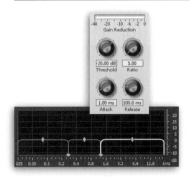

18 Authoring DVDs with Premiere Pro and Encore DVD 2.0

Adobe

Giles Baker
Premiere Pro Product Manager
Adobe Systems, Inc.

Greetings from the Adobe Premiere Pro team.

Thank you for choosing this book. Whether you are a longtime Premiere Pro user or someone just entering the world of professional video editing, this book will give you everything you need to get started with the application and to discover the new features that we've worked so hard to deliver.

We appreciate your interest and support of Adobe Premiere Pro.

Giles Baker
Premiere Pro Product Manager

Getting Started

Adobe® Premiere Pro 2.0, the essential editing tool for video enthusiasts and professionals, enhances your creative power and freedom. Adobe Premiere Pro is the most scalable, efficient, and precise video editing tool available. Whether you're working with DV, HD, HDV, or any other format, Premiere Pro's superior performance lets you work faster and more creatively. The complete set of powerful and exclusive tools lets you overcome any editorial, production, and workflow challenge to deliver the quality work you demand.

About Classroom in a Book

Adobe Premiere Pro 2.0 Classroom in a Book® is part of the official training series for Adobe graphics and publishing software. The lessons are designed so that you can learn at your own pace. If you're new to Adobe Premiere Pro, you'll learn the fundamental concepts and features you'll need to use the program. Classroom in a Book also teaches many advanced features, including tips and techniques for using the latest version of this application.

The lessons in this edition include opportunities to use new features, such as improved animation tools, multi-camera switching, professional color correction, DVD authoring from the Timeline, Adobe Acrobat® Clip Notes client reviw, and the Adobe Bridge® visual file browser. All these features are further enhanced through the inclusion of a redesigned interface with new conveniences.

Prerequisites

Before beginning to use *Adobe Premiere Pro 2.0 Classroom in a Book*, make sure that your system is set up correctly and that you've installed the required software and hardware. You should have a working knowledge of your computer and operating system. You should know how to use the mouse and standard menus and commands, and also how to open, save, and close files. If you need to review these techniques, see the printed or online documentation included with your Microsoft® Windows®.

Installing Adobe Premiere Pro

You must purchase the Adobe Premiere Pro 2.0 software separately. For system requirements and complete instructions on installing the software, see the Adobe Premiere Pro ReadMe.html on the application DVD.

Install Premiere Pro from the Adobe Premiere Pro 2.0 application DVD onto your hard disk; you cannot run the program from the DVD. Follow the on-screen instructions.

Make sure that your serial number is accessible before installing the application; you can find the serial number on the registration card or on the back of the DVD case.

Optimizing performance

Editing videos is memory-and processor-intensive work for a desktop computer. Premiere Pro 2.0 requires a minimum of 512 MB of RAM; 2 GB is recommended for high-definition video editing. The more RAM that is available to Premiere Pro, the faster the application will work for you. Premiere Pro takes advantage of multiple and Hyper-threading processors. The minimum requirement is a Pentium 4 (or equivalent) 1.4GHz processor. A Pentium 4 3.0GHz CPU with Hyper-threading is recommended.

Copying the lesson files

The lessons in *Adobe Premiere Pro 2.0 Classroom in a Book* use specific source files, such as image files created in Adobe Photoshop® and Adobe Illustrator®, audio files prepared in Adobe Audition® and videos. To complete the lessons in this book, you must copy all the files from the *Adobe Premiere Pro 2.0 Classroom in a Book* DVD (inside the back cover of this book) to your hard drive. You will need about 3.5 GB of storage space in addition to at least 6 GB you'll need to operate Premiere Pro 2.0.

While each lesson stands alone, some lessons use files from other lessons, so you'll need to keep the entire collection of lesson assets on your hard drive as you work through the lessons in this book. Here's how to copy those assets from the DVD to your hard drive.

1   Open the Classroom in a Book DVD in My Computer or Windows Explorer.

2   Right-click on the P Pro 2.0 CIB Assets file folder and select Copy.

3   Navigate to the location you set to store your Adobe Premiere Pro 2.0 projects.
The default location is My Documents\Adobe\Premiere Pro\2.0.

4   Right-click on the 2.0 file folder and select Paste.
That will load all the lesson assets to that file folder. It'll take a couple of minutes to finish this, depending on the speed of your DVD drive.

5   Open the P Pro 2.0 CIB Assets file folder on your hard drive, right-click on P Pro 2.0 CIB Workspace.layout, and select Copy,

6   Press Backspace to move back one file folder to the Premiere Pro\2.0 folder.

7   Right-click on the Layouts file folder and select Paste.
That loads a customized Premiere Pro 2.0 workspace to that folder. You can open that workspace whenever you find that your own workspace has become a bit cluttered.

About the lesson introductory videos

When you copied and pasted the P Pro 2.0 CIB Assets folder from this book's companion DVD to your hard drive, you also installed a collection of lesson introductory videos; one for each lesson. They are Windows Media Video files and are meant to play in the Windows Media Player. We recommend that before you start a lesson, you view that lesson's video. You will find the videos in the Lesson Intro Videos folder in the P Pro 2.0 CIB Assets file folder.

How to use these lessons

Each lesson in this book provides step-by-step instructions for creating one or more specific elements of a real-world project. The lessons stand alone but most of the them build on previous lessons in terms of concepts and skills. So the best way to learn from this book is to proceed through the lessons in sequential order.

The organization of the lessons is workflow-oriented rather than feature-oriented. The lessons follow the typical sequential steps video editors use to complete a project starting with laying down a cuts-only video to applying special effects. This real world approach differs from the reference manual approach you'll find in the Premiere Pro 2.0 User Guide.

Note: Many aspects of Premiere Pro 2.0 can be controlled by multiple techniques, such as menu commands, right-click context menus, and keyboard shortcuts. Sometimes more than one of the methods is described in any given procedure so that you can learn different ways of working, even when the task is one you've done before.

Additional resources

Adobe Premiere Pro 2.0 Classroom in a Book is not meant to replace documentation that comes with the program. This book explains only the commands and options actually used in the lessons, so there's much more to learn about Premiere Pro. Classroom in a Book aims to give you confidence and skills so that you can start creating your own projects. For more comprehensive information about program features, see:

• The Adobe Premiere Pro 2.0 User Guide, which is included with the Adobe Premiere Pro 2.0 software and contains descriptions of all features.

• Online Help, an online version of the user guide, which you can view by starting Premiere Pro and then choosing Help > Adobe Premiere Pro Help.

• The Adobe website (www.adobe.com), which you can explore by choosing Help > Online Support if you have a connection to the World Wide Web.

• Adobe Resource Center (http://studio.adobe.com), where you can find a wealth of tips, tutorials, plug-ins, actions, and other design inspiration and instructional content.

Adobe Certification

The Adobe Training and Certification Programs are designed to help Adobe customers improve and promote their product-proficiency skills. There are three levels of certification:

- Adobe Certified Expert (ACE)
- Adobe Certified Instructor (ACI)
- Adobe Authorized Training Center (AATC)

The Adobe Certified Expert (ACE) program is a way for expert users to upgrade their credentials. You can use Adobe certification as a catalyst for getting a raise, finding a job, or promoting your expertise.

If you are an ACE-level instructor, the Adobe Certified Instructor program takes your skills to the next level and gives you access to a wide range of Adobe resources.

Adobe Authorized Training Centers offer instructor-led courses and training on Adobe products, employing only Adobe Certified Instructors. A director of AATCs is available at http://partners.adobe.com.

For information on the Adobe Certified programs review the sample exam and other material in the Adobe Certified file folder on this book's companion DVD and visit http://www.adobe.com/support/certification/main.html

workflow

workspace

Timeline

It's time to roll up your sleeves and dive into Premiere Pro 2.0. But before you make your first edit or apply your first transition, I want to present a brief overview of video editing and how Premiere Pro fits into the video production workflow. Then I'll introduce you to its completely revamped workspace. Even those who are old hands at editing videos on a PC will find the new workspace features in Premiere Pro 2.0 worthy of exploration.

1 | Touring Premiere Pro 2.0

Topics covered in this lesson:

- Video editing: then and now.
- Premiere Pro 2.0: a non-linear editor.
- Presenting the standard digital video workflow.
- Enhancing the workflow with high-level features.
- Incorporating Adobe Creative Suite Production Studio Premium® into the workflow.
- Touring the Premiere Pro workspace.
- Customizing the workspace.

Getting started

We've come a long way from clunky old videotape machines and expensive production equipment to professional-level editing on a PC. In this lesson I want to give you some video editing history. Knowing what came before can help make where we are now look that much better. Following that overview, I go over the basic workflow most video editors follow and explain how Premiere Pro fits in the eight-product Adobe Creative Suite Production Studio Premium. Finally I introduce you to unique and revamped workspace in Premiere Pro. You'll begin actual video editing in Lesson 2.

Video editing: Then and now

Thirty years ago, engineers acted as video editors. They had to. Only they knew how to handle massive, unruly, and complex tape machines. They had to monitor things such as color framing, sync timing, and blanking. Back then videotape editing was a technical task, not an artistic endeavor.

As editing machines became smaller and easier to use, engineers gave way to artists, but editing on analog (non-digital) videotape still had its limitations. Each edit resulted in "generation loss," a reduction in visual quality caused by the less-than-perfect copying of the analog signal from the original videotape.

Transitions, such as cross-dissolves, required the use of three VCRs and expensive switchers. Frequently the VCRs did not synch-up properly, leading to a flicker or jump-cut at the edit point.

Thanks to the advent of digital videotape and software video editors, generation loss, jumpy transitions—and expensive tape machines and editing hardware—are things of the past. Now, anyone with a PC, or even a laptop, can do broadcast-quality video editing.

Premiere Pro 2.0—A nonlinear editor

Premiere Pro is a nonlinear editor (NLE). Unlike older videotape editing systems where you generally need to lay down edits consecutively and contiguously, Premiere Pro lets you place, replace, trim and move clips anywhere you want in your final edited video.

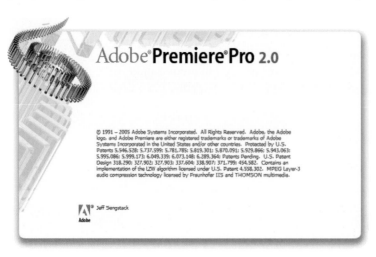

On videotape systems, if you decide to insert a sound bite in the middle of a story already edited on tape, you need to insert that sound bite over your existing edits and re-edit everything after it. Or you can make a dub (copy) of the story segment after the new edit point and re-record that part after adding the sound bite (causing generation quality loss in the process).

With Premiere Pro and other NLEs you can make changes by simply clicking and dragging clips or segments around within your final video. You can edit video segments separately and tie them together later. You can even edit the closing sequence first.

Premiere Pro lets you do things non-sequentially.

NLEs have another huge benefit over videotape-editing systems: immediate access to your video clips. No longer do you need to endlessly fast forward or rewind through tons of tape to find that one elusive-but-essential shot. With Premiere Pro, it's a mouse click away.

Presenting the standard digital video workflow

There is a basic workflow to creating videos with NLEs like Premiere Pro. After a while, it'll become second nature. Generally that workflow follows these steps:

1   Shoot the video.

2   Capture (transfer) the video to your PC's hard drive.

3   Build your edited video by selecting, trimming and adding clips to a timeline.

4   Place transitions between clips, apply video effects to clips, and composite (layer) clips.

5   Create text, credits or basic graphics and apply them to your project.

6   Add audio—be it narration, music or sound effects.

Note: Audio can also be the first thing you lay down when editing a video.

7   Mix multiple audio tracks and use transitions and special effects on your audio clips.

8   Export your finished project to videotape, a PC file, streaming video for Internet playback, or to a DVD.

Premiere Pro supports each of these steps with industry-leading tools. Since this book is geared to the beginning and intermediate video editor, becoming facile with these standard workflow tools is the primary goal of the upcoming lessons.

Enhancing the workflow with high-level features

Premiere Pro goes well beyond providing a full-featured toolset for standard digital video editing. It is loaded with extra features that can enhance the video production process and improve the quality of your finished product.

You are not likely to incorporate many of these in your first few video projects. But as you ramp up your skills and expectations, you will begin to tap these high productivity features. I will cover the following topics in this book:

• **Advanced Audio Editing**—Premiere Pro provides audio effects and editing unequaled by any other nonlinear editor, and by most audio software. Create and place 5.1 surround-sound audio channels, make sample-level edits, apply multiple audio effects to any audio clip or track, use the included state-of-the-art plug-ins and other VST (Virtual Studio Technology) plug-ins.

• **Advanced Color Correction**—Correct and enhance the look of your footage with two new color correctors.

• **Advanced Keyframe Controls**—Premiere Pro 2.0 gives you the precise control you need to fine-tune your visual and motion effects without requiring you to export to a compositing application.

• **Broad Hardware Support**—Choose from a wide range of capture cards and other hardware to best fit your needs and budget. Premiere Pro 2.0 support extends from low-cost computers for DV (digital video) and HDV (a compressed high definition video format) editing, up to high-performance workstations capturing high definition (HD) video. Further, when it's time to upgrade your hardware to work with HD and film, you don't need to leave the familiar Premiere Pro interface—unlike with some proprietary systems that provide different interfaces for different formats.

• **eReview**—Speed your client review and approval process by embedding Premiere Pro projects in PDF documents. Your client watches the video with Adobe Reader, enters comments into the PDFs feedback form, and then emails the comments to you.

• **GPU-accelerated Video Effects**—Use the Graphics Processing Units (GPU) on modern graphics cards to create real-time page curls, page rolls, spheres with video mapped on them, and other image distortion effects that typically require expensive hardware or long render times.

- **High-definition Video Support**—Work with every high-definition format including HDV, HDCAM, DVCPRO HD, D5-HD, and 4K film scans. Premiere Pro 2.0 supports these formats at any resolution (720p, 1080i, 1080p) and frame rate (24, 23.98, 30, 60fps, etc.).

- **Multicam Editing**—You can easily and quickly edit any production shot with multiple cameras. Premiere Pro displays all the camera tracks in a split-view monitor, and you set the edits by clicking in the appropriate screen or by making single keystrokes.

- **Project Manager**—Manage your media through a single dialog box. View, delete, move, search for, and reorganize clips and bins. Consolidate your projects by moving just the media actually used in a project, and copying that media to a single location. Then reclaim drive space media by deleting unused media.

Incorporating the Adobe Creative Suite Production Studio Premium into the workflow

Even with all of the exciting extra features in Premiere Pro, there are some digital video production tasks that it cannot do. For example:

- High-end 3D motion effects

- Detailed text animations

- Professional DVD authoring

- Layered graphics

- Vector artwork

- Music creation

- Advanced audio mixing, editing, and effects processing

To incorporate one or more of these features into a production I suggest you turn to the Adobe Creative Suite Production Studio Premium. It has all the tools you need to produce some absolutely amazing videos, including:

- Adobe Premiere Pro 2.0
- After Effects 7.0 Professional
- Adobe Photoshop CS2
- Adobe Audition 2.0
- Adobe Encore DVD 2.0
- Adobe Illustrator CS2
- Adobe Dynamic Link
- Adobe Bridge

The hub of the Adobe Creative Suite Production Studio Premium

Premiere Pro 2.0 is the hub of the eight-product Adobe Creative Suite Production Studio Premium (the three-product, Standard version consists of Premiere Pro 2.0, After Effects Professional 7.0 and Photoshop CS2). All eight tools feature tight integration to complement and enhance each other.

Here's a brief rundown of Premiere Pro's seven Production Studio Premium teammates:

- **Adobe After Effects Professional 7.0**—The tool-of-choice for motion graphics and visual effects artists.

- **Adobe Photoshop CS2**—The industry standard image-editing and graphic creation product.

- **Adobe Audition 2.0**—A professional-level audio recording, editing and sweetening product that also ships with more than 5,000 loops—music snippets that editors can use to create entire musical selections.

- **Adobe Encore DVD 2.0**—A high-quality DVD-authoring product designed to work closely with Premiere Pro, After Effects, and Photoshop CS.

- **Adobe Illustrator CS2**—Professional vector graphics creation software for print, video production and the Web.

- **Adobe Dynamic Link**—This cross-product connection allows you to work in real time with native After Effects files in Premiere Pro and Encore DVD without rendering first.

- **Adobe Bridge**—A visual file browser that provides centralized access to your suite project files, applications, and settings.

Adobe Creative Suite Production Studio Premium workflow

Your Premiere Pro/Adobe Creative Suite Production Studio Premium workflow will vary depending on your production needs. Here are a few mini-workflow scenarios:

- Use Photoshop CS to touch-up still images from a digital camera, a scanner or a Premiere Pro video clip. Then export them to Premiere Pro.

- Create layered graphics in Photoshop CS and then open them in Premiere Pro. You can opt to have each layer appear on a separate track in a timeline, allowing you to apply effects and motion to selected layers.

- Build custom music tracks using Audition music loops, then export them to Premiere Pro.

- Use Audition to do professional quality audio editing and sweetening on an existing Premiere Pro video or a separate audio file.

- Using Dynamic Link, open Premiere Pro video sequences in After Effects 7. Apply complex motion and animation, then send those updated motion sequences back to Premiere Pro. You can play After Effects compositions in Premiere Pro 2.0 without first waiting to render them.

- Use After Effects 7 to create and animate text in ways far beyond the capabilities of Premiere Pro. Export those compositions to Premiere Pro.

- Import Premiere Pro-created video projects into Encore DVD to use in DVD projects. You can use those videos as the foundation of a project or as motion menus.

Most of this book will focus on the standard, Premiere Pro-only workflow. However I will present several lessons that demonstrate how you can incorporate Adobe Creative Suite Production Studio Premium products within your workflow for even more spectacular results.

Touring the Premiere Pro workspace: Lesson 1-1

You'll dive into nonlinear editing in the next lesson. At this point I want to give you a brief tour of the video editing workspace. In this lesson you will use a Premiere Pro project from this book's companion DVD.

1   Make sure you've copied all the lesson folders and contents from the DVD to your hard drive. The default directory is: My Documents\Adobe\Premiere Pro\2.0\P Pro 2.0 CIB Assets\.

Note: *It's best to copy all the lesson assets from this book's DVD to your hard drive and leave them there until you complete this book because some lessons refer back to previous lessons' assets.*

2   You should have copied the P Pro 2.0 CIB Workspace.layout from the P Pro 2.0 CIB Assets folder on the DVD into the Premiere Pro 2.0 Layouts folder at: My Documents\Adobe\Premiere Pro\2.0\Layouts.

3 — You should have copied the Lesson Intro Videos file folder and its 18 video files to the same place you copied the lesson assets folders. Play this lesson's introductory video by opening Windows Media Player, selecting File > Open, navigating to the P Pro 2.0 CIB Assets\Lesson Intro Videos file folder and double-clicking Lesson 1 Intro.wmv.

More Info on the introductory videos

I created brief, introductory videos for this book's lessons to give you a feel for what's to come, and make it easier to learn these new concepts.

They are WMV (Windows Media Video) files that you can play in Premiere Pro or the Windows Media Player. The Media Player's viewing area is larger than the Program Monitor in Premiere Pro so I recommend you view these videos in Media Player.

I created these videos in a resolution of 1024x768 so they will look sharp running in the Windows Media Player's full-screen mode. I recorded them at 10 frames per second (about one-third the regular digital video frame rate so there is some occasional minor blurring during any kind of action).

When you finish viewing an intro video, simply close Media Player and move on to the next step in the lesson. If you need a quick review of a lesson, feel free to watch a video again.

4   Start Premiere Pro.

5   Click Open Project.

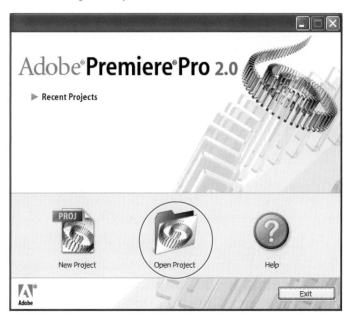

6   In the Open Project window, navigate to the P Pro CIB Assets > Lesson 1 file folder and double-click Lesson 1.prproj. That opens the user interface.

The workspace layout

If you've never seen a nonlinear editor, this workspace might overwhelm you. Not to worry. A lot of careful consideration went into its design and layout. I've identified its principal elements in the next figure.

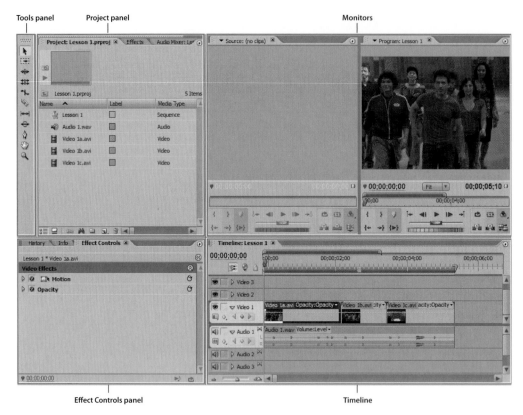

The Premiere Pro workspace might seem daunting to first-time NLE users, but you'll soon see the logic behind its layout.

Premiere Pro 2.0 sports a revamped workspace with many new features that I cover in this lesson. With this update comes some new nomenclature. Gone are palettes and most windows. Added are panels, frames and floating panels.

Each workspace item appears in its own panel. And you can dock multiple panels in a single frame. Some items with common industry terms stand alone, such as Timeline, Audio Mixer, and Program Monitor. I list all the new (and some old) names in the following workspace descriptions.

- **Timeline**—This is where you'll do most of your actual editing. You create sequences (Adobe's term for edited video segments or entire projects) in the Timeline. One strength of sequences is that you can nest them—place sequences in other sequences. In this way you can break up a production into manageable chunks.

More tracks than you can use

You can layer—composite—video clips, images, graphics, and titles in an unlimited number of tracks. Video clips in higher-numbered tracks cover whatever is directly below them on the timeline. Therefore, you need to give clips in higher-numbered tracks some kind of transparency or reduce their size if you want to let clips in lower tracks show through. I cover compositing in several upcoming lessons.

- **Monitors**—You use the Source Monitor (on the left) to view and trim raw clips (your original footage). To place a clip in the Source Monitor, double-click Video 1a in the Project panel. The Program Monitor (on the right) is for viewing your project-in-progress.

Single or dual monitor view

Some editors prefer working with only one monitor screen. I prefer two and the lessons throughout this book will reflect that. You can change to a single monitor view if you choose. Click the little 'x' in the Source tab to close that monitor. In the Main Menu, select Window > Source Monitor to open it again.

- **Project panel**—This is where you place links to your project's assets: video clips, audio files, graphics, still images and sequences. You use bins—file folders—to organize your assets.

- **Effects panel**—Click the Effects tab at the top of the Project panel to open the Effects panel (on the left, below). Effects are organized by Presets, Audio Effects, Audio Transitions, Video Effects and Video Transitions. If you open the various effects bins you'll note that they include numerous audio effects to spice up your sound; two audio crossfade transitions; video scene transitions, such as dissolves and wipes; and many video effects to alter the appearance of your clips.

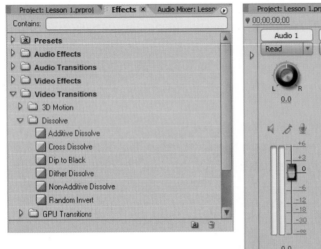 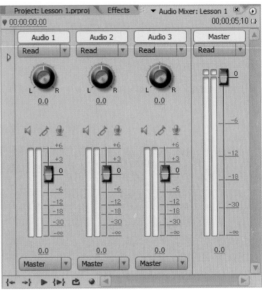

Effects panel (left) and Audio Mixer (right).

- **Audio Mixer**—Click the Audio Mixer tab to the right of the Effects tab (on the right, above). This interface looks a lot like audio production studio hardware with its volume sliders and panning knobs—one set of controls for each audio track in the Timeline plus a Master track.

- **Tools panel**—Each icon in this panel (on the right, below) represents a tool that performs a specific function, typically a type of edit. Older versions of Premiere had many more tools but now the Selection tool ( ) is context-sensitive. It changes appearance to indicate the function that matches the circumstances.

- **Effect Controls panel**—Click the Effect Controls panel (on the left below) to open it and then click on any clip in the Timeline. That will display that clip's effect parameters in the Effect Controls panel. This will give you a small taste of many lessons to come. Two video effects are always present for every video, still or graphic: Motion and Opacity. Each effect parameter (in the case of Motion: Position, Scale Height and Width, Rotation and Anchor Point) is adjustable over time using keyframes. The Effect Controls panel is an immensely powerful tool that gives you incredible creative latitude. It comes up in many of this book's lessons.

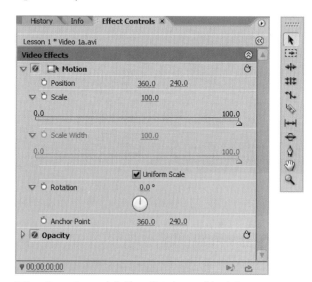

Effect Controls panel (left) and Tools panel (right).

- **Info panel**—Click the Info tab (left of the Effect Controls tab). Info presents a data snapshot of any asset you've currently selected in the Project panel or any clip or transition selected in a sequence.

- **History panel**—Click the History tab (left of the Info tab). History tracks every step you take in your video production and lets you back up if you don't like your latest efforts. When you back up to a previous condition, all steps that came after that point are also undone. You cannot extract a single misstep buried within the current list.

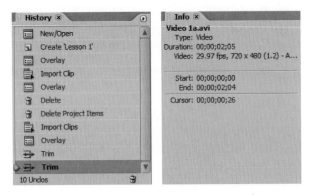

History panel (left) and Info panel (right).

Customizing the workspace: Lesson 1-2

Adobe revamped the user interface of Premiere Pro 2.0 and several other products in the Adobe Creative Suite Production Studio Premium. Here's what's new:

- As you change the size of one frame, other frames change size to compensate

- All panels within frames are accessible via tabs

- All panels are dockable—you can drag a panel from one frame to another as a means to customize your workspace

- You can peel away a panel into its own separate floating panel

In this lesson you'll try out all of those functions and save a customized workspace. You'll continue where you left off at the end of Lesson 1-1. Before changing the interface layout you'll adjust its brightness.

1 Select Edit > Preferences > User Interface.

2 Slide the Brightness slider to the left or right to suit your needs. When done, click OK.

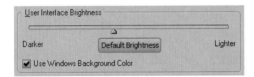

💡 **Cave-like editing bays**

As you approach the darkest setting, the text switches to white on gray. This is to accommodate those editors who work in editing bays in darkened rooms.

3 Place your cursor on the vertical divider between the Effect Controls panel and the Timeline. Click and drag left and right to change the sizes of those frames.

Note: The cursor stops briefly as the vertical divider between the two frames snaps to—lines up with—the divider above it between the Project and Source Monitors (holding down the Shift key as you drag a divider temporarily turns off the Snap function).

4 Use the Snap feature to adjust those frames so those dividers line up. Those four frame corners should like this next figure.

💡 Premiere's context help

Premiere Pro provides immediate context help in two ways: tool tips and messages displayed along the bottom of the interface. For example, as you click on a frame divider, a message appears at the bottom letting you know about the Snap feature. If you hover the cursor over the Program Monitor controls, tool tips pop up.

5 Place the cursor on the horizontal divider between the Effect Controls panel and the Project panel and slide them up and down.

6 Click on the History panel tab's upper left corner (its drag handle) and drag it to the top of the interface, next to the Project tab, to dock it in that frame.

Note: As you move a panel around, Premiere Pro displays a drop zone. If it's a rectangle, the panel will go into the selected frame. If it's a trapezoid, it'll go into its own frame.

💡 Dealing with a crowded frame

With the History panel added to the frame with the Project panel, you cannot see all the tabs. In this case a slider appears above the tabs. Slide it left or right to reveal all the tabs. You can also open a hidden (or any other) panel from the Main Menu by selecting Window and then clicking on a panel name.

7 Click and drag the Effect Controls drag handle to a point about mid-way up into the Project panel to place it in its own frame.

As shown in the following figure on the left, the drop zone is a trapezoid that covers the lower portion of the Project panel. Release the mouse button and your workspace should look something like the following figure on the right.

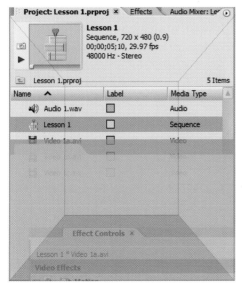
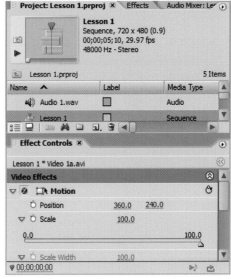

8   Click on the Program Monitor's drag handle and hold down the Ctrl key while dragging it out of its frame. Its drop zone image is much more distinct, indicating you are about to create a floating panel.

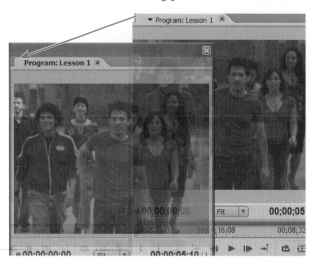

9   Drop the Program Monitor anywhere, creating a floating panel. Expand it by dragging one of its corners.

Use a floating panel to increase the viewing area of a panel beyond its frame's borders. This can come in handy when adjusting the many parameters in the Audio Mixer, Effect Controls, and Program Monitor.

10   As you gain editing acumen, you might want to create and save a customized workspace. To do that, select Window > Workspace > Save Workspace. Type in a workspace name and click Save.

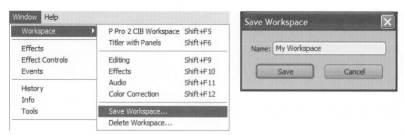

11   Open the workspace created for this lesson by selecting Window > Workspace > P Pro 2.0 CIB Workspace. This is a great way to get back to square one if your workspace customizing efforts run amok.

Review

▶ **Review questions**

1 Why is Premiere Pro considered a non-linear editor?

2 Describe the basic video editing workflow.

3 What purpose does the Project panel serve?

4 How can nested sequences simplify your editing?

5 What goes on in the Monitors?

6 How and why do you create a floating window?

▶ **Review answers**

1 Premiere Pro lets you place video, audio, and graphics anywhere on a sequence (timeline), rearrange media clips within a sequence, add transitions, apply effects, and do any number of other video editing steps in just about any order that suits you.

2 Shoot your video; transfer it to your PC; create a sequence of video, audio and still clips on the timeline; apply effects and transitions; add text and graphics; edit your audio; and export the finished product.

3 You store and organize links to your media assets in the Project panel.

4 A sequence can be an entire project or a project segment. Sometimes it's easier to work on one segment of a larger project, then nest that sequence into the final project sequence. Breaking up your project into constituent parts can make your work easier.

5 You use the Monitors to view your project and your original clips. When working with two Monitors—Source and Program—you can view and trim your raw footage in the Source Monitor and use the Program Monitor to view the timeline sequence as you build it.

6 Frequently you need much more real estate when working in a panel. The Effect Controls panel can display enough parameters to fill a full screen. To expand your view of a panel, hold down the Ctrl key while dragging a panel tab to create a floating window.

transition

effects

trimming

sequence

Premiere Pro 2.0 makes video editing enjoyable. Its full range of editing features gives you unlimited opportunities to create some great videos. This book will go over each major feature in detail later. In this Lesson you get to take a brief and fun look at a whole bunch of them.

2 | Taking a Quick Run-through of Premiere Pro 2.0

Topics covered in this lesson:

- Placing clips on a sequence.
- Arranging and trimming clips.
- Adding a transition.
- Applying a video effect.
- Editing a Photoshop layered graphic.
- Compositing graphics using a nested sequence.
- Editing rules of thumb from an expert.

Getting started

You're ready to dive into editing and this lesson gives you free rein to do that. We will cover a slew of editing tasks intended to give you a feel for the standard editing workflow. The caveat is: we will only scratch the surface of each of those tasks. All have extra features and functionality that give wide creative options and ease-of-use. We'll cover those extra goodies in later lessons.

I begin the lesson by presenting a finished video. You get to take a look at it on the Timeline and see how I put it together. Then you get to edit that video from scratch. By the end of this lesson, I think you will begin to see what you can create with Premiere Pro 2.0. It is an exciting product with limitless possibilities.

Placing clips on a sequence: Lesson 2-1

The purpose here is to give you a taste of what it's like to edit videos in Premiere Pro. We will bypass numerous options as well as some mundane things like project settings and preferences (saving them for Lesson 4) and dive right into basic editing.

Before you start this lesson, use Windows Media Player to view the Lesson 2 introductory video. As was the case in Lesson 1, and will be the case for the rest of the book, you'll find this Lesson's introductory video in this Lesson Intro Videos file folder. In Media Player, navigate to the P Pro 2.0 CIB Assets\Lesson Intro Videos file folder and double-click Lesson 2 Intro.wmv.

1 Start Premiere Pro 2.0.

2 Click Open Project, navigate to the Lesson 2 folder and open Lesson 2-1.prproj.

This project opens with assets (video clips, an audio file and a Photoshop graphic) loaded in the Project panel and four sequences in the Timeline.

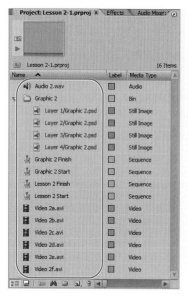
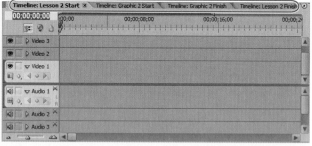

3　In the Timeline, click the tab for Lesson 2 Finish (the last tab on the right) to open that sequence. This collection of clips shows how your finished project will look at the end of this lesson.

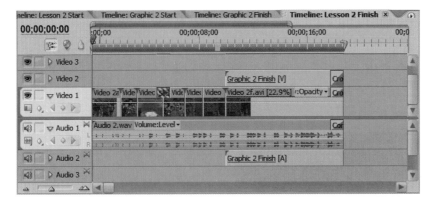

4　Check that the Current Time Indicator (CTI), highlighted in the next figure, is at the beginning of this sequence. If not, press the Home shortcut key to move it there (you can also simply click and drag the CTI all the way to the left).

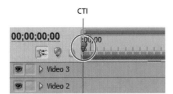

Timeline navigation keyboard shortcuts

In addition to the Home keyboard shortcut, pressing the End key moves the CTI to the end of the last clip in the sequence, and pressing the Page Up or Page Down keys moves you backward or forward respectively through a sequence, one clip at a time. I suggest you give these shortcuts a dry run since you will use them all the time while editing.

If pressing a shortcut key has no effect it's because the Timeline is not the active frame. Click somewhere inside the Timeline to make it active (an orange border appears around whichever frame is active) and then press the keyboard shortcut.

5 Press the Spacebar shortcut key to play this sequence (you can also click the VCR-style Play control at the bottom of the Program Monitor and highlighted in the next figure).

Watch the video in the Program Monitor. It's a series of short video clips with a music bed that finishes with a superimposed graphic. Note that there is a Slide transition between the third and fourth clips, and the last clip becomes a freeze frame, then gets blurry as text and a graphic fade up over the still shot.

Now you will start creating the video you just watched.

6 In the Timeline, click the Lesson 2 Start tab (the first tab on the left) to open that empty sequence. This will be where you'll do most of your work.

There are several ways to add clips to a timeline. For now, we'll use only one.

7 Click and drag Video 2a from the Project panel (you might need to scroll down the Project panel to access it) to the Video 1 track on the Timeline and line up its left edge along the left side—the beginning—of the track. Release the mouse button.

Note that as you drag the clip into the Timeline, it becomes a gray rectangle (indicating its relative size and which track it's hovering over) and a little blue *insert* edit icon appears on the clip (highlighted in the next figure) indicating the action you are about to take.

Also, as you move the clip near the left side of the track a vertical black line appears below the CTI, indicating that the first frame of the clip will start at the CTI's current position (the beginning of this sequence).

💡 **Fixing goofs**

As you click and drag clips to and within the Timeline, you invariably will drag a clip to the wrong place. The quick fix for a single goof is the standard Windows Undo keyboard shortcut: Ctrl+Z. You can also select Edit > Undo. If you totally mess up, you can start the project all over by selecting File > Open Recent Project, selecting the current project, and when asked whether to Save changes, clicking No.

8 Drag the next video clip in the Project panel—Video 2b—to the Timeline directly after Video 2a on the Video 1 track. When the vertical black line appears at the end of the first clip, release the mouse button.

That black line indicates the first frame of this second video clip will start immediately after the last frame of the previous clip.

Helpful black vertical line

You'll encounter that vertical black line many times in the coming lessons. It's part of the Snap function and is there to help you align clips with the CTI or other clips. You can turn off the Snap function. I explain more about it in Lesson 5.

9 Repeat these steps for the remaining four video clips. And then add another instance of the last video clip—Video 2f—to the end of the sequence.

You will turn that repeated clip into the freeze frame that you saw earlier. Your sequence should look like the following figure.

10 Drag Audio 2.wav to the beginning of the Audio 1 track.

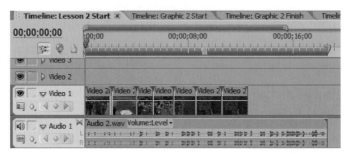

11 Click somewhere in the Timeline to make it the active frame (an orange border will appear around it).

12 Press the Home key, then press the spacebar to watch and listen to your work.

Arranging and trimming clips: Lesson 2-2

As you play the sequence you just built you might notice a few things. The second and third clips are out of order, the edit between the two sliding door shots is awkward, the sequence is missing the graphic at the end, and at least one edit is a bit abrupt. You'll fix these items and do a few other cool things in the remaining mini-lessons.

You have a choice at this point (depending on how confident you are that you followed Lesson 2-1 to a 'T'): either make a clean start to this lesson by opening Lesson 2-2.prproj or save your work and continue.

Starting fresh

If you choose start fresh, select File > Open Project, double-click Lesson 2-2.prproj in the Lesson 2 folder, and when asked if you want to save the changes click No.

Staying the course

If you want to continue working in your current project, then first save your work. Select File > Save As. You can name your project anything you want but for consistency's sake I suggest you name it Lesson 2 *[your name]*. Click Save.

You'll start this lesson by rearranging two clips. The second and third video clips in the sequence are out of order. It's a simple matter to drag Clip 3 in front of Clip 2 but it takes a specialized keyboard shortcut. First we'll do it the wrong way.

1   Click and drag the third clip along the Video 1 track so that its left edge lines up with the left edge of the second clip. Release the mouse button. Your sequence should end up with a gap in it as in the next figure.

You just did an overlay edit. The third clip covered the second clip rather than swapped places with it.

2 Press Ctrl+Z to undo that faux pas.

3 Drag the third clip to the same spot and before releasing the mouse button, hold down the Ctrl+Alt keys. Now release the mouse button.

Note: You just did a type of insert edit called an extract and move (note the curved arrow icon highlighted in the next figure). Instead of doing an overlay edit that covers up what was on the video track at the point of the edit, holding down the Ctrl+Alt keys did several things. Holding down Ctrl filled the gap you created when you extracted the third clip and slid the rest of the clips over to make room. Holding down Alt "unlinked" the audio track from the Insert function (Insert normally moves clips on both the video and audio tracks) so the audio clip did not slide along the track along with the video clips above it.

4 Play that section of the video. You'll see that the clip sequence makes more sense: the actor now stops, glances down, and then you see the tight shot of him unfolding the paper.

5 Drag the CTI through the fifth and sixth clips. Note that the sliding door opens twice. This is a jump cut and it's easy to fix.

6 Position the CTI on the edit point between the two clips (use the Page Up or Page Down keys). It doesn't have to be exactly on the edit point, merely close to it.

7 Click the Trim button (▨) in the lower right corner of the Program Monitor—highlighted in the next figure—or press Ctrl+T to open the Trim panel.

8 Hover your cursor over the left screen until it turns into a left-facing bracket (see next figure).

9 Drag that left-facing bracket to the left until the door is opened slightly past the main actor's face.

The Out Shift blue timecode below that screen should be at about –00;00;00;10 (-10 frames -- hours;minutes;seconds;frames). You've trimmed the end of the left clip by one-third of a second (NTSC is 30 fps).

10 Hover the cursor over the right screen until it turns into a right-facing bracket and drag until the door widths match—about +00;00;00;09 (9 frames) in the right screen's In Shift timecode display.

You trimmed nearly a third of a second from the beginning of the right clip.

11 Click the Play Edit button (▶️▶) in the Trim frame to check out your handiwork.

12 Close the Trim frame by clicking the 'X' in the upper right corner.

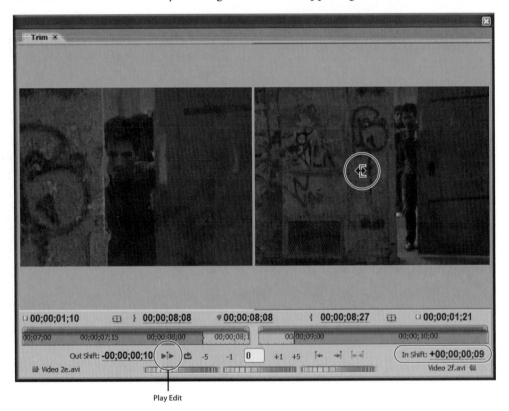

Play Edit

13 Select the Rate Stretch Tool (↖) from the Tools panel (keyboard shortcut X).

14 Click and drag the right edge of the last clip until it lines up with the end of the audio clip below it.

That Rate Stretch move puts that final clip into slow motion. But the real purpose is to make it fit the length of the piece and then to turn that stretched clip into a freeze frame.

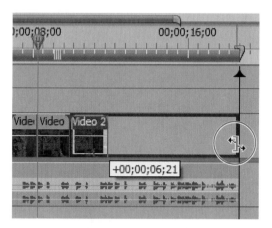

15 Switch back to the Selection tool by clicking its icon (↖) in the Tools panel or using the keyboard shortcut V.

16 Right-click anywhere on that stretched clip to open a lengthy, context menu and select Frame Hold. That opens the Frame Hold Options dialog box.

17 Check Hold On, select Out Point from the drop-down list and click OK.

That creates a freeze frame that matches the final frame of the preceding clip (since both clips have the same final frame).

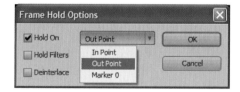

18 Feel free to save your work. If you already did a Save As, this time simply select File > Save. Or you can start fresh in Lesson 2-3 with a pre-built project.

Adding a transition: Lesson 2-3

View your sequence now. The clips move in a logical order, the sliding door jump cut is gone, and the sequence ends with a nice freeze frame. What you'll do now is add a transition to fix an abrupt edit between the third and fourth clips—the tight shot of the yellow flyer and the medium shot of the actor holding the flyer.

In clip three the actor is holding the flyer horizontally over a box and in the fourth clip the paper is vertical and in front of the actor's face. There is no way to match the action, as you did with the sliding door, but applying a video transition can make that edit less abrupt.

Either continue with your current project or open Lesson 2-3.

1　Click the Effects tab to open that panel.

2　Click the triangle next to Video Transitions to *twirl down* or open that file folder.

There are dozens of transitions in the folders. Selecting one to suit a situation can take some trial and error. In this case, I've done that work for you. I think the Slide transition works well here.

3　Twirl down the Slide folder. Your Effects panel should look like the following figure (you might need to expand the Effects panel by dragging its border down a bit).

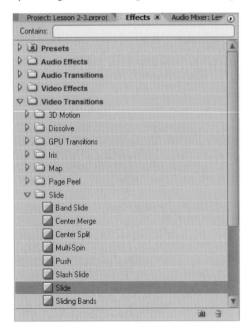

4   Click and drag the Slide transition to the edit point between Clips 3 and 4.

5   Hover the transition over that edit point. A little transition icon (⬚) appears and the edit point becomes highlighted. Drop the transition there.

Note: If you drag the transition slightly to the left or right of the edit point, the icon will change to show a transition that ends or starts at the edit point. That's no big deal but for our purposes, try to center the transition on the edit line.

An Information message pops up noting "Insufficient Media." These clips do not have any extra head or tail frames (a concept I explain later in the book) to use for a transition. But Premiere Pro can deal with that by repeating frames from the clips.

6   Click OK to close the "Insufficient Media" information window.

7   Click the little transition rectangle (highlighted in the next figure) that now resides at the top of the edit point between the two clips. That displays the transition's parameters in the Effect Controls panel.

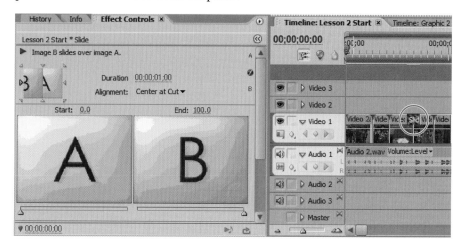

8 Drag the CTI through the edit point in the Timeline to preview the transition. The fourth clip slides in from the left over the third. I'd prefer that it slide up from the bottom, since that follows the flow of the edit.

9 Click the little "South to North" triangle below the transition preview screen at the top of the Effect Controls panel (highlighted in the following figure) to change the transition's direction. The preview screen changes accordingly.

10 Drag the CTI through the edit to preview your work.

Transition experimentation

Feel free to experiment with the Slide transition parameters in the Effect Controls panel. You can change the duration of the transition by clicking and dragging left or right on the Duration time. The default time is 1 second and zero frames.

If you scroll down the Effect Controls panel you'll see some extra features. You can see the actual video clips (instead of the blue 'A' and green 'B' displays) and you can put a color border on the edge of the sliding clip.

Feel free to use any transition. Simply drag a transition from the Effects panel to the current transition at the edit point to change to that new transition. Then double-click that little purple transition box to display its parameters in the Effect Controls panel. WARNING—this might lead to hours of goofing off.

Applying a video effect: Lesson 2-4

Now you'll apply a video effect to the freeze frame. You'll use a Blur effect that I customized for this lesson. Either continue with your current project or open Lesson 2-4.

1 Open the Effects panel by clicking its tab.

2 Open the fly-out menu by clicking the little triangle in the upper right corner of the Effects panel.

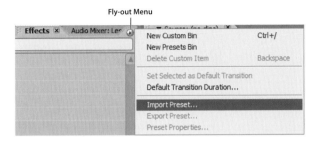

3 Select Import Preset, navigate to the Lesson 2 folder and double-click Lesson 2 Gradual Blur.prfpset.

4 Twirl down the Presets folder to reveal the newly-added Lesson 2 Gradual Blur.

5 Drag Lesson 2 Gradual Blur onto the final video clip of your sequence, the freeze frame.

6 Place the CTI ahead of the freeze frame and play the sequence.

Note: The freeze frame plays for a moment then gradually gets blurry. Look at the Effect Controls panel. The Fast Blur effect has been added below the Motion and Opacity effects (it's called Fast Blur but by using keyframes I applied it gradually).

7 Click the Show/Hide Timeline View chevron (⊗) (highlighted in the figure on the next page.)

To open the timeline portion of the Effect Controls panel (the chevron will switch directions when you open the timeline).

That shows how I customized this effect using keyframes (the little diamond-shaped icons highlighted in the following figure). This ability to change an effect's parameters over time is an incredibly powerful feature of Premiere Pro. I will cover it in depth in several upcoming lessons.

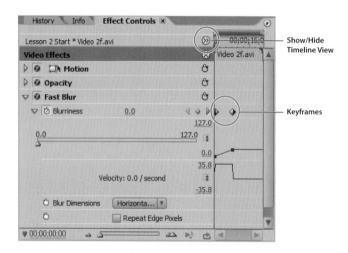

Editing a Photoshop layered graphic: Lesson 2-5

Now you'll edit the graphic and then put a few finishing touches on the entire project. The purpose is to have each layer of the Photoshop graphic fade-up on screen one graphic element at a time.

I saved you a couple steps by putting the Photoshop graphic in a sequence—Graphic 2 Start—in the Timeline. Later in the book you'll take a more detailed look at how to set up a sequence using a Photoshop graphic. For now you should know that I chose to import this layered graphic as a sequence with each of its layers in separate tracks. That is a powerful feature in Premiere Pro that lets you animate Photoshop graphics on a layer-by-layer basis.

Either continue with your current project or open Lesson 2-5.

1   In the Timeline, click the Graphic 2 Start tab to open that sequence.

You could simply slide each clip to the right so they appeared one at a time, but I want you to set specific times so they will appear in time to the music (did you notice how the drum beats match the actor's actions as he opens and closes the invitation?)

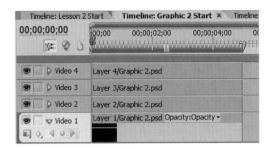

2   Drag the CTI to the 2-second position (you can see its exact time in the readout in the Program Monitor).

3   Click inside the Layer 3 clip and drag the entire clip (rather than trimming its beginning or end) so its first frame lines up with the CTI line at the 2-second mark.

You'll know it's lined up when that black, vertical line appears. Also a little pop-up timecode (highlighted in the next figure) tells you how far you have moved the clip from its original position.

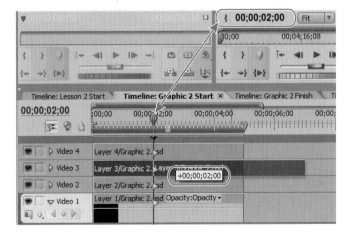

4   Move the CTI to 4 seconds and drag Layer 4 (you might need to move the video tracks scroll bar to see it) so it starts at the 4-second mark.

Since it (and all other graphics) are 5 seconds long by default, Layer 4 should now end at 9 seconds.

Note: I skipped Layer 1 because it's simply a black background. In the next mini-lesson you'll see how it covers up what's below it on the timeline. You will remove it later to fix that issue. So, for now, do nothing to it.

5   Click and drag the ends of Layers 2 and 3 to line up with the end of Layer 4.

That black, vertical line will appear at the end of the Layer 4 clip at the 9-second point. Reminder: you're ignoring Layer 1 because you're going to delete it later.

In the next step you'll add the Cross Dissolve transition to the beginning of Layers 2 and 3 to have them gradually fade onscreen one after the other.

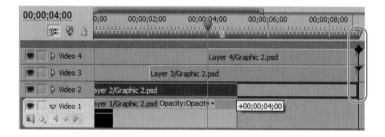

6   In the Effects panel, under Video Transitions, twirl down Dissolve and drag Cross Dissolve to the beginning of each of the Layer 2 and 3 clips.

If you want, you can use a different transition such as Slide. Feel free to experiment.

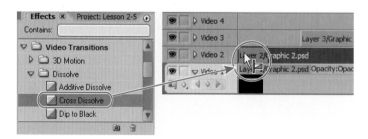

Why the red box around Cross Dissolve?

The red box around the Cross Dissolve icon in the Effects panel indicates it is the default transition. You can quickly apply it to any edit between two clips by placing the CTI at that edit point and using the keyboard shortcut Ctrl+D to add the default transition.

You can set any transition as the default transition simply by clicking on a transition in the Effects panel, opening the fly-out menu and clicking Set Selected As Default Transition. You can also change the Default Transition Time via the same fly-out menu.

Applying one more video effect preset

Now you'll apply another Preset video effect, this time to the Layer 4 graphic clip. In this case I customized the Motion effect to have the round logo in Layer 4 spin onscreen.

1   Open the Effects panel by clicking its tab.

2   Open the fly-out menu by clicking the little triangle in the upper right corner of the Effects panel.

3   Select Import Preset, navigate to the Lesson 2 folder and double-click Lesson 2 Logo Motion.prfpset.

4   Twirl down the Presets folder to reveal the newly-added Lesson 2 Logo Motion and drag it onto the Layer 4 clip on the Video 4 track of your sequence.

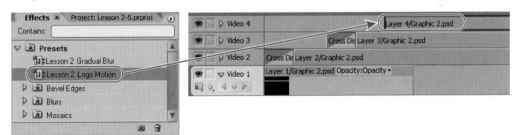

5   Click the Effect Controls tab, twirl down the Motion effect and open the Timeline View by clicking the chevron in the upper right corner.

Note: Take a look at the keyframes. Three have hourglass icons indicating I added Bezier motion to them (the spinning icon decelerates as it approaches full size).

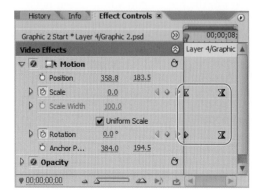

6   Play this sequence. The first two graphics will fade up, one at a time, and the third graphic, the circular logo, will grow and rotate into place. The sequence should play for 9 seconds.

Compositing graphics using a nested sequence: Lesson 2-6

Layering or compositing videos, graphics, and text is a very important feature of Premiere Pro. There are about a dozen ways to composite clips. I cover them in several upcoming lessons. For now, we'll stick with one simple method: compositing a graphic using its built-in transparent layer.

To do that you'll use a nested sequence. That's kind of a high-level editing concept but when you see it in use, I think you'll see how nested sequences work, and will have a greater comfort level with them when I go over them in detail later in the book.

Either continue with your current project or open Lesson 2-6.

1   Click the Lesson 2 Start tab in the Timeline to open that sequence.

2   Click the Project tab to open that panel.

3   Drag the Graphic 2 Start sequence clip from the Project panel to the Video 2 track so its first frame lines up with the beginning of the last clip in the sequence (the freeze frame).

Despite this sequence being a collection of four layered graphics, it shows up simply as a clip. This is the beauty of a nested sequence.

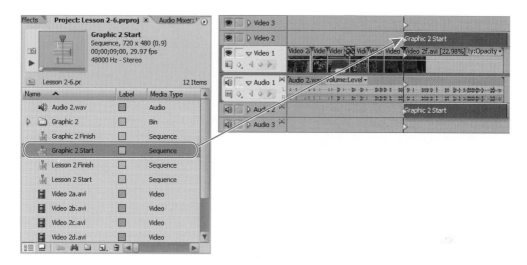

💡 Why is there audio?

If you scroll down in the audio track section of the Timeline you'll note that the Graphic 2 Start sequence has an audio clip associated with it even though it is only a collection of graphics. That is standard Premiere Pro behavior. For now you can ignore that audio clip but there are ways to remove it to avoid confusion.

4   View that portion of the Lesson 2 Start sequence.

You'll note that the graphic covers up the freeze frame below it in the timeline for the first few seconds, then reveals the freeze frame toward the end. The reason? The black Layer 1 clip in the nested sequence plays for the first 5 seconds of the 9-second clip.

It's another great feature of nested sequences that this is easy to fix. You simply go back to the original sequence and make the necessary changes. Those changes will show up immediately in the nested versions of that sequence.

5   Click the Graphic 2 Start tab in the Timeline to open up that sequence again.

6   Click on the Layer 1 clip to highlight it and press the Delete key to remove it (you also can right-click on it and select Cut).

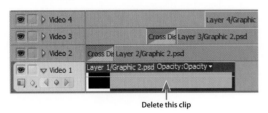

Delete this clip

7   Click the Lesson 2 Start tab and play that last segment again. Now the freeze frame shows through for the entire length of the nested sequence.

8   Drag the right end of the nested sequence clip to the left (it runs a bit too long) to line it up with the end of the freeze frame and audio clip.

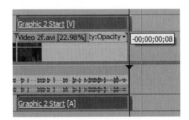

9   Drag the Cross Dissolve video transition from the Effects panel—Video Transitions/Dissolve folder— to the end of the Graphic 2 Start nested sequence clip and again to the end of the freeze frame clip. That will fade all the clips to black at the end.

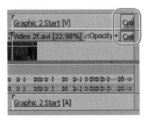

Nested sequence simplifies effects

When you apply the Cross Dissolve to the nested sequence clip, all three graphic clips in that sequence fade to black . That is a huge advantage to a nested sequence. Instead of applying an effect or transition to each layer of a sequence you can apply it only once to the nested version of that sequence. This is one reason you'll come to rely on nested sequences, a powerful Premiere Pro feature.

10 Drag the Constant Power audio transition from the Effects panel—Audio Transitions > Crossfade folder—to the end of the Audio 2.wav clip to have the drum track fade out with the video and graphics.

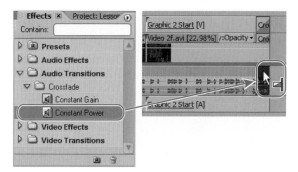

11 Press the Home key and the spacebar to view your finished project.

It should look and sound the same as the Lesson 2 Finish sequence you played at the beginning of this lesson. Congratulations!

John Crossman, owner, Crossman Post Production

EDITING "RULES OF THUMB" FROM AN EXPERT

I had the good fortune of being a reporter at KSL-TV in Salt Lake City in the mid-1980s when it was awarded the national TV news station of the year two years in a row and had the highest-rated (by percentage of viewers) news shows in the country.

John Crossman was the chief editor. He helped create the news operation's overall look and performed video magic, editing stunning pieces for our long-format, "magazine-style" show.

John now runs Crossman Post Production (www.crossmanpost.com) just outside of Salt Lake City. He provides video editing, graphics, and computer-generated animation for a lengthy list of corporate, educational, and broadcast clients.

John has won bushels of awards and is a wonderfully talented guy who has a true passion for the art of editing. Here are his editing "rules of thumb":

▶ **Good editors need certain basic talents:**

• **Rhythm**—Life has a rhythm, and so does editing. If you can't feel it, it's very hard to learn.

• **Visualization**—Good editors can see the completed project before they start. The actual editing is just the detail work.

• **Patience**—Even when you can see it in your mind's eye, you'll have to make compromises on every project. The true test of an editor is whether he can make compromises work well.

• **Positive attitude**—Your attitude will go a long, long way toward determining your success. You'll spend numberless hours editing in a small dark space, usually on a deadline, and always with budget pressure, client pressure, spouse pressure—you name it. The better the attitude, the better the job will go.

• **Team player**—You're part of a team. Try not to criticize the other members. Remember, you didn't have your eye in the viewfinder when the bomb went off. Thinking you could have had that shot when you're looking at the tape hours and miles away is easy, but not productive.

▶ **To edit well, you need to do the following:**

• **Use motivation and logic.** This is the most important concept in editing. Your editing should be motivated. You should have a reason for the shots you select and the order in which you select them. There should be a purpose to why you dissolve, why you use a wipe, as well as why you cut.

• **Comunicate clearly what has happened.** Your shot selection and the time spent on each shot should reinforce the narration while conveying information.

• **Plan as you capture.** As you transfer the video, you should see in your mind's eye how the pictures are going to line up to get you to where you want to be at the end. Is the shot a great scene-setter (beginning)? Is it incredibly beautiful (possible closing shot)? Is it self-explanatory or incomprehensible (possible cutting-room floor material)?

• **Build new skills.** If you're in the professional ranks, or want to be, you must budget a considerable amount of time and money toward keeping current. At the very least, you're going to need to learn about how to incorporate graphics, animation, compositing, and special effects into your editing to serve the demands of your clients.

• **Attitude makes a difference.** In the world of broadcast television, I was surrounded by people who knew how to create good stories. In corporate production, you might be working with someone who has no clue. At this point, you become 90% teacher and 10% editor. Your attitude will win you a loyal client or lose you a lifetime customer.

• **Editing is not the message.** Like music in a movie, good editing helps communicate your message and shouldn't really stand out to the viewer. Editing make the message work or not work.

Review

▶ **Review questions**

1　What's an advantage of the Snap function?

2　What's the principal difference between an Overlay edit and an Insert edit?

3　Name a few Timeline navigation keyboard shortcuts.

4　How do you swap one transition with another?

5　What's an advantage of working with a Photoshop layered graphic?

6　How does a nested sequence work?

▶ **Review answers**

1　It helps you place clips at an exact point, be it the CTI or next to the in- or out-point of an adjacent clip.

2　An Overlay edit covers whatever is on the Timeline at the point of the edit. An Insert slides everything to the right to make room for the inserted clip.

3　Page Up and Page Down move back and forward, one edit point at a time. Home takes you to the first frame. End takes you to the last frame of the last clip in the sequence. Spacebar = play.

4　Simply drag the new transition onto the existing transition in the sequence. Click the transition box at the edit point to display its parameters in the Effect Controls panel.

5　You can automatically put that graphic in its own sequence with each layer on a separate video track, thereby enabling you to apply motion or other effects to each layer individually.

6　You can nest an entire sequence in another sequence and it will behave as if it were a single video clip. If you go back to the original sequence and make a change, that change will show up immediately in its nested version. Finally, rather than applying the same effect—like a Cross Dissolve—to each clip in each layer of a sequence, you can apply that effect only once to the nested version of the sequence.

cutaways

1/3 1/3 1/3

Capture ✕

Paused...

capture

00;00;00

scene detection

▼ 00;14;19;29   { 00;00;00;00   00;00;00;00   00;00;00;01 }

It's time to do some work with your own videos. You've heard of garbage in, garbage out? That truism also applies to video editing. So, your first task is to shoot some great looking video. Then use Premiere Pro 2.0 to capture that video—transfer it from your camcorder or VCR to your PC's hard drive. Premiere Pro offers several ways to do that. Each is easy and fast.

3 Shooting and Capturing Great Video Assets

Topics covered in this lesson:

- Twenty tips for shooting great video.
- Advice from a TV-news chief photographer.
- Capturing an entire videotape.
- Using batch capture and scene detection.
- Tackling manual analog video capture.

Getting started

The purpose of this book is to help you use Premiere Pro to make professional-looking videos. To do that you need to start with high quality raw material. So in this lesson I give you my top 20 tips for shooting great video. I call on a friend who is a TV-news chief photographer to pony up his advice. And I show you four methods to transfer or capture your video to your PC. This is the first lesson to address Adobe Certified Expert exam objectives. I point them out as we encounter their applicable topics.

Twenty tips for shooting great video

With your camcorder of choice in hand, it's time to venture off and shoot videos. If you're new to videography, following these tips will help you create better videos. If you're an old hand, think of this list as a way to snap out of your routine and juice things up a bit. Here are my shooting axioms:

- Get a closing shot
- Get an establishing shot
- Shoot plenty of video
- Adhere to the "rule of thirds"
- Keep your shots steady
- Follow action
- Use trucking shots
- Find unusual angles
- Lean forward or backward
- Get wide and tight shots
- Shoot matched action
- Get sequences
- Avoid fast pans and snap zooms
- Shoot cutaways
- Don't break the "plane"
- Use lights
- Grab good "bites"
- Get plenty of natural sound
- Stripe your tapes
- Plan your shoot

Get a closing shot

Your closing images are what stick in people's minds. You should be constantly on the lookout for that one shot or sequence that best wraps up your story.

NBC-TV feature reporter Bob Dotson (see Lesson 5 for his story creation tips) and his photographer never fail to find a closing shot. It could be as simple as someone closing a door, capping a pen, petting a dog, turning out the lights, or releasing a butterfly from their cupped hands. If you happen to see a Dotson feature story, consider its close. It's sure to be memorable.

Get an establishing shot

An establishing shot sets a scene in one image. Although super-wide shots work well (aerials in particular), consider other points of view: from the cockpit of a race car, a close-up of a scalpel with light glinting off its surface, or paddles dipping frantically in roaring white water. Each grabs the viewer's attention and helps tell your story.

The establishing shot sets the scene: an isolated peninsula jutting into the ocean. The second tells the story: a thriving gannet colony.

Shoot plenty of video

Videotape is cheap and expendable. Shoot a whole lot more raw footage than you'll put in your final production. Five times as much is not unusual. Giving yourself that latitude might help you grab shots you would have missed otherwise.

Adhere to the rule of thirds

It's called the "Rule of Thirds" but it's more like the rule of four intersecting lines. When composing your shot, think of your viewfinder as being crisscrossed by two horizontal and two vertical lines. The center of interest should fall along those lines or near one of the four intersections, not the center of the image.

Consider all those family photos where the subject's eyes are smack dab in the center of the photo. Those are *not* examples of good composition.

Another way to follow the rule of thirds is to look around the viewfinder as you shoot, not just stare at its center. Check the edges to see whether you're filling the frame with interesting images. Avoid large areas of blank space.

The rule of thirds: Putting your image's most important elements along the lines or at their intersections will make it more pleasing to the eye.

Keep your shots steady

You want to give viewers the sense that they're looking through a window or, better yet, are there on location. A shaky camera shatters that illusion.

When possible, use a tripod. The best *sticks* have fluid heads that enable you to make smooth pans or tilts.

If it's impractical to use a tripod try to find some way to stabilize the shot: lean against a wall, put your elbows on a table, or place the camcorder on a solid object.

Follow action

This might seem obvious, but keep your viewfinder on the ball (or sprinter, speeding police car, surfer, conveyor belt, and so on). Your viewers' eyes will want to follow the action, so give them what they want.

One nifty trick is to use directed movement as a pan motivator. That is, follow a leaf's progress as it floats down a stream and then continue your camera motion past the leaf—panning—and widen out to show something unexpected: a waterfall, a huge industrial complex, or a fisherman.

Use trucking shots

Trucking or dolly shots move with the action. For example: hold the camera at arm's length right behind a toddler as he motors around the house, put the camera in a grocery cart as it winds through the aisles, or shoot out the window of a speeding train.

Find unusual angles

Getting your camcorder off your shoulder, away from eye level, leads to more interesting and enjoyable shots. Ground-level shots are great for gamboling lambs or cavorting puppies. Shoot up from a low angle and down from a high angle. Shoot through objects or people while keeping the focus on your subject.

Lean forward or backward

The zoom lens can be a crutch. A better way to move in close or away from a subject is simply to lean in or out. For example, start by leaning way in with a tight shot of someone's hands as he works on a wood carving; then, while still recording, lean way back (perhaps widening your zoom lens as well) to reveal that he is working in a sweatshop full of folks hunched over their handiwork.

Get wide and tight shots

Our eyes work like medium angle lenses. So we tend to shoot video that way. Instead, grab wide shots and tight shots of your subjects. If practical, get close to your subject to get the tight shot rather than use the zoom lens. Not only does it look better but that proximity leads to clearer audio.

Using a wide and a tight shot can create greater interest.

Shoot matched action

Consider a shot from behind a pitcher as he throws a fastball. He releases it, then it smacks into the catcher's glove. Instead of a single shot, grab two shots: a medium shot from behind the pitcher showing the pitch and the ball's flight toward the catcher, and a tight shot of the catcher's glove. Same concept for an artist: get a wide shot of her applying a paint stroke to a canvas, then move in for a close shot of the same action. You'll edit them together to match the action.

Matched action keeps the story flowing smoothly while helping to illustrate a point.

Get sequences

Shooting repetitive action in a sequence is another way to tell a story, build interest or create suspense. A bowler wipes his hands on a rosin bag, dries them over a blower, wipes the ball with a towel, picks the ball up, fixes his gaze on the pins, steps forward, swings the ball back, releases it, slides to the foul line, watches the ball's trajectory, and then reacts to the shot. Instead of simply capturing all this in one long shot, piecing these actions together in a sequence of edits is much more compelling. You can easily combine wide and tight shots, trucking moves, and matched action to turn repetitive material into attention-grabbing sequences.

Avoid fast pans and snap zooms

These moves fall into MTV and amateur video territory. Few circumstances call for such stomach-churning camerawork. In general, it's best to minimize all pans and zooms. As with a shaky camera, they remind viewers that they're watching TV.

If you do zoom or pan, do it for a purpose: to reveal something, to follow someone's gaze from his or her eyes to the subject of interest, or to continue the flow of action (as in the floating leaf example earlier). A slow zoom in, with only a minimal change to the focal length, can add drama to a sound bite. Again, do it sparingly.

> 💡 **Keep on rolling along**
>
> *Don't let this no-fast-moves admonition force you to stop rolling while you zoom or pan. If you see something that warrants a quick close-up shot or you need to suddenly pan to grab some possibly fleeting footage, keep rolling. You can always edit around that sudden movement later.*
>
> *If you stop recording to make the pan or zoom or adjust the focus, you might lose some or all of whatever it was you were trying so desperately to shoot. You will also miss any accompanying natural sound.*

Shoot cutaways

Avoid jump cuts by shooting cutaways. A jump cut is an edit that creates a disconnect in the viewer's mind. A cutaway—literally a shot that cuts away from the current shot—fixes jump cuts.

Cutaways are common in interviews where you might want to edit together two 10-second sound bites from the same person. Doing so would mean the interviewee would look like he suddenly moved. To avoid that jump cut—that sudden disconcerting shift—you make a cutaway of the interview. That could be a wide shot, a hand shot, or a reverse-angle shot of the interviewer over the interviewee's shoulder. You then edit in the cutaway over the juncture of the two sound bites to cover the jump cut.

The same holds true for a soccer game. It can be disconcerting simply to cut from one wide shot of players on the field to another. If you shoot some crowd reactions or the scoreboard, you can use those cutaways to cover up what would have been jump cuts.

A crowd reaction shot works well as a cutaway from this bloodless bullfight in Sumatra

Don't break the plane

This avoids another viewer disconnect. If you're shooting in one direction, you don't want your next shot to be looking back at your previous camera location. For instance, if you're shooting an interview with the camera peering over the left shoulder of the interviewer, you want to shoot your reverse cutaways behind the interviewee and over his right shoulder. That keeps the camera on the same side of the plane—an imaginary vertical flat surface running through the interviewer and interviewee.

To shoot over your interviewee's left shoulder would break that plane, meaning the viewer would think the camera that took the previous shot should somehow be in view.

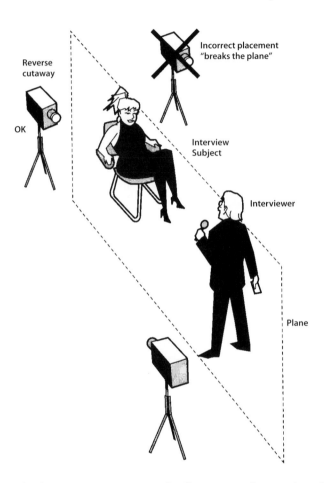

The plane is an imaginary vertical wall running, in this case, through the reporter and interviewee. Breaking the plane—particularly when shooting a reverse cutaway—leads to camera shots that cause viewer disconnects.

In general, you want to keep all your camera positions on one side of that plane, even when shooting large-scale events like football games. Otherwise viewers may lose track of the direction of play

There are exceptions. Consider videotaping a rock group performance. Camera crewmembers typically scramble all over the stage, grabbing shots from multiple angles, and frequently appear on camera themselves.

Switch sides

If you conduct formal, sit-down interviews with more than one person for the same piece, consider shooting each subject from a different side of the interviewer. Shoot one subject with the camera positioned over the left shoulder of the reporter, and for the next interview position the camera over the right shoulder of the reporter. That avoids a subtle jump cut that happens when you edit two bites from two individuals who are both facing the same way.

Use lights

Lights add brilliance, dazzle, and depth to otherwise bland and flat scenes. Consider using an onboard camcorder fill light and, if you have the time, money, patience, or personnel, a full lighting kit with a few colored gels. In a pinch, do whatever you can to increase available light. Open curtains, turn on all the lights, or bring a couple of desk lamps into the room. One caveat: Low-light situations can be dramatic, and flipping on a few desk lamps can destroy that mood in a moment.

Image courtesy of Lowel-Light Mfg.

Grab good "bites"

Your narrator presents the facts. The people in your story present the emotions, feelings, and opinions. Don't rely on interview sound bites to tell the who, what, where, when and how. Let those bites explain the "why."

In a corporate backgrounder, have the narrator say what a product does and let the employees or customers say how enthusiastic they are about that product.

Your narrator should be the one to say, "It was opening night and this was her first solo." Let the singer, who is recalling this dramatic moment, say, "My throat was tight and my stomach was tied in knots."

In general, even though your interviews might take forever, use only short sound bites in your final production. Use those bites as punctuation marks, not paragraphs.

 Exceptions for idiosyncratic characters

None of these admonitions are carved in stone. Some characters you'll videotape are so compelling, quirky, or humorous that your best bet is to let them be the primary narrator. Then you'll want to consider what scenes you can use to illustrate their commentary. You don't want to fill your entire video with a "talking head."

Get plenty of natural sound

Think beyond images. Sound is tremendously important. Listen for sounds you can use in your project. Even if the video quality is mediocre, grab that audio. Your camcorder's onboard mic is not much more than a fallback. Consider using additional mics: shotgun mics to narrow the focus of your sound and avoid extraneous noise, lavalieres tucked out of sight for interviews, and wireless mics when your camera can't be close enough to get just what you need.

Stripe your tapes

Premiere Pro can automate much of the video capture process. But if your DV (digital video) tape has a gap in its timecode, automated capture might not work.

Gaps typically occur when you eject a partially recorded tape and then reinsert it. That resets the timecode to zero and can leave an unrecorded portion on the tape. Either of these means Premiere Pro won't be able to automatically capture clips you've logged.

Striping your tapes before shooting resolves this issue. You can stripe tapes by placing a fresh tape in your camcorder, capping your lens, pressing Record, and waiting for your camcorder to record the entire tape.

This lays down a continuous timecode from beginning to end and ensures that there will be no duplicate timecodes or breaks in the timecode on the tape.

Rewind the tape and you're ready to go. Now, as you use your camcorder, it'll record new video over the black video you taped but won't change the timecode.

Plan your shoot

When you consider a video project, plan what you need to shoot to tell the story. Videotaping your kid's soccer championship match, a corporate backgrounder, or a medical procedure each require planning to ensure success. Know what you want your final video project to say and think of what you need to videotape to tell that story.

Even the best-laid plans and most carefully scripted projects might need some adjusting once you start recording in the field. No matter how you envision the finished project, be willing to make changes as the situation warrants.

Karl Petersen—Chief Photographer, KGW-TV, Portland, OR

ADVICE FROM A TV-NEWS CHIEF PHOTOGRAPHER

Karl Petersen is my favorite TV news photographer. We worked together at KSL-TV in Salt Lake City and formed a video production company in Oregon called Glint Video (we always tried to get a "glint" shot—a little flash of reflected light—in all our videos). Karl now is chief photographer at KGW-TV in Portland. Here are his tips:

• My first shooting advice is, don't do it. Pursue a career of doctor, lawyer, teamster, stevedore, bordello piano player, whatever.

• Having failed that, my next tip is always to shoot as an editor. Always think about how to get from one shot to the next. Try to get some kind of transition shot with either an entry or exit. Close-ups are especially helpful in editing to get from point A to point B.

• Get a good shot mix—wide, medium, close-up (extreme close-ups work well), and unusual angles. Get lots of shots. Variety is an editor's friend.

• Get an establishing shot that tells viewers where you are.

• Fundamentals: Make sure that you have freshly charged batteries, always monitor audio by wearing an earpiece (if you don't you're guaranteed to get burned), and watch your color balance.

• For all indoor interviews, I recommend using at least two lights. If I'm to the reporter's right, I place a light with an umbrella reflector slightly to his left. That means the interviewee is looking toward the light. I place a light with "barn doors" (to keep it from shining into the lens) behind and over the left shoulder of the interview subject (that is, to my right). This adds nice highlights. If I have time, I place a third umbrella well behind the camera to add fill.

• If I'm shooting in a room with sunlight coming in a window, I use blue gels that are especially balanced for daylight, and then color balance for sunlight

▶ **Shooting aerials**

If you like to do things on a grander scale you might get the opportunity to shoot from a helicopter. When shooting from KGW-TV's helicopter, "Sky 8," I sit in the warmth and comfort of the back seat and operate the cameras with a laptop and a joystick. Not many video producers have this luxury. For those who must shoot from a side window, here are some tips:

• Think safety first. Make sure that nothing can fall off the camera—such as a lens shade—or out of the back seat and possibly hit the rotor. That makes the chopper spin like crazy, so you get real dizzy before you die.

• Shooting with the door off is ideal (remove it before you take off).

• Try to keep the camera slightly inside the doorframe to keep it out of the wind.

• Have the pilot "crab" (fly sort of sideways) so that you can shoot straight ahead. That's much more dramatic. It's a great way to fly along a river for instance.

• Have the pilot fly low. This allows cool reveal shots, such as flying over a ridge to reveal an expansive vista.

Finally, don't forget to grab that "glint" shot.

Capturing video

Before you can edit your own video you need to transfer it to your PC's hard drive. In NLE parlance, you need to capture it. Capture is a somewhat-misleading term used throughout the NLE world. All that Premiere Pro does during DV capture is to place the video data in a Windows AVI file "wrapper" without changing the original DV data.

The capture process in the analog world takes several steps: transfer, conversion, compression and wrapping. Your camcorder transfers the video and audio as analog data to a video capture card. That card's built-in hardware converts the waveform signal to a digital form, compresses it using a codec (Compression/Decompression) process, and then wraps it in the AVI file format.

Three DV capturing scenarios

Premiere Pro offers tools to take some of the manual labor out of the capturing process. There are three basic approaches. I'll take you through all of them:

• Capture your entire videotape as one long clip

• Log clips' in- and out-points for automated, batch capturing

• Use the scene detection feature in Premiere Pro to automatically create separate clips whenever you pressed the pause/record button on your camcorder

To do this and the following mini-lessons, you need a DV camcorder. Most DV camcorders have a FireWire (IEEE 1394) cable that you hook up to your PC's FireWire connector. If your PC does not have a FireWire connector, I recommend you buy a FireWire/USB combination card. Decent ones cost less than $20.

You can work with HDV (a compressed high definition video format) or with a professional-level camcorder with an SDI (Serial Digital Interface) connector and a specialized video capture card.

Premiere Pro handles HDV and SDI capture with the same kind of software device controls used with a standard DV camcorder. SDI requires an extra set-up procedure. Refer to Premiere Pro Help for more on that.

If you have an analog camcorder, you need a video capture card that can handle S-Video or Composite video connectors. Your only option with most analog camcorders is to manually start and stop recording. Most don't work with remote device control or have timecode readout so you cannot log tapes, do batch capture devices and most do not use the scene detection feature.

Adobe Certified Expert exam objectives

Completing all the lessons in this book will go a long way toward preparing you for the Adobe Certified Expert (ACE) exam for Premiere Pro 2.0. I have included the exam objectives in the P Pro ACE Objectives.pdf file on this book's companion DVD in the Adobe Certified folder. And I state the objectives individually in lessons as they come up. I have also included a collection of sample questions in the Adobe Certified folder.

Here is the first objective: Describe the process, tools and options Adobe Premiere Pro provides for capturing digital video by using device control.

Capturing an entire tape: Lesson 3-1

1   View the Lesson 3 Intro video.

2   Connect the camcorder to your PC.

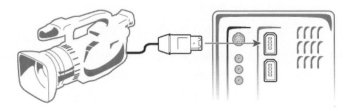

3   Turn on your camcorder and set it to the playback mode: VTR or VCR. Do not set it to the Camera mode.

Note: Windows might note that you've powered up your camcorder by popping up a Digital Video Device connection message.

 Use AC, not a battery

When capturing video, use your camcorder's AC adapter, not its battery. Here's why: When using a battery, camcorders can go into sleep mode. And the battery will often run out before you're done.

4   If the Digital Video Device window did pop up, click Take No Action, check the Always Perform the Selected Action checkbox and click OK.

Next time you fire up your camcorder, you should not see this connection query.

💡 **Project settings for SDI or HDV**

This project assumes you are recording from a DV camcorder: standard 4:3 format or widescreen anamorphic 16:9 screen ratio. If you are working with SDI or HDV, you need to Start Premiere Pro, click New Project and select the preset Project Settings that match your camcorder.

5   Start Premiere Pro, click Open Project, navigate to the Lesson 3 folder and double-click Lesson 3-1.prproj.

6   From the Main Menu, select File > Capture to open the Capture panel.

7   Look above the Capture panel preview pane to make sure your camcorder is connected properly.

Note: *If a message says No Device Control or Capture Device Offline, you'll need to do some troubleshooting. The most obvious fix is to make sure the camcorder is turned on and the cables are connected. For more troubleshooting tips refer to the Premiere Pro help files.*

8   Insert a tape into your camcorder. Premiere Pro will prompt you to give the tape a name.

9   Type in a name for your tape in that text box. Be sure not to give any two tapes the same name. Premiere Pro remembers clip in/out data based on tape names.

10   Use the VCR-style device controls in the Capture panel to play, fast forward, rewind, pause and stop your tape. If you have never used a PC to control a camcorder, this will seem pretty cool.

Capture panel playback controls: **A.** *Next scene* **B.** *Set In point* **C.** *Set Out point* **D.** *Rewind* **E.** *Step back* **F.** *Play* **G.** *Step forward* **H.** *Fast forward* **I.** *Pause* **J.** *Stop* **K.** *Record* **L.** *Previous scene* **M.** *Go To In point* **N.** *Go To Out point* **O.** *Jog* **P.** *Shuttle* **Q.** *Slow reverse* **R.** *Slow play* **S.** *Scene detect*

11   Try some of the other VCR-style buttons (if you need help identifying these buttons, Tool tips pop up as you hover your cursor over them):

• Shuttle (the slider toward the bottom) enables you to move slowly or zip quickly—depending on how far you move the slider off center—forward or backward through your tape.

• Single-frame Jog control (below the Shuttle)

• Step Forward and Backward, one frame at a time

• Slow Reverse and Slow Play

12 Rewind the tape to its beginning or to wherever you want to start recording.

13 In the Setup area of the Logging tab note that Audio and Video is the default setting. If you want to capture only audio or video, change that setting.

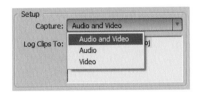

14 Click the Tape button or the Record button to start recording.

You'll see the video (and hear it) within the Capture panel and on your camcorder. Since there is a slight delay during capture, you'll hear what sounds like an echo. Feel free to turn down either your camcorder's speaker or your PC's.

15 Click the red Record button or the black Stop button when you want to stop recording. That pops up the Save Captured Clip dialog box.

16 Give your clip a name (add descriptive information if you want) and click OK.

Premiere Pro will store this clip and all other clips you capture during this lesson in the Lesson 3 file folder on your hard drive. You can change that to another location by selecting Edit > Preferences > Scratch Disks. I cover Preferences in the next lesson.

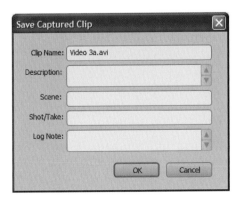

Using batch capture and scene detection: Lesson 3-2

When you perform a batch capture, you log the in- and out-points of a number of clips and then have Premiere Pro automatically transfer them to your PC.

Use the logging process to critically view your raw footage. You want to look for "keeper" video, the best interview sound bites, and any natural sound that will enhance your production.

The purpose of using a batch capture is threefold: to better manage your media assets, to speed up the video capture process and to save hard disk space (since one hour of DV consumes 13 GB).

Use a clip naming convention

Think through how you're going to name your clips. You might end up with dozens of clips, and if you don't give them descriptive names, it'll slow down editing.

You might use a naming convention for sound bites such as Bite-1, Bite-2, and so forth. Adding a brief descriptive comment, such as Bite-1 Laugh, will help.

Here are the steps to follow:

1   In the Capture panel Setup area, click the Logging tab.

2   Change the Handles setting (in lower right corner of the Capture panel) to 30 Frames.

This adds one second to the start and finish of each captured clip, which will give you enough head and tail frames to add transitions without covering up important elements of the clip (and you won't get that little "Insufficient Media" message you saw in Lesson 2-3).

Using the mouse drag method to change numeric values

When changing the Handles value, you can click on the current number and type in a new figure, or simply place your cursor over the Handles number and drag it left or right to lower or raise the value. This method of changing a numeric value works throughout Premiere Pro.

3   In the Clip Data section, give your tape a unique name.

4   Log your tape by rewinding and then playing it.

When you see the start of a segment you want to transfer to your PC, stop the tape, rewind to that spot and click the Set In button.

5   When you get to the end of that segment (you can use Fast-forward or simply Play to get there), click Set Out. The in/out times will display as well as the clip length.

Three other ways to set in/out points

There are other means to set in-points and out-points for selected clips: click the brackets ({ or }) on the play controls, use the keyboard shortcuts—I for In and O for Out—or change the in/out time directly in the Timecode area by clicking on the timecode and dragging your cursor left or right.

6   Click Log Clip to open the Clip Data dialog box.

7 Change the clip name, if needed, add appropriate notes if you want, and then click OK.

That adds this clip's name with its in/out times and tape name info to the Project panel (with the word "Offline" next to it). You'll go there later to do the actual capture.

8 Log clips for the rest of your tape using the same method.

Each time you click Log Clip, Premiere Pro automatically adds a number to the end of your previous clip's name. You can accept or override this automated naming feature.

9 When you've completed logging your clips, close the Capture panel.

All your logged clips will be in the Project panel with the word "Offline" after each.

10 Select all the clips in the Project panel that you want to capture (see following Tip for three methods to do that).

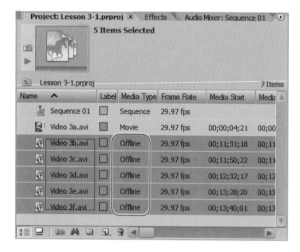

> ## Three ways to select more than one item
>
> *Windows and Premiere Pro offer three ways to select more than one file in a window.*
> *If the file names are contiguous, mouse-click on the top one and Shift+click on the last*
> *one in the group, or click off to one side and above the top clip and drag down to the*
> *last one to marquee select a group (I used the marquee select method—creating the gray*
> *rectangle—in the previous figure). If the file names are scattered about, click first one and*
> *then Ctrl+click on each additional one in turn.*

11   Select File > Batch Capture.

That opens a very simple Batch Capture dialog box that allows you to override the camcorder settings or add more handle frames.

12   Leave the Batch Capture boxes unchecked and click OK.

The Capture panel opens, as does another little dialog box telling you to insert the proper tape (in your case, it's probably still in the camcorder).

13   Insert the tape and click OK.

Premiere Pro now takes control of your camcorder, cues up the tape to the first clip and transfers that clip and all other clips to your hard drive.

14   When completed, take a look at your Project panel to see the results. Offline files have become movies.

Using scene detection

Instead of manually logging in- and out-points, you might want to use the Scene Detect feature. Scene Detect analyzes your tape's Time/Date stamp looking for breaks such as those caused when you press the camcorder's pause button while recording.

When Scene Detect is on and you perform a capture, Premiere Pro automatically captures a separate file at each scene break it detects. Scene Detect works whether you are capturing an entire tape or just a section between specific in- and out-points.

To turn on Scene Detect, in the Capture panel, do either of the following:

• Click the Scene Detect button below the record button.

• Check the Scene Detect checkbox in the Capture panel.

Then you can either set in- and out-points and click Record, or cue your tape to wherever you want to start capturing and click Record. In the latter case, click Stop when done.

Your clips will show up in the Project panel. No need to batch capture them—Premiere Pro captures each clip "on the fly." Premiere Pro will name the first captured clip by putting a 01 after the name you put in the Clip Name box and then increment each new clip by one.

Tackling manual analog movie capture

If you need to transfer analog video—consumer-level VHS, SVHS, Hi-8, or professional-grade video such as Beta-SP—you need a video capture card with analog inputs. Most such cards have consumer-quality composite connectors as well as S-video and sometimes top-of-the-line component plugs.

Adobe Certified Expert exam objective

Describe the process required to capture analog video.

Check your card's documentation for set-up and compatibility issues.

With analog video, you have only one capture option — to do it manually:

1   Open the Capture panel (File > Capture).

2   Use the controls on the camcorder to move the videotape to a point several seconds before the frame you want to begin capturing.

3   Press the Play button on the camcorder, then click the red Record button in the Capture panel.

4   When your clip has been captured, click the Stop button in the Capture panel and on the camcorder. Your clip will show up in the Project panel.

Review

▶ **Review questions**

1   Why is getting the closing shot so important?

2   If you're shooting a formal sit-down interview and the camera is positioned over the left shoulder of the interviewer, where should you place the camera for reverse cutaways?

3   Why should you stripe your tapes?

4   When you open the Capture panel, you don't see an image in the video monitor and you can't control your DV camcorder. What could be going on?

5   During the capture process, how do you add extra frames to ensure you have enough footage to do transitions?

6   You want to capture a clip for its video plus a portion of that clip for a snippet of natural sound. How do you do that?

▶ **Review answers**

1   Your closing shot is what viewers take away from your video. You want to do what you can to make it memorable.

2   Place the camera behind the interview subject and shoot over his right shoulder.

3   Striping your tapes ensures a distinct and uninterrupted timecode.

4   This could be one of several things: Your camcorder is not turned on (or if you're using a battery, it might be in sleep mode); you have it in Camera mode instead of VCR/VTR; or you haven't inserted your tape.

5   Put a number of frames in the Handles option in the Capture section of the Capture panel.

6   Simply log that entire clip and then go back and log the audio portion.

preferences

Bridge

assets

settings

Premiere Pro 2.0 is eminently customizable and adaptable. It accepts just about any moving or still image you throw at it. All you need to do is adjust the Project Settings and Preferences. Managing all your media assets is easy thanks to Project panel in Premiere Pro and the stand-alone file browser, Adobe Bridge.

4 Selecting Settings, Adjusting Preferences and Managing Assets

Topics covered in this lesson:

- Selecting project settings.
- Adjusting user preferences.
- Importing assets.
- Taking a closer look at still images.
- Managing media in the Project panel.
- Working with assets in Adobe Bridge.

Getting started

For the most part, you won't give more than a passing notice to Project Settings and Preferences. Nevertheless it's good to know the options available to you, and they do factor into the Adobe Certified Expert exam. So you'll take a brief look at them in this lesson. In addition you'll learn how to manage your assets from within the Project panel. Finally, you'll delve into Adobe Bridge: a full-scale asset browser that works with all products and file types in the Adobe Creative Suite Production Studio Premium.

Selecting project settings: Lesson 4-1

Up to this point you've been working on projects I've started for you. This time you will start a project from scratch. That will give you an opportunity to see the many ways you can configure your project as well as set user preferences once you've started the project.

The basic rule of thumb when selecting project settings is to match the settings to your source material and not to the final output. Maintaining the original quality of source material means you'll have more options later. Even if your goal is to create a low-resolution video to play on the Internet, wait until you *finish* editing and then reduce the *output* quality settings.

It's possible you might have a mix of source media—widescreen and standard, for example. The best approach here is to set up your project to match the majority of footage it will contain or to match the look you want to achieve. For example, choose a widescreen setting for a project with mostly widescreen videos that contains some standard definition video that you'll place in a "pillar box"—a black frame within the 16:9 aspect ratio widescreen.

Two types of settings menus

Premiere Pro has two settings menus: Project Settings and Preferences. Their similarities can lead to some confusion. For example, both contain General and Capture submenus. The Project Settings menu is also called the Custom Settings menu in the New Project window.

Project Settings apply to your current project. Your first step before opening a new project is to select that project's settings. Once you start a project you can't change many of the Project Settings.

Preferences, on the other hand, generally apply to all projects, and you can change them at any time.

We'll start with a brief lesson on Project Settings. The purpose is simply to check out the various Project Settings options and consider under what circumstances you'd use them.

1 View the Lesson 4 Intro video.

2 Open Premiere Pro 2.0.

That pops up the opening screen. Its Recent Projects list should be fully populated with the projects you worked on in the previous three lessons. In this case you want to start fresh.

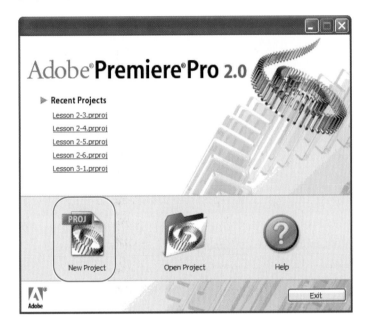

3 Click New Project to open the New Project window.

This screen offers six Project Setting file folders with presets that match virtually all the types of source media you'll work with. I will explain them below.

4   Click the Custom Settings tab highlighted in the next figure.

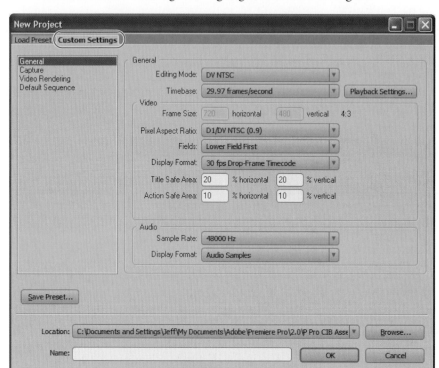

Custom settings—project settings—overview

When you start a new project, you can review and change project settings in this Custom Settings window. You should do so only if none of the available presets match the specifications of your source media.

Later, you can open Project Settings from within the Premiere Pro workspace. The interface is virtually identical to the Custom Settings window. The only difference is that the Project Settings menu does not have the file location and name section at the bottom.

Since some settings can't be changed after a project is created, confirm all project settings in the Custom Settings window before starting a project.

Adobe Certified Expert exam objectives

Given an option from the General submenu of the Project Settings dialog box, describe or explain the purpose of that option.

Given a scenario, select the appropriate project settings (settings include Capture, Video Rendering, Default Sequence).

The Custom Settings window has four submenus: General, Capture, Video Rendering and Default Sequence. Click on each in turn. Here are some brief explanations (refer to Premiere Pro Help for further details):

• **General**—Adjust these settings to match the specifications of the most significant source media in your project. There are six general sub-categories. I explain them on the next page. Usually, the editing mode you select at the top of the menu determines most of the settings in this window.

• **Capture**—This submenu has only three options: DV, Adobe HD-SDI and HDV. The editing mode you select in the General submenu auto-selects the correct capture format, so this is essentially a redundant submenu.

• **Video Rendering**—If you select DV in the General submenu, there are no preview options. Preview options appear only if your source media are Adobe HD-SDI or SD-SDI (both require AJA Xena HS video capture hardware).

• **Default Sequence**—Each time you add a sequence to a project, Premiere Pro displays a menu that lets you select the number of video tracks and the number and type of audio tracks. When it pops up you will generally accept the default values. This menu lets you set those defaults.

💡 **Creating a custom preset for new projects**

You can create a customized new project preset: simply make your choices in the four submenus and then click the Save Preset button. Give your customized project settings preset a name and click OK. It will show up in the New Project > Load Preset menu.

Checking out the new project presets

5   Click the Load Preset tab to return to that window.

6 Open each of the Available Presets file folders and click through the presets. Note the explanation of each preset in the New Project Description window:

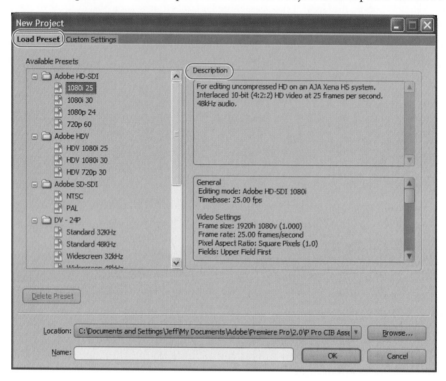

- **Adobe HD-SDI**—For editing high definition (HD) video only on AJA Xena HS System (www.aja.com).

- **Adobe HDV**—A compressed HD-style format that records to standard DV cassettes.

- **Adobe SD-SDI**—For editing high-quality DV in a standard definition (SD) format. This works only on AJA Xena HS systems.

- **DV-24p**—This preset was created for use with 24p DV cameras like the Panasonic AG-DVX100 and Canon XL224p. It's sometimes used for film that has been shot at the film-standard 24 frames per second and transferred to DV.

- **DV-NTSC**—What most Premiere Pro users work with. NTSC is the TV display standard for North and South America and Japan.

- **DV-PAL**—The TV display standard for most of Western Europe and Australia.

Note: *For more information on the many flavors of digital video, check out "A Digital Video Primer" on this book's companion DVD.*

Adjusting user preferences: Lesson 4-2

Preferences are different than Project Settings in that you typically set Preferences once and have them apply to all your projects. You can change Preferences and have them take immediate effect at any time.

Preferences include such things as: default transition times, timing and number of auto saves, Project panel clip label colors, file folder location for captured video, and the user interface brightness (you adjusted this in Lesson 1).

Note: *There are no Adobe Certified Expert Exam objectives for Preferences.*

Continue where you left off in Lesson 4-1. You should be in the New Project menu, with the Load Preset window open.

If you continued past this point and are already in the Premiere Pro workspace, and you selected a DV preset that matches your source material, fine. Otherwise, return to the New Project menu by selecting File > New > Project.

1   Select a DV preset that matches your source material (probably DV-NTSC—Standard or Widescreen—48kHz).

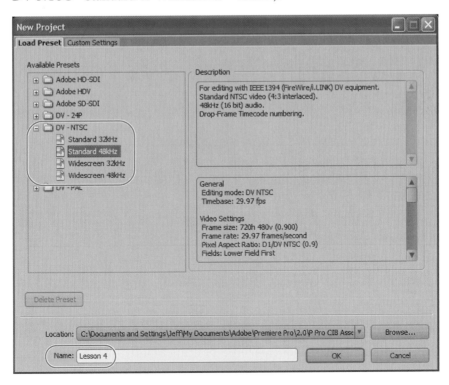

2 Click Browse and navigate to the Lesson 4 folder.

3 Give your project a name—I suggest *Lesson 4 [your name]*—and click OK.
That takes you to the Premiere Pro 2.0 user interface.

4 Select Edit > Preferences > General from the Main Menu.

Note: You can select any of the Preferences submenus. All choices take you to the main Preferences menu with the submenu you selected open. You can easily move from one submenu to another by clicking the submenu name.

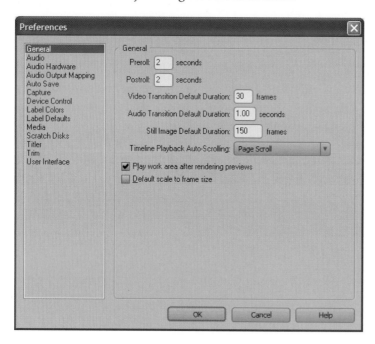

5 Click each submenu name in turn to check out the Preferences options. You will encounter some fairly obscure possibilities here.

Preferences submenus

These rarely come into play in the early stages of Premiere Pro usage, and most are self-explanatory. I'll leave it to you to look up specifics in the Premiere Pro Help files. Here's a brief run-through:

• **General**—Primarily default times for audio and video transitions, still image duration, and preroll/postroll for camcorders during capture.

- **Audio**—Automation Keyframe Optimization is relevant when you use the Audio Mixer to change volume or panning. Selecting Thinning and a Minimum Time Interval of greater than 30 msec makes it easier to edit the changes later.

- **Audio Hardware**—The default audio hardware device.

- **Audio Output Mapping**—Specifies how each audio hardware device channel corresponds to an Adobe Premiere Pro audio output channel. Generally the default settings will work fine.

- **Auto Save**—Set the frequency and number of Auto Saves. To open an auto-saved project select File > Open, navigate to the Premiere Pro Auto Save folder and double-click on a project.

- **Capture**—Four basic capture parameters.

- **Device Control**—Preroll (which you can set in General Preferences) and Timecode Offset (usually used only during analog video capture).

- **Label Colors**—Lets you change the default Project panel media link label colors.

- **Label Defaults**—This is where you can assign specific label colors to different media types.

- **Media**—Use this to empty the cache folders.

- **Scratch Disks**—Set file folder locations for seven items including captured video and preview files. The default location for all such files is your current project file folder.

- **Titler**—This is where you specify the characters used for font and style samples in the Adobe Titler frame.

- **Trim**—Adjusts how many frames and audio units are trimmed if you select the Large Trim Offset (a quick way to chop off chunks of video) in the Trim frame.

- **User Interface**—You saw this in Lesson 1. Set the interface brightness here.

Any changes you make in the user Preferences take effect immediately and will remain in effect the next time you open Premiere Pro. You can change them again at any time.

Note: When you finish reviewing the various options, click Cancel, or click OK if you made any changes that you want to keep.

Importing assets: Lesson 4-3

In this book's Lessons 1-3 your projects started with links to assets that I had already placed in the Project panel. Adding those links to the Project panel—*importing assets,* in Premiere Pro parlance—is easy. But there are a few issues to keep in mind. This lesson will cover importing how-tos and the issues you're most likely to encounter.

Adobe Certified Expert exam objectives

Discuss considerations related to using and importing still images and digital audio.

In this mini-lesson you will import all four standard media types: video, audio, graphics and stills. I will show you two importing methods. And you will take a look at the properties of audio and graphic files. In Lesson 4-4 you'll look more closely at image files.

You can continue where you left off in Lesson 4-2, or open Lesson 4-3.prproj from the Lesson 4 folder.

You should see the standard Premiere Pro opening workspace. All the frames should be empty except for the Sequence 01 item in the Project panel and in the Timeline.

1   Select File > Import.

2   Navigate to the Lesson 4 folder, select the two audio clips, the graphic file, the two stills, and the video (see next tip if you don't know how to select multiple files), and then click Open.

Selecting all but one (or more) files

Use the group select method here (plus one additional step) to select all but one (or more) files. As I explained earlier in the book, select a group of contiguous files using the marquee select—click and drag—method or the Shift+click method. Then press Ctrl+click to deselect one (or more) of them. In this case deselect the three Lesson 4.prproj files.

3   Double click inside the Project panel, in the empty space below the newly added clips.

Note: This is a different and faster way to open the Import window. You could also use the keyboard shortcut: Ctrl+I.

You will import files from a different file folder, demonstrating that you don't have to keep all your assets in the same place. The Project panel simply lists links to your assets, wherever they may be.

4   Navigate to the Lesson 2 folder, select Audio 2.wav and Graphic 2.psd (the audio clip and Photoshop layered graphic you worked on in Lesson 2), and click Open.

Premiere Pro imports the WAV file without a hiccup. For the Photoshop file, Premiere Pro pops up an Import Layered File dialog box.

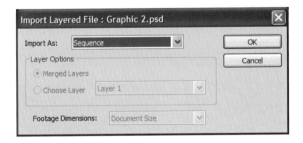

5   Select Import As: Sequence and click OK.

You could have selected Import As: Footage and then had the option of merging all the layers into a single graphic or selecting a specific layer. Choosing Import As: Sequence does two things:

•   Adds a file folder to your Project panel with all the Photoshop layers listed as separate clips

•   Creates a new sequence with all the layers on separate video tracks

6 Right-click Audio 4b.mp3 in the Project panel and select Properties from the context-sensitive menu.

Note: The Source Audio Format is 44100 Hz - 16 bit Stereo (standard CD audio quality) and the Project Audio Format is 48000 Hz - 32-bit floating point Stereo. Premiere Pro upconverts all audio to the project setting, thereby ensuring no quality is lost during editing. Floating point data allow for even more precise and smoother edits.

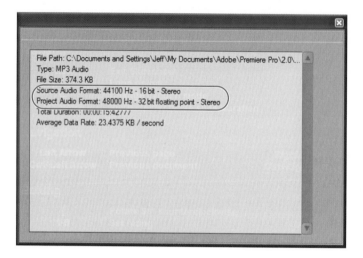

7 Close the Properties window.

Image and graphics issues: Lesson 4-4

Premiere Pro can import just about any image and graphic file type. You've already seen how Premiere Pro handles Photoshop layered files—giving you the option to import the layers as separate graphics within a sequence, as single layers, or by merging the entire file into one graphic clip.

What's left to cover is how Premiere Pro handles Adobe Illustrator files and image files. We'll start this lesson where we left off at the end of Lesson 4-3. If you need to start fresh, open Lesson 4-4.prproj from the Lesson 4 folder.

Note: When you open Lesson 4-4, Premiere Pro will ask "Where is the File [file name]." This project uses files from a folder other than the Lesson 4 folder. Navigate to the missing file (in this case Graphic 2.psd in Lesson 2) and double-click it. This will happen later in this lesson if you open the Lesson 4-5 project.

1   Right-click Graphic 4.ai in the Project panel and select Properties from the context-sensitive menu.

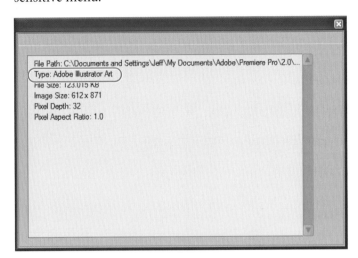

This file type is Adobe Illustrator Art. Here's how Premiere Pro deals with Illustrator files:

• Like the Photoshop file you imported in step 4, this is a layered graphic file. However, Premiere Pro does not give you the option to import Illustrator files in separate layers. It merges them.

• It also uses a process called *rasterization* to convert the vector—path-based—Illustrator art into the pixel-based image format used by Premiere Pro.

• Premiere automatically *anti-aliases*, or smoothes edges of the Illustrator art.

• Premiere converts all empty areas into a transparent alpha channel, so that clips below those areas on the Timeline can show through if you choose.

2   Close the Properties window.

 Edit Illustrator files in Illustrator

If you right-click Graphic 4.ai again, you'll note that one option is Edit Original. If you have Adobe Illustrator loaded on your PC, selecting Edit Original will open Illustrator with this graphic ready to edit. So, even though the layers are merged in Premiere Pro, you can go back to Illustrator, edit the original layered file, save it, and the changes will immediately show up in Premiere Pro.

3 Convert the Project panel into a floating window by Ctrl+clicking on its drag
handle and dragging it out of its frame.

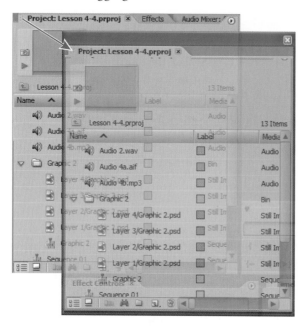

4 Expand the Project panel's floating window as wide as you can and twirl down the
Graphic 2 disclosure triangle to display all the Photoshop graphic layers.

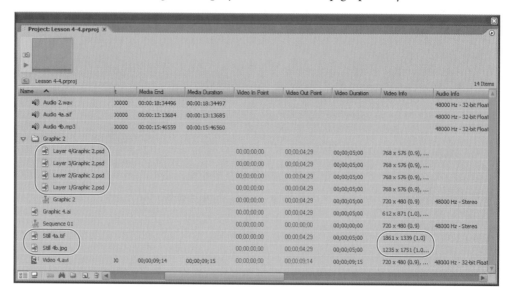

5   Drag the scroll bar along the bottom of the Project panel noting all the various descriptive columns and types of media they apply to.

In particular note the *Video Info* for the two still images. These are image resolutions, and are much larger than standard DV: 720x480. I'll show you how Premiere Pro deals with that in the next steps.

6   Drag the Project panel back to its original frame next to the Effects tab.

Note: If you have trouble re-docking that floating window back in its frame, select Window > Workspace > P Pro 2.0 CIB Workspace to get it into place.

7   Drag the two still images—Still 4a.tif and Still 4b.jpg—to the Video 1 track in the Timeline.

8   Press the backward slash (\) key. That is the keyboard shortcut to expand the Timeline view to match the length of the clips in it. Your Timeline should look like the next figure.

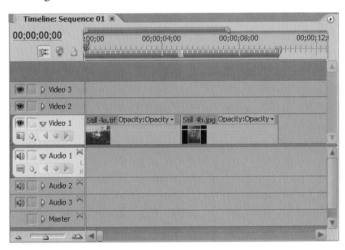

9 Drag the CTI through the two clips.

Note: *As you drag the CTI, look in the Program Monitor. You will see only a portion of each image. The center 720x480 pixels. Both clips have resolutions that are much larger than the standard DV screen size. By default Premiere Pro centers them in the screen and displays them in their original resolution. The next step explains how to view them in their entirety, without changing the aspect ratio of the images.*

10 Right-click the first clip—Still 4a—in the Timeline and click Scale to Frame Size in the context menu to turn on that feature.

Now, you see the entire image.

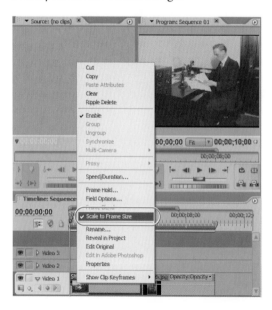

11 Right-click on that same clip and click Scale to Frame Size to un-enable that feature so it returns to its original full resolution display (so you see only a portion of the image).

I will show you the advantage of working with oversize, high-resolution images. You can pan or zoom in on them while retaining a resolution high enough to look crisp on a TV set.

12 Import two Effect Presets I created for this exercise.

To do that, repeat the steps you followed in Lesson 2: Click the Effects tab, open the Fly-out Menu, select Import Preset, navigate to the Lesson 4 folder and double-click (one at a time) Lesson 4 Image Pan.prfpset and Lesson 4 Image Zoom.prfpset.

Note: Another way to import a preset is to open the Effects panel, right-click on Presets and select Import Presets.

13 Open the Presets folder in the Effects panel and drag Lesson 4 Image Pan to that first clip.

Note: Take a look at the Effect Controls panel. Twirl down the Motion effect disclosure triangle and you'll see those hourglass keyframes you saw in Lesson 2. In this case they change the position and scale of the clip over time.

14 Play that clip and note how it starts on the two old telephones and pans to the accountant's face.

15 Drag the Lesson 4 Image Zoom preset effect to the second clip and play it.

Note how it starts as a full image then zooms in to the two young men.

Image tips

Here are a few image importing tips:

• You can import images up to 4,096x4,096 pixels.

• If you don't plan to zoom or pan, try to create files with a frame size at least as large as the frame size of the project—720x534 for NTSC DV (see Square Versus Rectangular Pixels Tip). Otherwise you have to scale up the image and it will lose some of its sharpness.

• If you plan to zoom or pan, try to create images such that the zoomed or panned area will have a frame size at least as large as the frame size of the project.

> 💡 **Square versus rectangular pixels**
>
> *TV sets display rectangular pixels—slightly vertical rectangles (.9 aspect ratio) for NTSC and slightly horizontal for PAL. PC monitors use square pixels. Images created in graphics software typically are square. Premiere Pro adjusts them to display properly by squashing and interpolating the square pixels to keep the images' original aspect ratios and to display them properly on TV sets. So when you create graphics or images with square pixels, create them with your TV standard in mind: 720x534 for NTSC (that resolution will become 720x480 after Premiere Pro squashes the square pixels into rectangles) and 768x576 for PAL (for other standards, including high definition, see the "About square-pixel footage" page in Premiere Pro Help).*

Managing media in the Project panel: Lesson 4-5

You used naming conventions to make accessing your video and other media assets easier. One additional step will enhance that ease of access: organizing your Project panel.

The Project panel is simply a means to access and organize your assets—video clips, audio files, still images, graphics and sequences. Each listed media asset is a link. The files themselves—the video clips and so on—remain in their file folders.

Importing and logically arranging your assets in the Project panel is simple. It's not much more than adding a few bins, then doing some dragging and dropping.

Adobe Certified Expert exam objective

Given an option from the Project panel, explain the purpose of that option.

In this lesson you will check out some of the Project panel options and then rearrange the clips you have been working with in Lessons 4-1 through 4-4. If you need to start fresh, open Project 4-5.

1 Click the Icon button in the lower-left corner of the Project panel (highlighted in the next figure).

That changes the Project panel display from a list to thumbnails and icons.

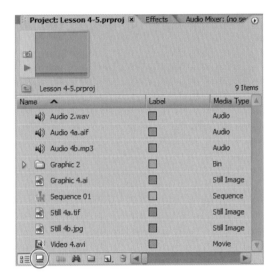

2 Expand the Project panel view by dragging its right edge to the right so you can see all nine items.

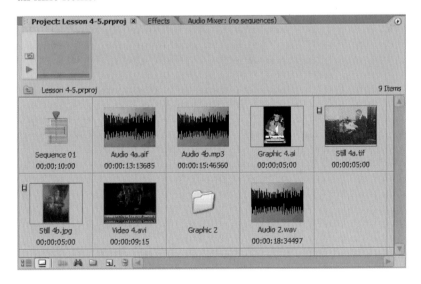

3   Click Audio 4a.aif to select it and then click the Play button next to the Preview screen (highlighted in the next figure) to play the eerie-sounding clip.

You can click any other asset and play it. The Play button will be inactive (grayed-out) for still images and graphics.

4   Click Video 4.avi and drag the slider under the Project Preview screen a few seconds into the clip.

5   Click the Poster Frame button next to the Preview screen to create a new thumbnail image for that clip.

Note: *That new thumbnail shows up immediately in the Project panel. The thumbnail view has an audio display in it indicating this is a video clip with audio.*

6   Double-click the Graphic 2 file folder icon thumbnail to view its five thumbnails—four graphic layers and a sequence.

7 Click the file folder with the up arrow (highlighted in the following figure) to return to the main Project panel view.

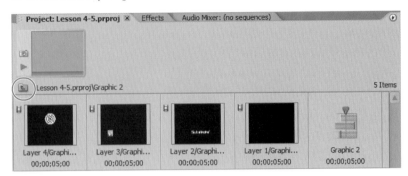

8 Click the Bin button to create a new file folder.

It shows up in the Project panel with its default name—*Bin 02*.

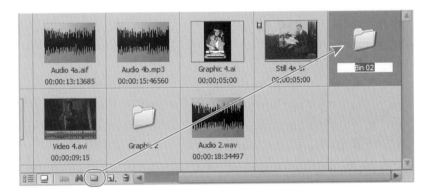

9 Type in *Audio* to replace *Bin 02* and press Enter.

10 Create one more bin and name it *Stills*.

11 Drag and drop the three audio clips onto the Audio file folder thumbnail.

12 Drag and drop the two stills into their folder.

13 Do some housecleaning by dragging the folders and remaining files into a tidy 3x2 grid as shown in the next figure.

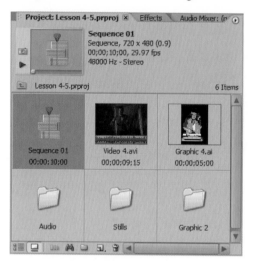

14 Return to the List view by clicking the List button (to the left of the Icon view button).

15 Click somewhere in the Project panel to deselect any bin that might be selected.

Note: You need to do this here so the bin you're about to add won't be a sub-folder inside another folder. There are instances when you might want to use sub-folders to help organize the Project panel.

16 Click the Bin button to create a new bin. Name it *Sequences*.

17 Open the Graphic 2 bin and drag and drop the Graphic 2 Sequence in the Sequences bin.

18 Drag Sequence 01 to that bin as well.

19 Click twice on Name at the top of the file link list in the Project panel to put all the asset links and bins in alphabetical order. Your Project panel should look like the following figure.

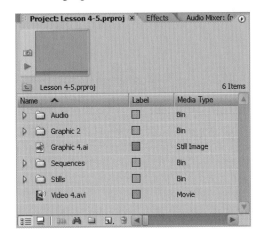

Working with assets in Adobe Bridge: Lesson 4-6

Adobe Bridge simplifies the everyday tasks of asset management by giving you a powerful way to browse and search your digital assets; view and edit metadata (extra file information such as contents, copyright status, origin, and history of documents); and add, rename, move, and delete files and folders.

Right-click an asset in the Project panel and select Reveal in Bridge. That will open Bridge and display the contents of the Lesson 4 folder.

Note: You can also open Bridge by selecting File > Browse. In that case it will open to the main Premiere Pro file folder: Premiere Pro\2.0.

The Adobe Bridge window is made up of several parts:

- **Favorites window**—Lists the folders you want quick access to, including Version Cue, Adobe Stock Photos, Collections, and Bridge Center. It's located on the left side of the Bridge window.

- **Folders panel**—Lists the folder hierarchy to help you navigate to the correct folder. It's located on the left side of the Bridge window along with the Favorites panel.

- **Preview panel**—Displays a thumbnail of the selected file. The panel is located on the left side of the Bridge window.

- **Metadata panel**—Contains metadata—text embedded in the file—for the selected file. Access its tab in the lower left corner of the Bridge interface.

- **Keywords panel**—Helps you organize your images by attaching keywords to them.

- **Content area**—Displays thumbnail previews of the items in the current folder, along with information about those items.

The bottom of the Bridge window displays status information and contains buttons for toggling the display of the panes, a slider for setting the size of thumbnails, and buttons for specifying the type of display in the content window.

Note: When working in Bridge, you'll notice references to Version Cue. Version Cue is a set of features that help manage design workflow and collaboration in the Adobe Creative Suite. The Version Cue features in Bridge are only compatible with files and projects created in Adobe Creative Suite applications: Adobe GoLive CS, Adobe Photoshop CS, Adobe Illustrator CS, and Adobe InDesign CS.

Managing files and folders in Bridge

Bridge lets you easily drag and drop files and move them between folders. You can use standard Windows commands to cut, copy, paste, or delete files. And you can create or delete new folders.

Drag files into Bridge by selecting one or more files on the desktop, in a folder, or in another application that supports drag and drop, and then dragging them into the content area in Bridge. The files are moved from their former folder into the one displayed in Bridge.

You can specify how you want to view files and folders in the content area, such as how big thumbnails should be, whether file information should be displayed, what type of files should be shown, and the order they should appear in.

Follow these steps to get a basic feel for Adobe Bridge:

1   Drag the Thumbnail slider at the bottom of the Bridge window to adjust the size of thumbnails.

2   Click the Video 4.avi thumbnail to select it.

3   Click the Play button in the Preview screen to view this video.

Note: *Bridge can play or display virtually any media asset.*

4   Click the Filmstrip View button in the bottom right corner of Bridge or select View > As Filmstrip to display thumbnails in a scrolling list along with an extra-large thumbnail of the currently selected item.

5   Click the Back button or Forward button directly below the extra large thumbnail to go to the previous or next thumbnail.

Note: You can click the Switch Filmstrip Orientation button (to the right of the Back/ Forward buttons) to change from a horizontal slideshow to a vertical one.

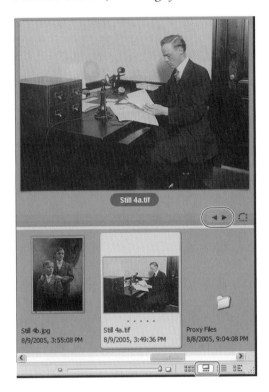

6   Select View > Sort and note the many sorting options.

Note: Selecting Manually will return the thumbnails to the last order in which you dragged the files.

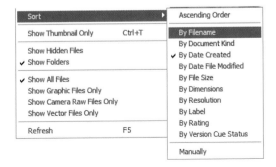

7   Select View > Slideshow to view thumbnails as a slideshow that takes over the entire screen.

This is useful when you want to work with large versions of all the graphics files within a folder. Instructions on how to use the slideshow are displayed on the screen when you choose this command.

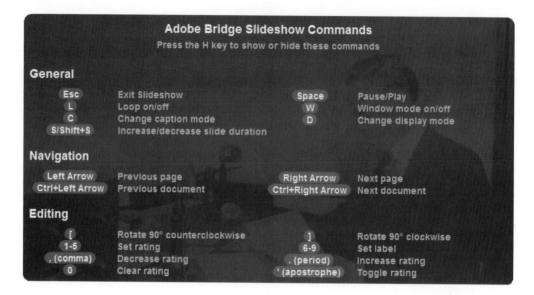

Adobe Bridge Slideshow Commands
Press the H key to show or hide these commands

General

Esc	Exit Slideshow	Space	Pause/Play
L	Loop on/off	W	Window mode on/off
C	Change caption mode	D	Change display mode
S/Shift+S	Increase/decrease slide duration		

Navigation

Left Arrow	Previous page	Right Arrow	Next page
Ctrl+Left Arrow	Previous document	Ctrl+Right Arrow	Next document

Editing

[	Rotate 90° counterclockwise	]	Rotate 90° clockwise
1-5	Set rating	6-9	Set label
, (comma)	Decrease rating	. (period)	Increase rating
0	Clear rating	' (apostrophe)	Toggle rating

Note: There are several other View options. For example, Show All Files displays all files regardless of type—even files Bridge can't open, such as spreadsheets—and Show Graphic Files Only displays only files using a graphic file format.

Using labels, ratings, and keywords to organize files

Labeling files allows you to quickly sort a large group of files. Labels are colors that you assign to individual files or groups of files. You can rate files from 0 to 5 stars. And you can apply keywords to files to help you identify files based on their content. Here's how to do all three tasks:

1   Return to the Thumbnail view by clicking that button at the bottom of the screen.

2   Select the Video 4a and Still 4b files (they should be next to each other in the Thumbnail view).

3   Select Label and choose one of the five colors.

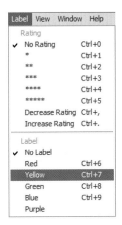

4   An information window about how Bridge will store that label information pops up. Check Don't Show Again and click OK.

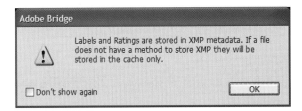

The two files now have a colored oval below their thumbnail images.

Note: *If you don't see any labels it's probably because the thumbnail images are too small. Move the slider on the bottom a bit to the right to enlarge the icons and the labels should display.*

Here are two other Label functions:

• To remove labels from files, select Label > No Label.

• To sort by label color, select View > Sort > By Label.

Using labels to purge assets

Suppose you've just imported a large number of files, and are viewing them in Bridge. As you review each new file, you can assign those you want to keep a green label. After this initial pass, you can use the Unfilter drop-down menu to view and work on just those files you've labeled green. Then you can discard the rest.

5　Click the Graphic 4.ai thumbnail to select it.

6　Click one of the dots representing the number of stars you want to give the file.

Note: *You can remove all stars by clicking to the left of the dots or stars. In addition, select Label and note how you can adjust star ratings via that menu.*

> 💡 **Rate new files to prioritize them**
>
> *Suppose you've just imported a large number of images, and are viewing them in Bridge. As you review each new image, you can rate those in priority from best to worst. After this initial pass, you can view only files you've rated with 4 or 5 stars and work on those.*

7   Click the Keywords tab to open that panel.

8   Open the Fly-out Menu, select New Keyword Set and type in *CIB Lesson 4*.

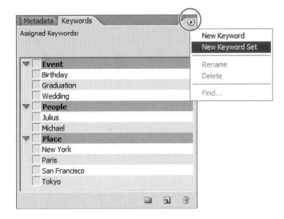

9   Click the newly added CIB Lesson 4 Keyword set to select it.

10   Open the Fly-out Menu again, select New Keyword and type in *Old Photo*.

11   Select the two photos and click the checkbox next to Old Photo in the Keywords panel.

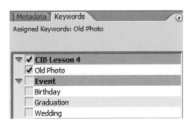

That will pop up an information window letting you know you are applying a keyword to multiple files. Click the Don't Show Again checkbox and click Yes.

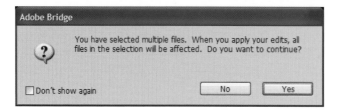

12   Select Edit > Find to open the Find window.

13   Change the Criteria to Keywords, in the Enter Text box type in *Old*, and click Find. That opens a new Find Results window that displays the two photos.

Note: *Take a look at the other Find parameters. This is a very helpful tool.*

Here are some other Keyword functions:

• To remove keywords from a file, select the file, and then click the box (removing the check mark) next to the name of the keyword or keyword set you want to remove.

• To rename a keyword or keyword set, select the keyword or keyword set and choose Rename from the palette menu. Type the new name over the old name in the palette and press Return on your keyboard.

Note: *When you rename a keyword, the keyword's name isn't changed in files that currently contain it. The original name stays in the file.*

• To move a keyword to a different keyword set, drag the keyword into the set you want.

• To delete a keyword, select the keyword by clicking its name, and then click the Delete Keyword button at the bottom of the palette. Or choose Delete from the palette menu.

Note: *Keywords that you get from other users appear in the Other Keywords category until you categorize them.*

Adding and editing metadata

Depending on the selected file, the following types of metadata appear in Bridge's Metadata palette:

• **File Properties**—Describes the characteristics of the file, including the size, creation date, and modification date.

• **IPTC Core**—Information about the file such as: creator, address, description, date created, captions and copyright information.

• **Camera Data**—Displays information assigned by digital cameras with an EXIF (Exchangeable Image File Format) feature. EXIF information includes the camera make/model, aperture and shutter speed settings when the picture was taken, and the date.

• **GPS**— Displays navigational information from cameras equipped with global positioning systems.

To edit metadata, select a file, click next to the metadata field you want to change and type in the information. When done, click the Apply button in the lower-right corner of the Metadata panel.

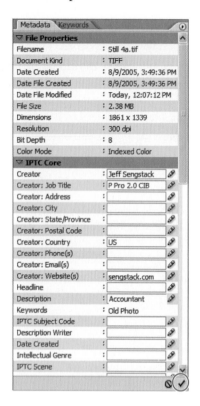

Review

▶ **Review questions**

1   What's the principal difference between Project Settings and Preferences?

2   What's the basic rule of thumb when selecting a Project Setting preset?

3   Describe two ways to open the Project panel Import window.

4   Premiere Pro handles Adobe Photoshop and Illustrator layered graphic files differently. Explain the differences.

5   What's the advantage of importing high-resolution photos?

6   In Bridge, how do you add a color label to a file, and why would you use label colors?

▶ **Review answers**

1   Project Settings apply to the current project and you select them before opening the project. They primarily refer to the specifications of your source media. Preferences apply to any project and you can change them at any time. They have more to do with overall functionality of your workspace.

2   Select a Preset that matches your source media. For most users that would be DV-NTSC Standard 48 kHz.

3   Select File > Import or double-click in an empty space in the Project panel.

4   Premiere Pro lets you import Photoshop files in one of three ways: as a sequence with individual layers on separate video tracks, on an individual-layer basis, or as a merged file. Premiere imports Illustrator layered graphics only as merged files. It rasterizes and anti-aliases Illustrator's vector-based art.

5   You can pan and zoom in on them and maintain a sharp-looking image. To see images at their full resolution, right-click on them in the Timeline and uncheck Scale to Frame Size.

6   Click a file, select Label and choose a color. This can come in handy when you are reviewing a lot of media and want to put them in categories.

storyboard

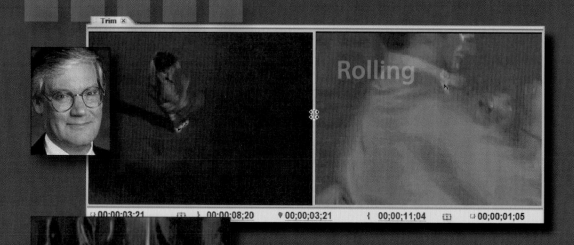

00;00;03;21   00;00;08;20   00;00;03;21   00;00;11;04   00;00;01;05

Rolling

Overlay

Extract

Video 5e.avi
00;00;02;19

Video 5g.avi
00;00;02;20

Video 5f.avi
00;00;02;10

Timeline: Lesson 5-1

00;00;00;00

:00;00

Snap

You will see very few transitions like dissolves or wipes in the video-editing world. Watch any TV news program and virtually every edit in every story is a cut edit with no transitions. There is an art to creating cuts-only videos, and Premiere Pro 2.0 gives you a full palette of cut edit tools and techniques.

5 | Creating Cuts-only Videos

Topics covered in this lesson:

- Using a storyboard to build a rough cut.
- Editing clips on the Timeline.
- Moving clips to, from and within the Timeline.
- Working with Source Monitor editing tools.
- Adjusting clips in the Trim panel.
- Using other editing tools.
- Story creation tips from NBC-TV correspondent Bob Dotson.

Getting started

You create a video by first laying down a cuts-only version. Later, you can apply transitions, effects, titles, motion and work on compositing. Whether or not you use those extra effects, there is a real art to building a cuts-only video. You want to create a logical flow to your clips, make matching edits, and avoid jump cuts.

Premiere Pro offers several means to those ends. Depending on your circumstances you might work in the Trim panel, use the Ripple Edit tool, or move clips on the Timeline using keyboard modifiers. I will show you all those techniques in this lesson.

I present a lot of techniques here. For instance, I cover four of the 27 Adobe Certified Expert Exam objectives in this lesson. By its conclusion you will have sampled the fundamentals of video editing. But to become truly proficient at the cuts-only part of non-linear video editing, you need to practice. I encourage you to experiment, to try things on your own, and use the techniques presented in this lesson over and over.

Using a storyboard to build a rough cut: Lesson 5-1

You've seen storyboards. Film directors and animators frequently use walls of photos and sketches to visualize story flow and camera angles.

Storyboards also help after the fact. In the case of Premiere Pro, you can arrange clip thumbnails in the Project panel to get a basic feel for how your finished video will work. Then you can move all those clips to the Timeline for more precise editing.

This approach can come in handy by revealing gaps in your story—places that need fleshing out with more video or graphics. It's also a way to note redundancy and a way to quickly place a whole bunch of ordered clips on a sequence. When confronted with a Project panel loaded with clips, storyboards can help you see the big picture.

After creating your storyboard, you can place several clips in a sequence on the Timeline at one time. This bypasses two other workflows: dragging clips from the Project panel to the Timeline, and using the Source Monitor's editing tools to drop clips on a sequence. I will cover those methods later in this lesson.

Before moving on to step 1, play the Lesson 5 Intro video.

1   Open Premiere Pro.

2   Click Open Project, navigate to the Lesson 5 folder and double-click Lesson 5-1.prproj.

Note: This is a DV-NTSC Standard 48kHz project.

3   Double-click on an empty space in the Project panel (or select File > Import) and import all the assets (except the project files) from the Lesson 5 folder: Audio 5a.wav, Lesson 5 Finish.wmv, and 14 video clips—Video 5a.avi-Video 5n.avi.

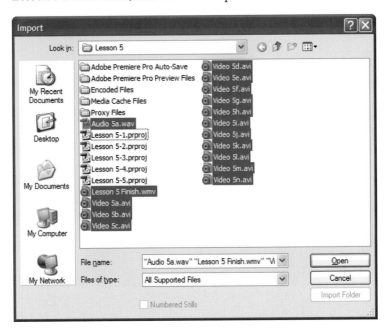

4   Double-click Lesson 5 Finish.wmv in the Project panel to put it in the Source Monitor. Play it.

Note: *This video shows how your project will look and sound by the end of Lesson 5-2 (if you do the brief extra credit work). It's a compressed WMV—Windows Media Video—file. It's a bit blurry and intended to run only in Premiere Pro's Program Monitor, or in Windows Media Player running in less than a full screen mode.*

5 Click the Bin button in the Project panel (keyboard shortcut: Ctrl+/) and name the new bin *Storyboard*.

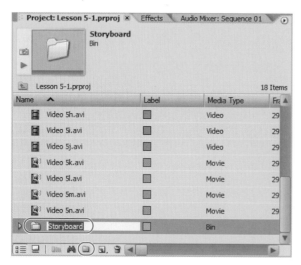

6   Use marquee select or Shift+click to select 10 video clips—Video 5a–Video 5j.

7   Right-click on one of the selected clips (you need to click on the clip name or you will deselect all the clips) to bring up the context menu, and select Copy.

Note: Selecting Copy when you've highlighted multiple clips will copy the entire collection of clips.

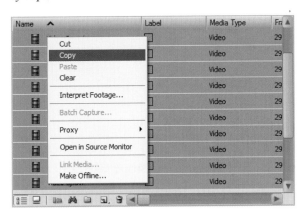

8   Right-click on the Storyboard bin and select Paste.

All 10 video files will show up under the Storyboard bin. They will remain in the main Project panel as well.

Note: I had you Copy/Paste the video files into the separate Storyboard bin because you will delete some of them. In this way, you delete them from the Storyboard bin but not from the Project panel.

9   Ctrl+click on the Project panel and drag it out of its frame to create a floating window.

10   Click the Icon button to switch to Icon view.

Note: Even though the Storyboard video files were highlighted, shifting to Icon view returns you to the top-level Project panel view.

11   Double-click the Storyboard file folder thumbnail to display its 10 videos.

12 Click the Fly-out Menu and select Thumbnails > Large.

13 Expand your Project panel view to display all ten clips.

As shown in the next figure, you'll end up with a 3x4 grid (depending on the size of your workspace and other factors, it could be a different shape, like 2x5).

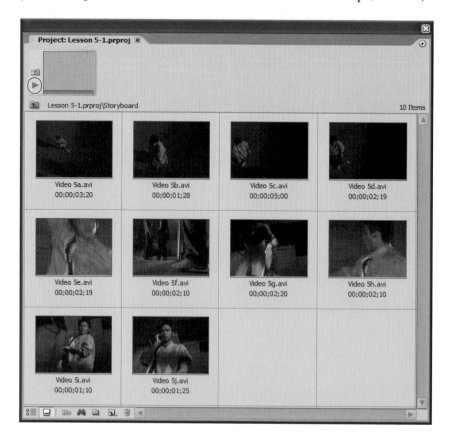

Arranging your storyboard

The purpose now is to arrange the thumbnails into a logical order. Before I tell you what I think that order should be, do the steps below to see what you can come up with. Keep in mind that you will trim some clips later to make the edits work more smoothly.

View each clip in the Preview monitor by clicking each clip to select it and then clicking the Preview monitor Play button (highlighted in the previous figure).

Decide which clips do not work in this sequence and settle on an order for the remaining clips. Take some time working on this before continuing with this lesson. Selecting an order for clips is something you will do time after time.

Note: Some of the videos are a little dark and can be hard to view critically in the Project panel Preview Monitor. In those cases, double-click on a clip and view it in the Source Monitor.

Here's the order that I think works well: Video 5f, 5e, 5c, 5h, 5i, 5b, and 5g. I think the following clips don't work in this sequence: Video 5a (one-handed break dance move doesn't match other clips), 5d (doesn't match other spinning moves) and 5j (hand by ear doesn't match other shots).

Here's how to create my recommended sequence:

1 Select Video 5a, 5d, and 5j (use the Ctrl+click selection method) and press the Delete key (or right-click and select Cut) to remove them from the Storyboard bin. They remain in the top-level view of the Project panel.

 No word wrap

The Project panel Icon view does not have the equivalent of Word Wrap. Removing clips leaves gaps in the Icon view. Newly added clips generally run past the right side of the panel, and when you resize the panel, the clips don't move to accommodate the change. To remedy these issues, open the Fly-out Menu and select Clean Up.

2   Drag the remaining clips to put them into this order: Video 5f, 5e, 5c, 5h, 5i, 5b, and 5g.

To move a clip, simply drag it to a new location. The cursor will change to this (🖟) and a black vertical line indicates the new placement location'

Note: As you drag clips, you will leave gaps. Use Clean Up to remove those gaps.

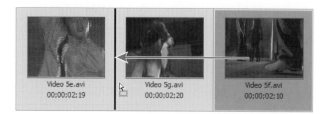

Your Storyboard should look like the next figure.

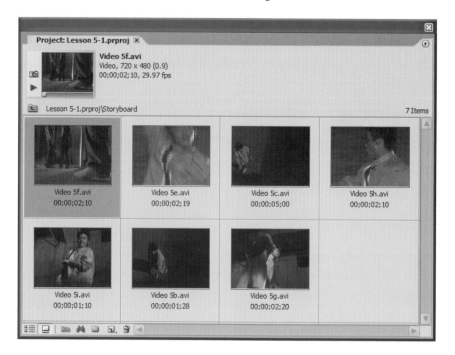

Automating your storyboard to a sequence

Now you're going to move your storyboard clips to the Timeline, placing them there contiguously, in sequential order. Premiere Pro calls this *Automate to Sequence*. Here's how you do it:

1 Make sure the CTI is at the beginning of the Timeline. Automate to Sequence places the clips starting at the CTI location.

2 Select Edit > Select All to highlight all the clips (you can also marquee select or use the Shift+click method).

3 Click the Automate to Sequence button in the lower-left corner of the Project panel. I highlighted it in the next figure.

Note: You can also open the Fly-out Menu and select Automate to Sequence.

In the newly opened Automate to Sequence dialog box you face several options (see figure on next page):

• **Ordering**—Sort Order puts clips on a sequence in the order you established in the Storyboard. Selection Order places them in the order you selected them if you Ctrl+clicked on individual clips.

• **Placement**—Places your clips sequentially on the Timeline as opposed to at unnumbered markers (something we haven't covered).

• **Method**—The choices are Insert or Overlay. I discuss both concepts later in this lesson. Because here you are placing the clips on an empty sequence, both methods will do the same thing.

• **Clip Overlap**—Overlap presumes that you'll put a transition such as a cross-dissolve between all clips. The goal in this lesson is to create a cuts-only video; that is, a video with no transitions. Set Clip Overlap to zero.

• **Apply Default Audio/Video Transition**—Because you'll opt for no transitions, uncheck these boxes.

• **Ignore Audio/Video**—These clips have no audio so these options are inactive.

4   Click OK. This places your clips in order on the sequence in the Timeline.

5   Drag the Project panel out of the way and play the Timeline by clicking inside the Timeline to activate it and pressing the space bar.

Note: View this sequence critically. Several edits are jump cuts or feel awkward. Some clips are too long. Your task in the next two lessons is to fix those flaws.

Editing clips on the Timeline: Lesson 5-2

You will use a variety of editing tools to improve this storyboard rough cut:

- Trim a clip by dragging its end.
- Ripple Delete a gap between clips.
- Ripple Edit clips to save a step.

Adobe Certified Expert exam objective

Given an option on the Timeline, explain the purpose of the option and when or how to use that option.

You can start where you left off in Lesson 5-1 or start fresh by opening Lesson 5-2.prproj from the Lesson 5 folder.

Trimming a clip

1 Select Window > Workspace > P Pro 2.0 CIB Workspace.

That puts the Project panel back in its regular spot next to the Effects and Audio Mixer panels.

Note: If you don't see the P Pro 2.0 CIB Workspace, you probably did not install it or put it in the correct file folder. Copy P Pro 2 CIB Workspace.layout from the P Pro 2.0 CIB Assets folder on the DVD into the Premiere Pro 2.0 Layouts folder on your hard drive at: My Documents\Adobe\Premiere Pro\2.0\Layouts.

2 Click the List button in the Project panel (lower left corner) to switch back to that mode.

3 Click in the Timeline to select it and press the backslash key (\) to expand the view of the clips to full Timeline width.

4 Expand that view a bit more by pressing the equal (=) key twice.

This expands the width of the clips to help you make a more accurate edit. Your Timeline should look like the next figure.

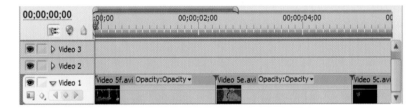

5 Hover the cursor over the left side of the second clip until you see the right-facing Trim bracket (⊕) highlighted in the next figure.

Note: As you move your cursor around you might notice it changes into a Pen Keyframe tool ( ) That happens when you hover the cursor over the thin yellow Opacity line. You'll work with the Opacity effect in upcoming lessons on compositing.

6 Drag the bracket to the right 14 frames (almost a half-second).

Use the timecode pop-up display in the Timeline and the Program Monitor display for reference. Release the mouse button. The purpose is to remove the first few frames where the dancer's arm is above his head.

Note: This trim edit will leave a gap between the two clips on the Timeline. You'll remove it later.

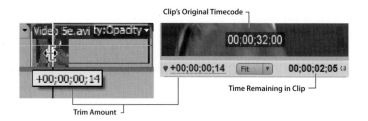

Step farther back using History

You will make multiple edits and therefore, a few mistakes. You know you can back up, one step at a time by pressing Ctrl+Z (or selecting Edit > Undo). You can also use the History panel to move back several steps at once—even as far back as the original Automate to Sequence.

7 Press the minus key (-) to shrink the view in the Timeline slightly, so you can see the entire third clip.

8 Move the CTI to 00;00;08;15 (read the time in the Program Monitor). That's just as the dancer begins his spin move.

9 Drag the right side of the third clip to the left until it reaches the CTI line.

That vertical black line you saw in Lesson 2 appears and the edit *snaps* to that point (see *Snap Feature* sidebar). Release the mouse button.

Snap feature

Premiere Pro has a tremendously useful attribute called Snap. It's a default setting, and in only a few instances will you want to deselect it. With Snap on, as you drag a clip toward another clip, it'll jump to the edge of the adjacent clip to make a clean, unbroken edit. With Snap turned off, you'd have to slide the new clip very carefully next to the other clip to ensure there is no gap.

Snap is also useful when making precise edits. Using the Selection tool (in its trim mode) to trim a clip is a bit clumsy, as you might have noted in Step 6 of this mini-lesson. Snap lets you make it frame-specific.

Locate the frame you want to edit to by dragging the CTI through your sequence to that frame's location (use the Right and Left Arrow Keys to move to the specific frame). Use the Selection tool and drag the edge of the clip toward the CTI line. When it gets near the line, it will snap to the CTI, and you'll have made a frame-specific edit. You can use this technique in all sorts of circumstances.

If you want to toggle the Snap function off or on, click the Snap button in the top left corner of the Timeline (highlighted in the next figure).

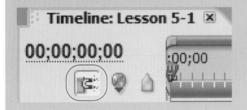

Closing the gaps—Ripple Delete

Trimming the two clips left two gaps in the sequence. You'll remove them using Ripple Delete.

1   Right-click the gap between the first and second clips and select Ripple Delete (your only "choice").

Ripple Delete removes the gap by sliding all the material after the gap to the left.

2   Repeat this for the gap between the third and fourth clips.

Note: You can also Ripple Delete a clip. Simply right-click on the clip and select Ripple Delete from the context menu.

Using the Ripple Edit tool

A way to avoid creating those gaps in the first place is to use the Ripple Edit tool (highlighted in the next figure). It's one of the eleven tools in the Tools panel.

Use the Ripple Edit tool to trim a clip in the same way you used the Selection Trim tool. The two differences are that the Ripple Edit tool does not leave a gap on the sequence and the display in the Program Monitor gives a clearer representation of how the edit will work.

When you use the Ripple Edit tool to lengthen or shorten a clip, your action ripples through the sequence. That is, all clips after that edit slide to the left to fill the gap, or slide to the right accommodate a longer clip.

3   Click the Ripple Edit tool (keyboard shortcut: B).

4   Hover it over the left edge of the fourth clip until it turns into a large, right-facing square bracket (⬥).

Note: Ripple Edit's cursor is larger than the Selection tool's Trim cursor.

5 Click and drag it to the right about eight frames.

Watch the moving edit position on the right half of the Program Monitor. Your goal is to move that clip until the dancer's head position on the right matches its position at the end of the previous clip (on the left).

6 Release the mouse button to complete the edit. The remaining part of the clip moves left to fill the gap, and slides the clips to its right over with it. Play that portion of the sequence to see if the edit works smoothly.

7 Move the CTI to about 10;10 (when the dancer's left shoulder is pointing toward the camera).

8 Use Ripple Edit to drag the left edge of the fifth clip to the right until it snaps to the CTI.

Once again, placing the CTI at your edit point with Snap turned on makes it easy to make accurate edits.

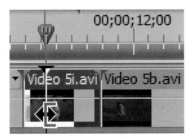

Take a look at the Program monitor and note that the dancer's arms are close to the same position in both frames—a matching edit.

9 Do one more Ripple Edit at 12;11.

Position the CTI there and drag the left edge of the sixth clip to the right until it snaps to the CTI.

10 View your sequence. It should flow fairly smoothly.

Complete the video: Extra credit exercise

Completing the work to match the Lesson 5 Finish.wmv video will take a few more steps that fall outside cuts-only editing. Use the figure of the completed sequence that follows these steps as a reference.

1 Drag Audio 5a.wav to the beginning of the Audio 1 track.

2 Move the CTI to 13;15.

3 Select the Razor tool (keyboard shortcut: C) and click on the CTI line to cut the clip.

4 Select the Rate Stretch tool (X) and drag the right end of the last clip to about a second past the end of the audio.

5 Move the CTI to 14;15 (just as the audio fades), select the Razor tool and do a Razor edit of the video clip there.

6 Right-click on that last video clip segment, select Frame Hold > Hold On > InPoint, and click OK.

7 Drag the Cross Dissolve from the Effects panel > Video Transitions > Dissolve bin to the end of the last video clip.

8 Play your video.

Moving clips to, from and within the Timeline: Lesson 5-3

One of the beauties of Premiere Pro is how easy it is to add clips anywhere in the project, move them around, and remove them altogether.

> ### Adobe Certified Expert exam objective
>
> Given a scenario, add clips to the Timeline.

There are two ways to place a clip in the Timeline (whether you drag it from the Project panel or from another location on the Timeline):

- **Overlay**—The newly placed clip and its audio replace what was on the sequence.

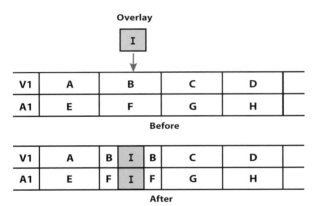

- **Insert**—The first frame of the newly placed clip cuts the current clip, and without covering up anything, slides the cut segment and all clips after it to the right. This requires holding down the Ctrl key—a *keyboard modifier*.

And there are two ways to move a clip from a location on the Timeline:

- **Lift**—Leaves a gap where the clip used to be.

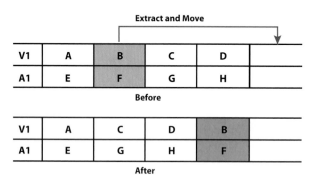

- **Extract**—Works like a Ripple Edit in that other clips move over to fill the gap. This move requires a keyboard modifier—holding down the Ctrl key *before* clicking on the clip to be removed.

Adding and moving clips on the Timeline

You'll start by setting up a new sequence with three clips on it.

1   Continue with Lesson 5-2 or open Lesson 5-3.

2   Select File > New > Sequence.

Note: The New Sequence menu displays the default values for numbers and types of tracks from the Project Settings Default Sequence submenu.

3   Name the Sequence Lesson 5-3 and click OK.

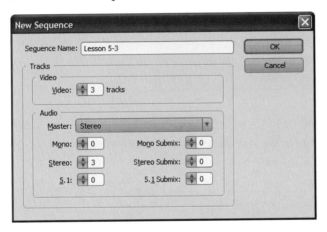

4   Select three video clips—Video 5k-Video 5m—and drag them to the newly created Sequence 5-3 in the Timeline.

5   Press backslash (\) to expand the view.

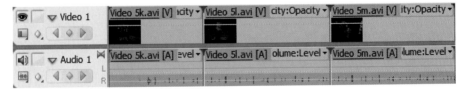

Overlay edit example

6   Drag Video 5n from the Project panel to the Timeline so its first frame is approximately in the middle of the first clip.

Note: the Program Monitor shows two images. The left view is the new out-point of the first clip that will precede the new clip. The right view is the new in-point of the next clip that will follow the newly placed clip.

7   Drop Video 5n on the sequence.

That is an Overlay edit. It covers the video and audio that was there before. It does not change the length of the sequence.

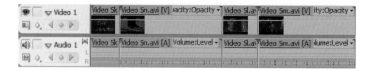

Insert edit example

8   Press Ctrl+Z to undo that edit.

9   Drag Video 5n to the same place, but this time hold down the Ctrl key *before releasing* the mouse button.

Video 5n will slice the first clip in two, sliding the second half of the first clip and all subsequent clips to the right and inserting Video 5n on the Timeline.

That is an Insert edit. Your sequence will now be longer.

Note: As you hold Video 5n over the first clip in the sequence, press and release the Ctrl key and note that the monitor display switches back and forth. It shows only one image for an insert edit—where you will cut clip one—and two images for an overlay—the new out-point for clip one and the new in-point for clip two.

Lift and Move edit example

10 Press Ctrl+Z to undo that edit.

11 Drag Video 5n from the Project panel to the end of the third clip to create a four-clip sequence: Video 5k-Video 5n. Press the backslash key (\) to see all the clips.

12 Drag the second clip to the end of the four clips on the Timeline.

That is a Lift and Move. There will be a gap where the second clip used to be, and the end of the sequence will extend beyond its former length.

Note: No keyboard modifier is needed as you place the clip at the end of the sequence since nothing comes after it.

Extract and Move edit example

13 Press Ctrl+Z to return to the original position.

14 Press the Ctrl key and then click and drag the second clip to the end of the sequence.

This is an Extract and Move. Because you held down the Ctrl key—a keyboard modifier—while removing the clip from its former position, you created the equivalent of a Ripple Delete. The sequence length will not change. The clip order will be Video 5k, 5m, 5n, and 5l.

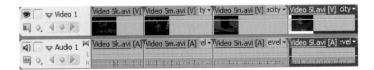

Extract and Overlay edit example

15 Press Ctrl+Z to return to the original position.

16 Click the S key to turn off the Snap feature (or click the Snap button in the upper left corner of the Timeline).

17 Press the Ctrl key and then click and drag the first clip to the center of the third clip, *release* the Ctrl key, and then drop the clip there.

That is an Extract and Overlay. Clips slide over to fill the gap left by the removed first clip (the Ctrl key *modifier* turned what would have been a Lift into an Extract). The sequence length will be shorter.

Note: If you had not used the Ctrl keyboard modifier when removing the clip from its original location, that would have left a gap there—a Lift and Overlay edit.

Extract and Insert edit example

18 Press Ctrl+Z to return to the original position.

19 Press the Ctrl key and then click and drag the first clip to the center of the third clip. Continue holding down the Ctrl key and drop the clip there.

That is an Extract and Insert. Clips slide over to fill the gap left by the removed first clip and the clips after the insert edit point slide to the right. The sequence length remains unchanged.

💡 **Modifier key feedback**

As you drag a clip from the Project panel to a sequence, or from one place on a sequence track to another, Premiere Pro displays a text message at the bottom of the user interface. If you are not using Ctrl, it'll say "Drop in Track to Overwrite. Use Ctrl to enable insert." Press Ctrl and Premiere Pro will let you know that you can use Alt to "limit the tracks that shift." I cover the Alt key modifier later in the book. Its primary use is to unlink a video clip from its associated audio clip so you can move them separately. You did a variation of that in Lesson 2.

Working with Source Monitor editing tools: Lesson 5-4

It's helpful to trim clips before moving them from the Project panel (or Storyboard) to the Timeline. Do that by double-clicking a file name or thumbnail to display it to the Source Monitor and trim it there.

> **Adobe Certified Expert exam objective**
>
> *Given an option in the Monitor panel, explain the purpose of the option or when to use that option.*

1   Continue with Lesson 5-3 or open Lesson 5-4.

2   Drag a marquee around all four clips in the Lesson 5-3 sequence in the Timeline and press Delete.

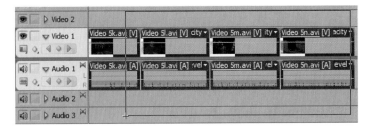

💡 **Selecting multiple clips**

Another way to select more than one clip in the Timeline is to Shift+click on clips, one at a time. This works the same way as the standard Windows Ctrl+click method for selecting a group of files one file at a time.

3   Double-click Video 5k to open it in the Source Monitor.

Note: You also can drag the clip from the Project panel and drop it on the Source Monitor.

4   Move the Source Monitor's CTI to 02;13, just before the dancer slams his foot to the floor. That's where you want this clip to start.

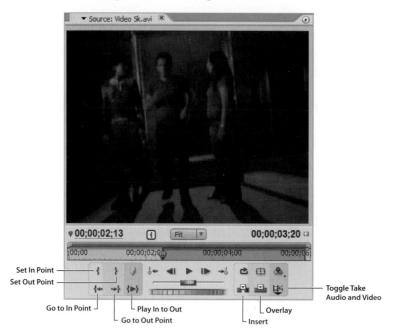

Source Monitor editing tools.

5   Click the Set In Point button.

Note: The Set In Point button is the same as that used in the Capture panel. It also has the same keyboard shortcut: I.

6   Play the clip, listen for a logical out-point and place the Source Monitor's CTI there. I would select 06;02.

> **Move to exact timecode**
>
> *Rather than slide to a location in the clip, you can type in a timecode and go there directly. In this case, click on the blue timecode (on the left side of the Source Monitor), type in 6;02 and press Enter.*

7   Click the Set Out Point button.

8   Navigate back and forth between the in- and out-points by clicking the Go to In Point (keyboard shortcut: Q) and Go to Out Point (V). And play that entire segment by clicking the Play In to Out button.

9   Move the Timeline CTI to the beginning of the sequence.

10   Check to see that the Video 1 and Audio 1 track headers (highlighted in the next figure) are selected—*targeted* in Premiere Pro parlance. If not, click on one or both to highlight them (their corners also become rounded).

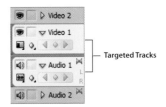

11   Click the Source Monitor Insert button to place this clip at the CTI line in the empty Lesson 5-3 Sequence.

Note: Clicking either Insert or Overlay will place the clip at the Timeline CTI.

12   Double-click Video 5l to put that clip in the Source monitor.

13   Twirl down the disclosure triangle at the top of the Source Monitor.

All clips viewed in the Source Monitor show up in this list. You can access them here and remove all or one of them at a time by selecting Close All or Close.

14   Play Video 5l in the Source Monitor and listen for edit points—the beginning or end of a rhythmic phrase. I suggest you put the In-point at 09;20 and the Out-point at 13;10.

15   See that the Timeline CTI is at the end of the first clip (it goes there automatically after an Insert of Overlay edit) and click the Insert button.

Play the Timeline to see how that edit works.

16 Use the Source Monitor to create in- and out-points for Video 5m. I suggest 16;27 and 20;15 (one frame shy of the entire clip).

17 Place the Timeline CTI between the first and second clips (use the Page Up key).

18 Click the Insert button.

That does a standard Insert edit. It places the new clip at the CTI and shoves the previous clip to its right farther down the sequence to make room.

19 Use the Source Monitor to create in- and out-points for Video 5n. I suggest 23;28 and 27;14 (the entire clip).

20 Place the Timeline CTI between the second and third clips.

21 Click the Toggle Take Audio and Video button until you see the filmstrip button (). You will lay down video-only without changing the existing audio.

22 Click the *Overlay* button.

That covers the video portion of the previously placed third clip with this new clip but does not change the audio. Play the sequence to see how the edit works.

Adjusting clips in the Trim panel: Lesson 5-5

The Trim panel is a very useful tool. You used it in Lesson 2 to do some quick Ripple Edits. It also performs a so-called Rolling Edit. Its value is its large preview monitors, precise controls and informative timecode displays.

> ### 💡 Rolling and Rippling Edit behaviors
>
> *You apply a Ripple Edit to only one clip. It changes the length of your project as the rest of the project slides over to accommodate the change. A Rolling Edit does not change the length of your project. It takes place at an edit point between two clips: shortening one and lengthening the other.*

1 Continue with Lesson 5-4 or open Lesson 5-5.

2 Marquee select the clips in the Lesson 5-3 Sequence and press Delete.

3 Drag Video 5c and Video 5h to the Lesson 5-3 Sequence in the Timeline. You worked with these clips in the Storyboard mini-lessons.

4 Place the CTI at the edit point between the two clips.

5   Click the Trim button (⊞—shortcut: Ctrl+T) in the lower right corner of the Program Monitor.

This opens the Trim panel.

6   Hover the cursor over the left preview screen until it turns into a left-facing Ripple Edit cursor (⬌).

7   Trim the right edge of clip (the out-point) by dragging it left to about one second (use the Out Shift timecode below the center of the left screen).

8   Use the same method to trim the right clip's in-point to the right to about one second (use the In Shift timecode beneath the center of the right screen—highlighted in the figure on the next page).

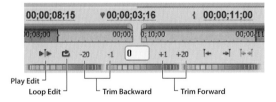

Trim panel editing tools.

9   Click the precision trimming tools—the –1 and +1 numbers (highlighted in the previous figure)—to trim or lengthen the clips a frame at a time until you have matched the position of the dancer in both preview screens. I trimmed 1;04 from the left clip and 0;24 from the right.

Note: Click in the left or right preview screen to make it active (so the precise trim tools apply to it). You can tell which preview screen is active by the thin blue line beneath it.

10   Click Play Edit to review your work.

11   Hover the cursor between the two preview screens. It will turn into a Rolling Edit tool ⚏ (highlighted in the next figure).

12   Drag it left and right to change the out- and in-points of the left and right clips respectively. Notice how both clips move and the dancer's motions remain matched.

13   See if you can find a better edit point. I ended up by trimming 1;02 from the left and 0;26 from the right.

14   Click Play Edit.

You might notice that you just gave the dancer one extra spin.

15   Close the Trim panel by clicking the little 'x' in its corner.

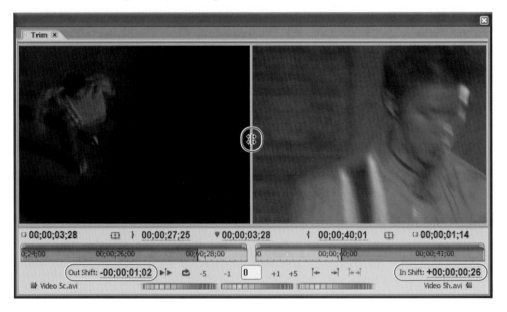

Using other editing tools

The Tools panel has lost weight in Premiere Pro. Previous versions of Premiere packed 18 tools into an even smaller space than the current Tools panel. Premiere Pro has only 11. The reason: context-sensitive tools. In particular the Selection tool changes to other tools depending on its location in the Timeline and elsewhere.

Adobe Certified Expert exam objective

Given an editing tool, explain the purpose of the editing tool.

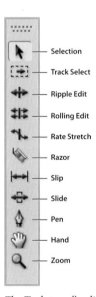

The Tools panel's editing tools.

Here's a brief rundown of all 11 tools:

- **Selection** (keyboard shortcut: V) ▷—Multipurpose, all-around aide. You use it frequently to drag, drop, select and trim clips.

- **Track Select** (M) ⊞—Not to be confused with the Selection tool, the Track Select tool enables you to select all clips to the right of wherever you position it on a video or audio track. You can Shift+click to select other tracks. After they've been selected, you can slide them, delete them, cut/paste them, or copy/paste them.

- **Ripple Edit** (B) ◂▸ —You've worked with this many times already. A Ripple Edit trims a clip and shifts subsequent clips in the track by the amount you trimmed.

- **Rolling Edit** (N) ⁍ —A Rolling Edit trims adjacent out- and in-points simultaneously and by the same number of frames. This effectively moves the edit point between clips, preserving other clips' positions in time and maintaining the total duration of the sequence. You just did this in the Trim panel.

- **Rate Stretch** (X) ⤚ —You used Rate Stretch in Lesson 2. You can stretch or shrink a clip, putting it in slow motion or speeding up the action.

- **Razor** (C) ◆—Razor slices a clip or clips in two. It can be useful when you want to use different effects that can't both be applied to a single clip, such as different speed settings. You used it in the extra credit section of Lesson 5-2.

- **Slip** (U) ⤙⤚—By dragging with the Slip tool, you can change a clip's starting and ending frames without changing its duration or affecting adjacent clips.

- **Slide** (Y) ⬌ —A Slide edit shifts a clip along the Timeline while trimming adjacent clips to compensate for the move. As you drag a clip left or right with the Slide tool, the out-point of the preceding clip and the in-point of the following clip are trimmed by the number of frames you move the clip. The clip's in- and out-points (and hence, its duration) remain unchanged. I cover this later in the book, along with the Slip tool.

- **Pen** (P) ✎—Use this to add, select, move, delete, or adjust keyframes on a sequence as well as create and adjust curves in the Titler, Effect Controls panel and Program Monitor. You use the keyframes to change audio volume levels and panning, to alter clip opacity, and to change video and audio effects over time.

- **Hand** (H) ✋—Use the Hand tool to move an entire sequence by grabbing a clip and sliding it and the rest of the sequence to one side. It works the same as moving the scrollbar at the bottom of the Timeline.

- **Zoom** (Z) ⚲ —This works like the Zoom In and Zoom Out buttons in the lower-left corner of the Timeline and the Viewing Area Bar at the top of the sequence above the Time Ruler. Default is Zoom In (⚲). Hold down Alt to change that to Zoom Out (⚲). When you want to expand the view of a set of clips in the sequence, click and drag the Zoom tool around those clips.

Bob Dotson, NBC-TV reporter.

▶ **STORY CREATION TIPS FROM NBC-TV'S BOB DOTSON**

NBC-TV Today Show correspondent Bob Dotson is, I think, the best human-interest feature-story TV reporter.

Although you probably aren't a TV newsperson, you'll likely create human-interest stories. If there's a storyteller out there you should emulate, he's the one. During my TV reporting days I tried to watch all his stories, and when a station I worked for offered me the chance to attend one of his seminars, I jumped at it.

I've reproduced my notes, with his approval, here. I took many things away from his class. Three points stand out:

• Give viewers a reason to remember the story.

• When interviewing people, try not to ask questions. Merely make observations. That loosens people up, letting them reveal their emotional, human side to you.

• Make sure that you get a closing shot. Most video producers look for dramatic opening shots or sequences (and that's still a good thing), but your viewers are more likely to remember the closing shot.

▶ **Bob Dotson Storyteller's Checklist**

Dotson has prepared his list with TV news reporters in mind, but his tips apply to professional, corporate, and home video producers as well:

• Always remember that the reporter is not the story.

• Decide early on what you want the audience to take away from the story—the commitment. Use that commitment to guide your story creation and use your images to prove that commitment visually.

• Write your pictures first. Give them a strong lead, preferably visual, that instantly telegraphs the story to come.

• The main body of the story should usually be no more than three to five main points, which you prove visually after you've identified them.

• Create a strong close that you can't top, something you build toward throughout the story. Ideally, the ending is also visual.

• Write loose. Be hard on yourself as a writer. Say nothing in the script that your viewers would already know or that the visuals say more eloquently.

• Throughout the story, build your report around sequences—two or three shots of matched action.

• Allow for moments of silence. Stop writing occasionally and let two or three seconds or more of compelling action occur without voiceover. For a writer, nothing is more difficult to write than silence. For viewers, sometimes nothing is more eloquent.

• Use strong natural sound to heighten realism, authenticity, believability and to heighten the viewer's sense of vicarious participation in the events you're showing. Some reports merely enable you to watch what happened. The best reports make it possible for you to experience what happened.

• Tell your story through people. People sell your story. Try to find strong central characters engaged in compelling action that is visual or picturesque.

• Build in surprises to sustain viewer involvement. Surprises help viewers feel something about the story; surprises lure uninterested viewers to the screen. Surprises can be visual, wild sounds, short bites, or poetic script. Surprises are little moments of drama.

• Short sound bites prove the story you are showing. Don't use sound bites as substitutes for more effective storytelling.

• Address the larger issue. "A trailer home burned down." Such a story fails to meet the "so what?" test. "The trailer home burned down because the walls are full of flammable insulation" describes the larger issue and meets the "so what?" test.

• Finally, make your story memorable. Can your viewers feel something about the story and its subjects? If feeling is present, the story will be memorable. It will stick in the viewer's minds.

Review

▶ **Review questions**

1   How can storyboards help?

2   What's the difference between a Trim and a Ripple Edit?

3   You want to drag a clip from the Project panel and place it between two clips in a sequence without covering them up. How do you do that?

4   How do you move a clip from one position on a sequence to another without covering up other clips and at the same time automatically filling the gap left by the removed clip?

5   How do you use the Source Monitor to do an Overlay, video-only edit?

6   How can the Trim panel's Rolling Edit tool help you?

7   What is the single most important concept in Bob Dotson's Storyteller's Checklist?

▶ **Review answers**

1   They can give you an overall feel for the flow of your project, reveal gaps, help you weed out weaker shots, and avoid redundancy.

2   Trims leave gaps where the trimmed video used to be (of if you lengthen a clip using the Trim tool, they cover that portion of the next clip). Ripple Edits automatically fill gaps by sliding the clips following the edit over to the left fill the space left by the edit (or slide them to the right to compensate for a lengthened clip).

3   Use an Insert edit. Before you drop the clip between the two clips in the sequence, hold down the Ctrl key to switch that edit from an Overlay to an Insert.

4   Use an Extract and Insert. Hold down the Ctrl key as you Extract the clip and hold down Ctrl as you place the clip in its new position.

5   Change the Toggle Take Audio and Video button to the video-only filmstrip icon, position the Timeline CTI to where you want to make the edit, target the audio and video tracks, and click the Overlay button in the Source Monitor.

6   Once you find a matching edit between two clips, you can fine-tune that edit using the Rolling Edit tool. It'll help you find just the right place to make a seamless edit.

7   This is a matter of opinion. I think it's "Make your stories memorable."

transitions

Cross Dissolve

GPU

Page Roll

A/B Mode

Transitions can make a video move more smoothly or snap the audience to attention. Some can be whimsical, others draw attention to a portion of the scene, and still others create a frantic mood. Premiere Pro 2.0 has nearly 80 transitions that are easy to use and customize. Fun stuff—but I suggest you use restraint.

6 | Adding Video Transitions

Topics covered in this lesson:

- Using transitions with restraint.
- Trying some transitions.
- Changing parameters in the Effect Controls panel.
- Using the A/B mode to fine-tune transitions.

Getting started

Applying transitions between clips—dissolves, page wipes, spinning screens and many more—is a nice way to ease viewers from one scene to the next or to grab their attention.

There's art to adding transitions to your project. Applying them starts simply enough: a mere drag and drop. The art comes in their placement, length, and parameters such as colored borders, motion, and start and end locations.

Most transition work takes place in the Effect Controls panel. In addition to the various options unique to each transition, that panel displays something called an A/B timeline. This feature makes it easy to move transitions relative to the edit point, change the transition duration, and apply transitions to clips that don't have sufficient head or tail frames.

Using transitions with restraint

Once you discover the cornucopia of possibilities that transitions in Premiere Pro offer, the temptation will be to use them for every edit. They can be great fun.

Despite that, I urge restraint.

Watch some TV news stories. Most use cuts-only edits. I'd be surprised if you see any transitions. Why? Time is a factor. But more and more stations these days have ready access to nonlinear editors (NLEs) such as Premiere Pro, and it takes almost no time to add a transition using an NLE.

The principal reason for the dearth of transitions is that they can be distracting. If a TV news editor uses one, it's for a purpose. Their most frequent newsroom editing bay use is to take what would have been a jarring edit—such as a major jump cut—and make it more palatable. An oft-heard newsroom phrase applies: "If you can't solve it, dissolve it."

That's not to say transitions don't have their place in carefully planned stories. Consider the Star Wars movies with all their highly stylized transitions like obvious, slow wipes. Each of those transitions has a purpose. George Lucas purposely created a look reminiscent of old serialized movies and TV shows. Specifically, they send a clear message to the audience: "Pay attention. We're transitioning across space and time."

Adding whimsy

Transitions can lighten up a story. Here are a few examples:

• Start on a tight hand shot of someone cutting a deck of cards and make a Swap transition—one image slides to one side and another slides over it—to another card-related shot.

• Start with a tight shot of a clock (analog, not digital) and use the aptly named Clock Wipe—a line centered on the screen sweeps around to reveal another image—to move to another setting and time.

• Get that James Bond, through-the-bloody-eye effect using the Iris Round transition.

• Take a medium shot of a garage door and use a Push—one image moves off the top while another replaces it from below—to transition to the next shot of the garage interior.

• With some planning and experimentation, you can videotape someone pushing against a wall while walking in place and use that same Push transition (after applying a horizontal direction to it) to have that person "slide" the old scene off screen.

Adding visual interest

Transitions can give your video some pizzazz:

- Take a shot of a car driving through the frame and use a wipe, synchronized with the speed of the car, to move to the next scene.

- Transition from a shot of driving rain or a waterfall using the Slash Slide transition, in which streaks, like driving rain, slice through an image revealing another image behind it.

- Use the Venetian Blinds transition as a great way to move from an interior to an exterior.

- A Page Peel transition works well with a piece of parchment.

During this lesson, I encourage you to experiment with all that Premiere Pro has to offer.

Trying some transitions: Lesson 6-1

Premiere Pro ships with nearly 80 video transitions (plus two audio transitions that I cover later in the book). Some are subtle, and some are "in your face." The more you experiment with them, the more likely you are to use them well.

Applying a transition between two clips starts with a simple drag-and-drop. That might be enough for many transitions, but Premiere Pro gives you a wide variety of options to fine tune transitions. Some transitions have a Custom button that opens a separate dialog box with sets of options unique to each. And most offer tools that allow you to position the transition precisely.

Adobe Certified Expert exam objective

Describe the tools, options, and process required to add transitions.

In Lesson 6-1 I show you some of the transitions in Premiere Pro. In subsequent mini-lessons I introduce you to some others that offer extra options. Before venturing off into this lesson, watch the Lesson 6 Intro video.

1   Open Premiere Pro and open the Lesson 6-1 project.

2   Select Windows > Workspace > Effects.

This changes the workspace to the preset that the Premiere Pro development team created to make it easier to work with transitions and effects.

3 Open the Lesson 6 Finish sequence in the Timeline and watch that sequence.

Note: I don't expect you to duplicate Lesson 6 Finish by the end of this lesson. It has too many frame-specific edits to be a practical learning tool. On the other hand, you will work with all the transitions and options I used to create it.

4 Click the Lesson 6-1 Start tab in the Timeline.

5 Drag and drop Video 6a and Video 6b to the Video 1 track and press the backslash key to expand the view.

Note: There are little triangles in the upper right and left corners of both clips (highlighted in the next figure). They indicate that the clips are at their original, full length. For transitions to work smoothly you need handles—some unused head and tail frames to overlap between the clips. Trimming both clips will give you those handles.

6 Select the Ripple Edit tool (shortcut B) and drag the end of the first clip to the left to shorten it by at about 2 seconds (note the time in the pop-up display).

7 Use the Ripple Edit tool to drag the beginning of the second clip to the right to the point where the dancer starts dancing (to create a match edit with the previous clip) at about 2 seconds into the clip.

8 Press the backslash key (\) to expand the Timeline view, and press V to switch back to the Selection tool.

Note: Since you used the Ripple Edit tool, these two trims should have no gap. If there is a gap, right-click it and select Ripple Delete.

9 Open the Effects panel and open the Video Transitions > Dissolve bin.

10 Drag Cross Dissolve to the edit between your two clips on the sequence, but do not release the mouse button just yet.

Note: As I mentioned in Lesson 2, Cross Dissolve has a red box around it indicating it's the default transition.

11 While still holding down the mouse button, move the cursor to the left and right and note how the cursor and the highlighted rectangle on the clips change (see next figure). You can place the transition such that it ends at the edit point, is centered on the edit point, or starts there.

12 Place the transition at the middle of the edit point and drop the transition there.

13 Put the CTI ahead of the transition and press the spacebar to play it.

The transition has a 1-second duration by default.

> ### Changing the default transition and duration
>
> *There are two primary uses for the default transition: when automating a storyboard to a sequence or as a quick means to add a transition using the keyboard shortcut—Ctrl+D. As I mentioned in Lesson 2, you can set a different default transition. To do that, select the transition you want to use, open the Effects panel's Fly-out Menu, and select Set Default Transition. A red box will appear around that transition. If you select Default Transition Duration, that opens the General Preferences dialog box where you can change that setting.*

14 Open the 3D Motion bin and drag Curtain to the beginning of the first clip. Note that the only placement option is to have the transition start at the edit point.

One very cool characteristic of transitions in Premiere Pro is that you can use them at the beginning or end of a video. This is called a single-sided transition (double-sided transtions go between clips).

15 Press Home to move the CTI to the beginning of the Timeline and play the transition. This is a slick way to start a video.

💡 Transitions on any track

Premiere Pro lets you place transitions between two clips (or at the beginnings or ends of clips) on any track in a sequence. Older versions of Premiere limited transitions to the Video 1 track. One very cool use of single-sided transitions is to put them in clips on higher tracks so they gradually reveal or cover up what's below them in the Timeline. I use only a single track in these lessons to simplify things and because transition behavior on the Video 1 track is the same as on any other track.

16 Drag the Curtain transition to the end of the second clip.

17 Click the Effect Controls tab to open the Effect Controls panel.

18 Click the Curtain transition rectangle at the end of the clip in the Timeline to switch on the display of its parameters in the Effect Controls panel.

19 Click the Reverse checkbox (highlighted in the next figure) to have the curtains close at the end of the clip. It's a slick finish.

Note: *I cover Effect Controls panel transition parameters in much greater detail in Lesson 6-2.*

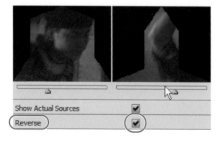

20 Open the Page Peel bin and drag Center Peel to the Cross Dissolve transition between the two clips. That replaces Cross Dissolve with Center Peel. Play that transition.

Note: The next step calls for the use of a GPU (graphics processor unit). If your PC does not have a GPU with enough horsepower to handle the GPU effects in Premiere Pro, those effects will not show up in the Effects panel. In that case, skip the next step.

21 Open the GPU Transitions bin and drag Center Peel (yes, it's the same name but a different effect) to the non-GPU version of the Center Peel transition in the Timeline. Play that transition.

Notice how different the GPU version looks from the non-GPU accelerated transition. In particular, the GPU version plays the video on the reverse side of the peel.

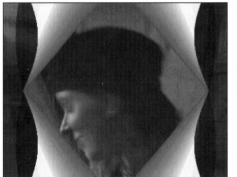 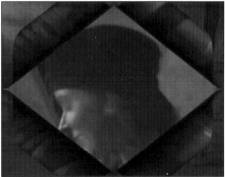

The standard Center Peel transition (left) versus the GPU-accelerated Center Peel transition (right).

22 Test out some other transitions. I suggest you try at least one from every bin (except Map—it's beyond the scope of this lesson).

Additional transitions to try out

Here are the transitions I used in the Lesson 6 Finish Sequence that you have not tried yet: Page Roll, Push, Three-D (the only one in the Special Effect bin relevant to this lesson), Wipe, Zoom Trails, Iris Round, Split, and Funnel. You will work in greater detail with most of these in Lesson 6-2.

To find them one at a time in the Effects panel, start typing their name in the Contains box and they'll appear as shown in the next figure.

Sequence display changes

When you add a transition to a sequence a short red horizontal line appears above that transition (highlighted in the next figure). That red line means that this portion of the sequence must be rendered before you can record it back to tape or create a file of your finished project.

Rendering happens automatically when you export your project, but you can choose to render selected portions of your sequence to make those sections display more smoothly on slower PCs. To do that, slide the handles of the Work Area Bar (highlighted below) to the ends of the red rendering line (they will snap to those points) and press Enter. Premiere Pro will create a video clip of that segment (tucked away in the Preview Files folder with an indecipherable file name) and will change the line from red to green.

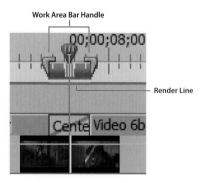

Changing parameters in the Effect Controls panel: Lesson 6-2

Up to this point you've seen the default action of each transition you've tested. That just scratches the surface of their possibilities. Tucked away in the Effect Controls panel is a passel of parameters, unique to each transition.

Adobe Certified Expert exam objective

Describe the available options for changing transition settings by using the Effect Controls panel.

You'll start with the Cross Dissolve transition, and then move on to most of the transitions I used in the Lesson 6 Finish sequence. Here's how you adjust transition characteristics:

1   Continue where you left off in Lesson 6-1 or open Lesson 6-2.

2   Click the Lesson 6-2 Start tab in the Timeline to open that sequence.

Here you'll find all the clips I used in the Lesson 6 Finish sequence with the transitions removed. The clips have been trimmed to match the music and to give you sufficient head and tail handle frames for transitions.

3   Drag the Cross Dissolve transition from the Effects > Video Transitions > Dissolve bin to the beginning of the first clip.

4   Click the transition rectangle in the upper left corner of the clip in the sequence to display its parameters in the Effect Controls panel.

Note: If the Effect Controls panel A/B timeline opens on the right side of the panel, it's OK to leave it that way though I won't refer to it until Lesson 6-3.

5 Click the Show Actual Sources checkbox (highlighted in the previous figure) and drag the sliders beneath the two preview screens.

You can use those sliders to have the transition start partially faded up, and end less than completely faded up.

6 Change the duration in the Effects Control panel to 2 seconds and play the transition in the Timeline.

7 Move the Timeline CTI to about 3 seconds (when the music really kicks in) and drag the right edge of the transition marker in the sequence to the CTI.

Note: Snap does not work when dragging the edges of transitions.

8 Play the transition now and notice how it fades up completely just as the music volume increases.

9   Drag the Page Roll transition from the GPU Transitions bin to the edit between the second and third clips.

Play it in the Timeline and note that it rolls in from the left.

Note: *This is another GPU-accelerated transition. If your PC can't handle this, skip to step 11.*

10   Change the direction to go from top to bottom by clicking the North to South triangle highlighted in the next figure.

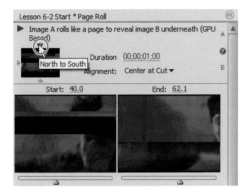

11   Apply the Wipe transition (Wipe bin) between the fourth and fifth clips.

Note that there are three new options: Border Width, Border Color and Anti-aliasing Quality.

12   Change the Border Width to 20.

13   Click the upper left direction triangle to change the direction to Northwest to Southeast.

14   Click the Eyedropper tool highlighted in the figure on the next page and click it on the dancer's hair to have the border match that shade of purple.

15 Set Anti-aliasing Quality to High (see "Clean Up the Jaggies with Anti-aliasing" below). Play that transition.

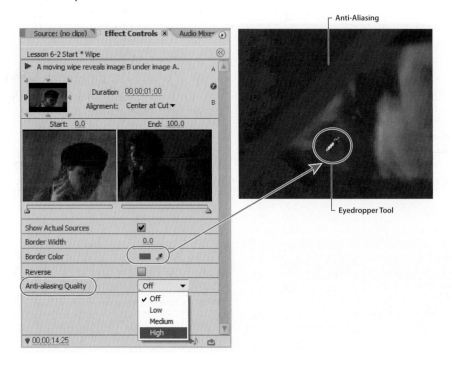

Clean up the jaggies with anti-aliasing

Every transition that offers a border option also has an anti-aliasing option. Aliasing is the jagged, stair step edge common along sharply defined diagonal lines in computer graphics and TV sets. To get rid of aliasing, you select Anti-Aliasing.

On an effect such as a vertical or horizontal wipe, there should be no noticeable aliasing, whether or not you've opted for anti-aliasing. But when you work with diagonal transitions, like Wipe, use anti-aliasing to take the stair-steps look out of the edges.

Note: By now you might want a break from the music. If so, click the Toggle Track Output speaker icon to the left of Audio 1 to turn off the sound.

16 Apply the Zoom Trails transition (Zoom bin) between the fifth and sixth clips. This has two new options: Custom and a little positioning circle.

17 Click custom and change the number of trails to 20.

18 Move the End preview screen slider to the left slightly so you can see how the transition will look as it finishes.

19 Move the positioning circle in the Start screen to have the transition finish on the dancer's face (watch the position of the transition change in the End screen).

Note: *You can also watch the end position in the Program Monitor. You need to drag the Timeline CTI through the transition to view it.*

20 When you settle on a location, return the End preview screen slider all the way back to the right. Play the transition.

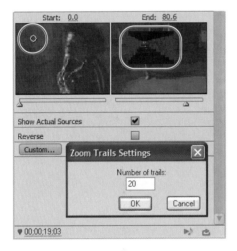

21 Apply Iris Round (Iris bin) between the sixth and seventh clips.

22 Click the Reverse button in the Effect Controls panel.

That will have the transition start as a large circle and shrink.

23 Move the finishing position to the dancer's left foot, set the border width to 20 and select a red color from the dancer's jacket. Play that transition.

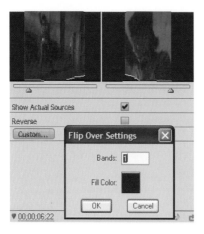

Extra credit: Apply the remaining transitions

I used three other transitions in Lesson 6 Finish: Split, Funnel and Three-D. You can check out their parameters in that sequence. With Split, I positioned it to start between the feet of the dancer. Funnel is a great way to end a piece. And Three-D is less a transition and more an effect in that it blends the two clips together.

Give the Flip Over transition a test drive. It's in the 3D Motion folder, a collection of transitions that use perspective to give your transitions greater depth. The Flip Over transition takes the A clip and spins it like a flat board horizontally or vertically and then reveals the B clip on the board's other side. That flipping motion briefly leaves an empty space behind the board. Click Custom to change the color of that space and split the board into as many as eight bands.

I've touched on most of the primary types of transitions, but have saved two for later: Image Mask and Gradient Wipe. I explain them in Lesson 8.

Using the A/B mode to fine-tune a transition: Lesson 6-3

Because the developers of Premiere Pro created version one of Premiere Pro from the ground up, they had the opportunity to make some fundamental decisions. One was to no longer include A/B editing in the Timeline.

A/B editing is old-school, linear, film-style editing. Film editors frequently use two reels of film: an A-roll and a B-roll, which are usually duplicates made from the same original. The two-reel approach permits cross-dissolves from the A track to the B track.

The advantage of A/B editing in older versions of Premiere was that it let you more easily modify transition positioning and start and end points than you could on single tracks NLEs.

Here's the good news for both A/B and single-track editing camps: Premiere Pro includes all of that functionality in its Effect Controls panel.

Working with the Effect Controls panel's A/B feature

The Effect Controls A/B editing mode splits a single video track into two sub-tracks. What would normally be two consecutive and contiguous clips on a single track now display as individual clips on separate sub-tracks, giving you the option to apply a transition between them, to manipulate their head and tail frames—or handles—and change other transition elements.

1   Continue where you left off in Lesson 6-2 or open Lesson 6-3.

2   Drag the Three-D transition (Special Effect bin) between the third and fourth clips.

3   Click on the transition in the Timeline to select it and display its parameters in the Effect Controls panel.

4   Open the A/B timeline in the Effect Controls panel by clicking the Show/Hide Timeline button in the upper right corner.

Note: You might need to expand the width of the Effect Controls panel to make the Show/Hide Timeline button active.

5 Drag the border (cursor highlighted in the next figure) between the A/B timeline and the transition parameters section to expand the view of the timeline.

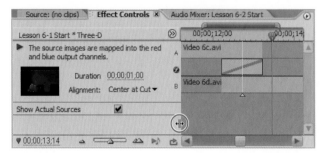

6 Hover the cursor over the white edit line at the center of the transition rectangle (highlighted in the next figure).

That's the edit point between the two clips, and the cursor that appears there is the Rolling Edit cursor (⁘)—the same Rolling Edit you encountered in the Trim panel.

7 Drag the Rolling Edit cursor left and right and note how the changing out-point of the left clip and the changing in-point of the right clip show up in the Program Monitor.

Note: As was the case when you used the Rolling Edit tool in the Trim panel, moving it left or right does not change the overall length of the sequence.

Rolling Edit

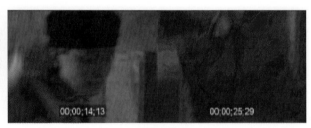

Program Montior

8 Move the cursor slightly left or right and note that it changes to a Slide tool (⬌).

9 Use the Slide tool to drag the transition rectangle left and right.

Note: That changes the start and end points of the transition without changing its overall length (default duration: 1 second). The new start and end points show up in the Program Monitor. But unlike the Rolling Edit, moving the transition rectangle does not change the edit point between the two clips.

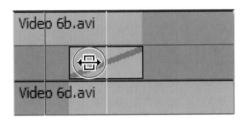

10 Click the drop-down Alignment list and click through the three available options: Center at Cut, Start at Cut and End at Cut.

Note: The transition rectangle moves to a new location as you make each change. These three locations mimic the options when you drag a transition to the Timeline. Additionally, if you manually change the transition location, the Custom Start alignment option becomes active.

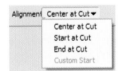

11 Drag an end (it doesn't matter which end) of the Viewing Area Bar to the edge of the A/B timeline.

As shown in the next figure, that expands your view of the two adjacent clips so you can see the beginning of the left clip and the end of the right clip.

12 Drag the right and left edge of the transition to lengthen it.

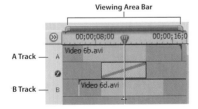

> ### 💡 Two other ways to change transition duration
>
> *As a reminder, you can also change the duration value by typing in a new time or by clicking on the duration time and dragging left or right to decrease or increase its value.*

As you drag notice the changing hue of the two sub-clips: labeled A and B. The lighter color blue represents the area of the clips within the transition and the darker blue areas represent the head and tail frames available for the overlap to give you a smooth transition.

Note: *As you lengthen the transition, the viewing area bar shrinks, thereby allowing you to drag its ends yet again to expand the area viewed in the A/B timeline.*

Dealing with inadequate (or no) head or tail handles

Eventually you will want to place transitions at edit points where you don't have adequate head or tail handles. This might be because you paused the camcorder too soon or didn't get it started fast enough. You might want to add a transition to ease what would be an abrupt cut edit. Premiere Pro deals with that elegantly.

You will set up that situation in the Lesson 6-1 Start sequence.

1   Click the Lesson 6-1 Start tab, marquee select the two clips in that sequence and press Delete.

2   Drag Video 6i and Video 6j to the Timeline.

This time you will not trim the clips to give them head and tail handle frames. Those little triangles that show there are no extra frames available will be in the upper corners at the edit point.

3   Drag the Wipe transition to that edit point.

You will get the "Insufficient Media" alert again. Click OK.

4   Click the transition to display it in the Effect Controls panel and note that the transition rectangle has parallel diagonal lines running through it, indicating the lack of head or tail frames.

5   Set the transition direction to go from South to North.

This direction will give you the clearest picture of how Premiere Pro deals with a lack of head or tail frames.

6   Lengthen the transition to about 3 seconds by dragging the right and left edge of the transition rectangle.

Note: The A and B clips retain their light blue color, indicating there are no head or tail frames available for overlap.

7   Drag the CTI slowly through the entire transition and watch how it works:

•   For the first half of the transition (up to the edit point) the B clip is a freeze frame while the A clip continues to play.

•   At the edit point, the A clip becomes a freeze frame and the B clip starts to play.

•   When played at regular speed (at the default 1 second duration), few viewers would notice the freeze frames.

When only one clip has no head or tail handles

In this lesson's example both the A and B clips have no head or tail handle frames. Frequently only one clip will have no head or tail room. In those cases Premiere Pro would have forced placement of the transition to start or end at the edit point depending on which clip was lacking extra frames for the overlap.

You can override that by dragging the transition into the clip lacking extra frames. The next figure shows examples of both circumstances with the transition centered. The diagonal lines indicate freeze frames will take the place of the head or tail frames.

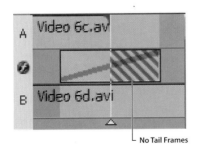
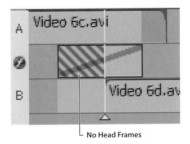

The transition on the left has no extra tail frames. The one on the right has no extra head frames.

Review

▶ Review questions

1 How do you change the default transition duration?

2 How do you track down a transition by name?

3 How do you replace a transition with another one?

4 You apply a transition but it does not show up in the Effect Controls panel. Why not?

5 Some transitions start as small squares, circles or other geometric shapes then grow to reveal the next clip. How to you get those transitions to start with large geometric shapes that shrink to reveal the next clip?

6 Explain three ways to change the duration of a transition.

7 You want your video to end with a 5 second curtain close over a freeze frame. How do you do that?

▶ Review answers

1 There are two ways to do that. 1: select Edit > Preferences > General and change the Video Transition Duration from the default 30 frames (one second) to whatever length you want. Two: with the Effects panel tab open, click the Fly-out Menu, select Default Transition Duration. That too opens the General Preferences dialog box.

2 Start typing the transition name in the Effects panel Contains: box. As you type, Premiere Pro will display all effects and transitions (audio and video) that have that letter combination anywhere within their name. Type more letters to narrow down your search.

3 Drag and drop the replacement transition on top of the transition you're rejecting. The new one automatically replaces the old one.

4 Click on the newly placed transition to select it. That displays its parameters in the Effect Controls panel.

5   Simple. Check the Reverse box in the Effect Controls panel. That switches the movement from starting small and ending full screen to starting full screen and ending small.

6   Drag the edge of the transition rectangle in the Timeline, do the same thing in the Effect Controls panel A/B timeline, or change the Duration value in the Effect Controls panel.

7   Apply a Frame Hold on the In Point or Out Point of the final clip. Use the Trim or Rate Stretch tool to adjust its length to 5 seconds. If you use the Trim tool and you selected Hold on the Out Point in the Frame Hold window, the out point will change as you trim away frames at the end of the clip. Using Rate Stretch retains the out-point. You then apply the Curtain transition to the end of that clip, click the Reverse check box, and stretch the transition rectangle so it covers the entire clip.

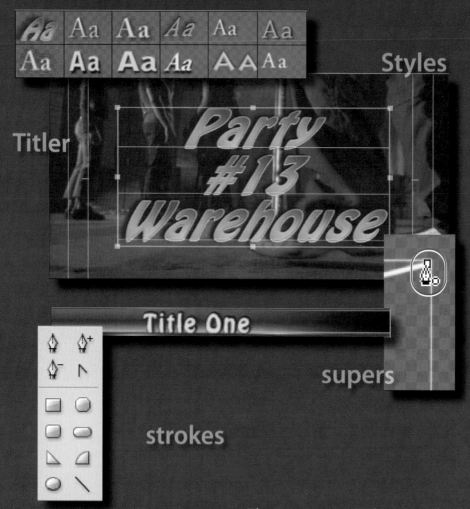

Styles

Titler

supers

strokes

The Premiere Pro Titler is a multi-faceted, feature-rich text and shape creation tool. You can use it to build text—of any size, color or style—with borders, beveled edges, shadows, textures, and sheens. Your Titler-designed text and objects can run superimposed over video as static titles, rolling credits, or as stand-alone clips.

7 | Creating Dynamic Titles

Topics covered in this lesson:

- Strengthen your project with supers.

- Changing text parameters.

- Building text from scratch.

- Putting text on a path.

- Creating shapes.

- Making text roll and crawl.

- Deconstructing effects: sheens, strokes, shadows and fill.

Getting started

On-screen text helps tell your story. Your message can be reinforced through supers (superimposed text), giving a location or an interviewee's name and title, on-screen bulleted points, opening titles and closing credits.

Text can present information much more succinctly and clearly than narration. It can also reinforce narrated and visual information by reminding viewers about the people in your piece and the message you're trying to convey.

The Premiere Pro Titler offers you a full range of text- and shape-creation options. You can use any font stored on your PC. Your text and objects can be any color (or multiple colors), any degree of transparency, and a multiplicity of shapes. Using the Path tool, you can place your text on the most convoluted curved line you can imagine. The Titler is an engaging and powerful tool.

Its infinite customizability means that you can create a look unique to your productions.

Strengthen your project with supers

Consider this opening sequence: a telephoto shot of scorched desert sand with rippling heat distorting the scene. Dry, desiccated, lifeless sagebrush. A lizard slowly seeking shade beneath a small stone. And a small plume of dust in the distance. Attention-getting stuff.

Now a narrator intones, "The summer heat beats down on the Bonneville Salt Flats." Effective. But even better is a super: Bonneville Salt Flats. Then, as the plume of dust moves toward the camera, another super: Speed Trials—Summer 2005. Then a rocket-shaped vehicle screams through the scene.

Rather than interrupt the building suspense with a sonorous narrator, save him for later. Instead, simply use supers to set up your story.

Here are other instances in which text can be an effective alternative to voice-overs:

• Instead of using a voice-over to say, "Sue Smith, vice president of manufacturing for Acme Industries," put that information in a super at the bottom of the screen.

• Instead of narrating a collection of statistics, use bulleted points that pop on screen with each new item.

Text strengthens your project.

Changing text parameters: Lesson 7-1

In this mini-lesson you start with some formatted text and then change its parameters. This approach is a good way to give you a quick overview of the powerful features of the Premiere Pro Titler. In Lesson 7-2, you build basic text from scratch. Take a moment to view the Lesson 7 Intro video. Then do the following.

1 Open Premiere Pro to the Lesson 7 project.

2 Double-click Lesson 7-1 Start Text in the Project panel.

That opens the Titler with a title already loaded over a video frame. Here's a quick rundown on the Titler's panels:

• **Title Designer**—The screen where you build and view text and graphics.

• **Title Properties**—Text and graphic options such as font characteristics and effects.

• **Title Styles**—Preset text styles. You can choose from several libraries of styles.

- **Title Actions**—Use to align, center or distribute text and groups of objects.
- **Title Tools**—Define text boundaries, set text paths, and select geometric shapes.

The Premiere Pro Titler

Adobe Certified Expert exam objective

Given a feature or function associated with the Titler, describe the purpose of that feature or function.

3   Click on several different Titler Styles thumbnails below the Titler screen.

They instantly change your text to the new style. When done, return to the original style selection: HoboStd Slant Gold 80 (highlighted in the next figure).

Note: Styles are fonts with preset properties like bold, italic, size, and slant, as well as effects such as fill color and style, stroke, sheen and shadow. You deconstruct those font effects in Lesson 7-6.

4 Click the Font Browser button (highlighted in the next figure). Note the current font is Hobo Std Medium.

5 Scroll through the fonts and note that as you click on a new font you see immediately how it'll work with your text.

6 Click Cancel.

7 Click the Font drop-down list in the Properties panel on the right side of the Titler.

Note: With all the clicking and testing you may have deselected the text. If there is no bounding box with handles around the text, select the text by clicking the Selection tool (upper left corner) and clicking anywhere in the text.

8 Change the font to Times New Roman Bold Italic.

The change will show up immediately in the Titler screen.

Note: To track down Times New Roman, roll your cursor over More (highlighted in the figure below) to open the additional groups of fonts until you get to Times New Roman.

9 Change the font size to 120 by dragging your mouse on the Font Size number or typing in the new value. Your screen should look like the next figure.

10 Change the Aspect to 70% to shrink the horizontal scale of the text so it fits within the width of the Safe Title Margin, defined by the smaller of the two rectangles (noted in the previous figure).

Note: NTSC TV sets cut off the edges of a video signal. Keeping text within the Safe Title Margin (also called the Title Safe Zone) ensures viewers will see all of your text.

11 Change Leading to –20 to shrink the distance between the lines of type so the text appears above the bottom of the Safe Title Margin line.

12 Check Small Caps and change the Small Caps size to 50%.

Note: Small Caps puts all selected objects into uppercase. Changing the size to less than 100% shrinks all but the first character of each word.

13 Check Underline.

14 Click the Vertical Center and Horizontal Center buttons in the Title Action panel.

15 Click the Titler Styles Fly-out Menu, select Replace Style Library and in the Open Style Library window double-click Default.prsl.

That loads several dozen text styles.

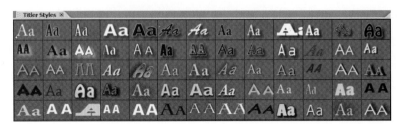

16 Click on a few and note that those styles immediately change the look of your text.

17 Click the Titler Styles Fly-out Menu, select Replace Style Library and in the Open Style Library window double-click Entertainment.prsl to return to the original Styles group.

18 Click on HoboStd Slant Gold 80 change your text back to its original Style.

Adobe Certified Expert exam objective
List and describe the options available for working with text in titles.

19 Drag the Titler panel to the right far enough to be able to see the Project panel.

20 Double-click Lesson 7-1 Finish Text to load it in the Titler.

21 Switch between the two titles using the drop-down list above the Browser button. You text should look the same as Lesson 7-1 Finish Text.

22 Close the Titler by clicking the little x in the upper right corner.

Note: Premiere Pro automatically saves your updated Lesson 7-1 Start Text in the project file. It does not show up as a separate file on your hard drive.

23 Drag Lesson 7-1 Start Text from the Project panel to the Video 2 track on the Timeline, trim it so it fits above the video clip, and drag the CTI through it to see how it looks over that video clip.

Note: You can apply transitions to titles to fade them up or move them on or off screen.

> ### Using titles in other projects
>
> *You will likely create title templates for location names and interviewee supers that you'll use in multiple projects. However Premiere Pro 2.0 does not automatically save titles as separate files. To make a title available for use in another project, select the title in the Project panel, select File > Export > Title, give your title a name, choose a file folder location, and click Save. Later you simply import that title file the same way you import any other asset.*

Extra credit: Other properties options

Double click Lesson 7-1 Start to reopen the Titler and then check out these four other Properties options by first selecting the text using the Selection tool, then adjusting these properties:

- **Kerning**—Adjusts spacing between selected character pairs.
- **Tracking**—Adjusts spacing for a group of characters.
- **Baseline Shift**—Specifies the distance of the characters from the baseline—the thin white line running through the bottoms of each line of characters. Raise or lower selected type to create superscripts or subscripts.
- **Distort**—Stretches text along its X and Y axes.

Building text from scratch: Lesson 7-2

The Adobe Titler offers three text creation approaches, each offering a horizontal and vertical text direction option:

- **Point Text**—Builds a text bounding box as you type. The text will run on one line until you press Enter or select Word Wrap from the Title menu on the Main Menu bar. Changing the shape and size of the box changes the shape and size of the text.

- **Paragraph (Area) Text**—You set the size and shape of your text box before entering text. Changing the box size later displays more or less text, but does not change the shape or size of the text.

- **Text on a Path**—You build a path for your text to follow by clicking points in the text screen to create curves, then adjusting the shape and direction of those curves.

Titler Text Tools. Selecting a tool from the left or right side determines whether the text will orient horizontally or vertically.

Adobe Certified Expert exam objective

Describe the process required to create a static title.

Since Premiere Pro 2.0 automatically saves text to the project file, you can switch to a new or different title and not lose whatever you've created in the current title. That's what you'll do now.

1   If the Titler is open, move the Titler floating window so you can access the Main Menu.

2   Select File > New > Title to open the Titler (F9).

3   Type Lesson 7-2 Text in the New Title box and click OK.

Note: Before version 2.0, Adobe Premiere Pro saved all titles as independent files separate from the project file. You can import titles created in older versions of Premiere Pro just as you import any asset. When you save the project, the imported titles are saved with the project, not as separate files. The old files remain unchanged.

4   Drag the Time Code (to the right of the Show Video checkbox) to change the video frame displayed in the text screen.

This can come in handy if you want to position text relative to the video contents or check how the text looks over your video.

5   Uncheck Show Video.

> ### 💡 Checkerboard pattern signifies transparency
>
> *The background now consists of a grayscale checkerboard. That signifies a transparency. That is, if you place text created in the Titler on a video track above other video clips, the video on lower tracks will be visible wherever you see that checkerboard. You can also create text or geometric objects with some transparency. In that case, you'll see the checkerboard through an object, which means the video will show through but it'll appear that it's covered with smoked or tinted glass.*

6 Click the GaramondPro OffWhite 28 style (sixth style of this eight-style group), click the Fly-out Menu and select Set Style As Default.

That places it at the head of the style line, puts a very tiny box with a red diagonal line next to it (highlighted in the next figure) to identify it as the default Style, and changes the thumbnail in the Title Tools panel to that style.

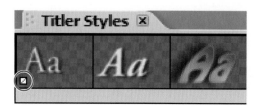

7 Click the Type tool (**T**)—shortcut T—and click anywhere in the Titler screen.

The Type tool creates Point Text.

8 Start typing. For the purposes of this exercise, type *Lesson 7-2.*

Note: If you continue typing, you will note that Point Text does not wrap. Your text will run off the screen to the right. To make it wrap when it reaches the Safe Title Margin, choose Title > Word Wrap. To begin a new line, press Enter.

9 Click the Selection tool (the black arrow in the top left corner of the Titler). That puts handles on the text bounding box.

Note: In this case the Selection tool keyboard shortcut V won't work since you are typing inside a text bounding box.

10 Drag the corners and edges of the text bounding box and note how the text changes size and shape accordingly.

11 Hover the cursor just outside a corner of the text bounding box until you see a curved line cursor () and then rotate the bounding box off its horizontal orientation.

> ### More than one way to move a box
>
> *Instead of dragging bounding box handles, you can change values in the Transform settings (in the Properties panel). Either type in new values or place your cursor on a value and drag left or right. Your changes will show up immediately in the bounding box.*

12 Click anywhere within the bounding box (the Selection tool is still active) and drag the angled text and its bounding box around the Titler screen.

13 Edit that text by double-clicking anywhere in the text and typing.

You can drag to select text you want to remove or replace.

14 Delete all the text by clicking the Selection tool, which puts handles on the text bounding box indicating it's selected, and pressing Delete.

15 Click the Style Fly-out Menu and select Apply Style with Font Size to revert back to the style's original size.

16 Click the Area Type tool () and drag a text bounding box into the Titler screen that nearly fills the Safe Title Margin.

The Area Type tool creates Paragraph Text.

> ### Turning off safe margin displays
>
> *You can turn off the Safe Title Margin and Safe Action Margin rectangles by opening the Title Designer's Fly-out Menu (or selecting Title > View from the Main Menu) and then clicking on either of those options.*

17 Start typing. This time type enough characters to go beyond the end of the bounding box.

Unlike Point Text, Area Text remains in the confines of the bounding box you defined. It wraps at the bounding box borders. Press Enter to go down a line.

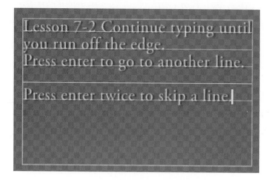

18 Click the Selection tool and change the size and shape of the bounding box.

The text does not change size. Instead it adjusts its position on the bounding box baselines. If you make the box too small for all your text, the extra text scrolls below the bounding box bottom edge. In that instance a little plus (+) appears in the lower-right corner outside the bounding box.

19 Double-click within the text to edit it.

20 Switch to the Selection tool, click anywhere in the text bounding box, and press Delete to remove the text.

 Vertical text

While you're testing your text, try the vertically-oriented Point and Area text tools. They create text where each character stands on top of the next one.

Putting text on a path: Lesson 7-3

The Path Text tool is both elegant and tricky. It enables you to build paths that are simple or complex, straight and/or curved, for your text to follow.

If you've worked with the Pen tool in Adobe Photoshop, you know how to use the Path Text tool. You define a path by clicking a number of locations in the Titler panel and dragging handles at each point to define the curves.

1   Select the Path Type tool (↖).

2   Click and drag anywhere in the text creation screen.

That creates an anchor point with handles. You'll use those handles to define the curve's characteristics. If you only click without dragging the cursor, you won't add handles. It's tricky to add them later.

3   Click and drag somewhere else to create another anchor point with handles.

The Titler automatically creates a curved path between the two anchor points.

Note: *You can add as many anchor points as you choose. Each new point outside the confines of the current bounding box expands the bounding box dimensions. Delete points by selecting the Delete Anchor Point tool (see next figure) and clicking on an anchor.*

4   Click the Pen tool (◊).

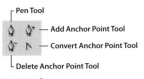

Pen Tools

5 Hover that cursor over the handles (as highlighted in the next figure, your cursor will change to a black arrow) and drag the handles.

Make them longer, shorter, or just move them around to see how they work.

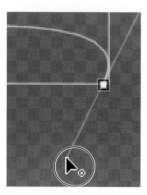

6 Drag the anchor points to lengthen or shorten the path.

7 Click anywhere inside the newly created bounding box.

That will place a blinking text cursor at the beginning of the curved line.

8 Type in some text. Your Titler screen should look something like the next figure. If you're having trouble with the Pen tool, double-click Lesson 7-3 Text in the Project panel and work with it.

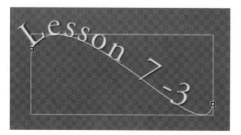

You will want to practice creating Path Text if you want to perfect it, but for now just try to get a basic idea of how it works.

Creating shapes: Lesson 7-4

If you've created shapes in graphics-editing software such as Photoshop or Illustrator, you know how to create geometric objects in Premiere Pro.

Simply select from the various shapes to the left of the text window, drag and draw the outline, and release the mouse.

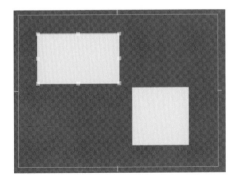

Shape drawing tools. **A.** *Pen* **B.** *Rectangle* **C.** *Rounded Corner Rectangle* **D.** *Wedge* **E.** *Ellipse*
F. *Clipped Corner Rectangle* **G.** *Rounded Rectangle* **H.** *Arc* **I.** *Line*

1   Press the F9 key, type *Shapes* in the New Title text box and click OK.

2   Open the Styles Fly-out Menu, select Replace Style Library and double-click default.prsl.

Note: *Switching to default styles and using its default style (Default Caslon Pro 68) means any shape you draw will be a simple white object with no effects. If you use any other style, the new shape will incorporate that style's features including borders, color, shadows and the like.*

3   Select the Rectangle tool (R) and drag in the Titler screen to create that shape.

4   Shift+drag in another location to constrain the shape's aspect ratio, making a square.

Note: *Pressing shift creates shapes with reflexive properties: circles, squares, and right angle triangles and arcs. To maintain the aspect ratio for a shape you've already made, hold the Shift key before resizing that shape.*

5   Click the Selection tool, drag it in the Titler screen to marquee select the two objects and press Delete to make a clean slate.

6   Select the Rounded Corner Rectangle tool and Alt+drag to draw from the center of the shape.

The center remains in the spot where you first clicked and the figure changes shape and size around that point as you drag the cursor.

Note: *Not all shape tools have keyboard shortcuts.*

7   Choose the Cropped Corner Rectangle tool and Shift+Alt+drag to constrain the aspect ratio and draw from the center.

8   Select the Arc tool (A) and drag diagonally across the corner points to flip the shape diagonally as you draw.

9   Click the Wedge tool (W) and drag across, up, or down to flip the shape horizontally or vertically as you draw.

Note: *To flip the shape after you've drawn it, use the Selection tool to drag a corner point in the direction you want it to flip.*

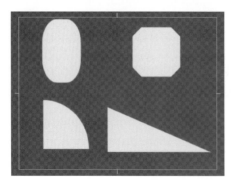

10   Marquee select those four objects and press Delete to make another clean slate.

11   Select the Line tool (L) and drag to create a single line.

Note: To connect another segment to the line you just drew you need to click on the end point of the line. It's an imprecise process. The Pen tool connects lines more elegantly.

12   Select the Pen tool and click to create an anchor point (don't drag to create handles).

13   Click again in the Titler screen where you want the segment to end (Shift+click to constrain the segment's angle to multiples of 45°). This creates another anchor point.

14   Continue clicking the Pen tool to create additional straight segments. The last anchor point you add appears as a large square, indicating that it is selected.

15   Complete the path by doing one of the following:

•   To close the path, move the Pen tool to the initial anchor point. When it is directly over the initial anchor point, a circle appears underneath the pen pointer (highlighted in the figure on the next page). Click to make the connection.

•   To leave the path open, Ctrl+click anywhere away from all objects, or select a different tool in the Tools panel.

Note: Open Lesson 7-4 Shapes in the Project panel to see a collection of shapes. I added strokes (borders) to two along with some transparency to give you an idea of the possibilities. I cover effects like stroke and opacity in Lesson 7-6.

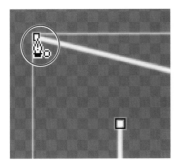

Making text roll and crawl: Lesson 7-5

Using the Titler you can make rolling text for opening and closing credits and crawling text for items like headline bulletins.

Adobe Certified Expert exam objective

Describe the process required to create rolling or crawling titles.

---

1 Select Title > New Title > Default Roll.

2 Name it *Rolling Credits* and click OK.

3 Type in text.

Create placeholder credits as in the figure on the next page, pressing enter after each line. Input enough text to more than fill the screen vertically.

Note: With Rolling Text selected the Titler automatically adds a scroll bar along the right side that enables you to view your text as it runs off the bottom of the screen. If you select the Crawl option, that scrollbar will appear at the bottom to enable you to view text running off the right or left edge of the window.

4   Click the Roll/Crawl Options button (highlighted in the previous figure). You have the following options (shown in the next figure):

•   **Start Off Screen**—Choose whether the credits start completely off the screen and roll on, or begin with the uppermost text item at the top or side of the screen.

•   **End Off Screen**—Indicates whether the credits roll completely off the screen.

•   **Pre-Roll**—Specify the number of frames before the first words appear on screen.

•   **Ease-In**—Number of frames before the first words appear.

•   **Ease-Out**—Frames to slow down the roll or crawl at its end.

•   **Post-Roll**—The number of frames that play after the roll or crawl ends.

•   **Crawl Left, Crawl Right**—The Crawl direction (Rolling text always moves up the screen).

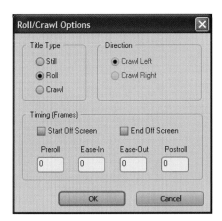

5   Check Start Off Screen, End Off Screen, and type in 5 frames each for Ease-In and Ease-Out.

6   Close the Titler.

7   Drag your newly created Rolling Credits to the Video 2 track of the Timeline above the video clip (if another title is there, drag this one directly on top of it to do an overlay edit).

Note: The default length of rolling or crawling credits is 5 seconds. If you change the length of the credits clip, that changes the speed. A longer clip length means slower rolling credits.

8   Press the spacebar to view your rolling credits.

Note: If you're having trouble with Rolling or Crawling text, open Lesson 7-5 Rolling Credits in the Titler or drag it from the Project panel to the Timeline.

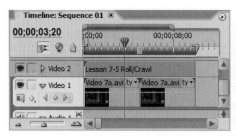
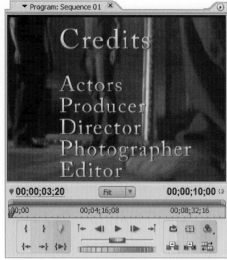

Deconstructing effects: Sheens, Strokes, Shadows and Fill: Lesson 7-6

Reverse enginering can be a good learning tool. So in this mini-lesson you will deconstruct one of the many built-in templates that come with Premiere Pro to learn how to work with Titler's effects..

Unlike Styles, Templates are a combination of background graphics, geometric shapes and placeholder text. They are organized into themes with enough variety for just about any circumstance.

They are tremendously useful. You can easily customize graphic themes to suit your needs or build your own templates from scratch and save them for future projects.

1   Select Title > New Title > Based on Template.

Note: You can also open the Titler and select Title > Templates to get to the same Templates screen.

2   Open as many template folders and click through as many templates as you like.

3   Open the Lower Thirds folder, select Lower Third 1026, and click Apply.

Note: I chose this template because it has a full range of effects including 4 Color Gradient, reduced opacity (transparency), sheen, stroke and shadows.

4   Click the Selection tool (V) and move it over the template.

Bounding boxes will appear, delineating the three components of this title: *Title One* text, a brown and yellow rectangle, and a black rectangle.

5 Drag each bounding box in turn up the screen so you can see the template's three components.

Your Titler should look something like the next figure.

Note: If you have trouble selecting the components, double-click Lesson 7-6 Template Test in the Project panel to open a disassembled version of the template.

6 Drag the brown and yellow rectangle's top edge to expand it.

That selects it and displays its characteristics in the Titler Properties panel.

7 Close Transform and Properties to make some room.

8 Twirl down Fill, Sheen (in the Fill section), Strokes, and Outer Strokes (there are no Inner Strokes used in this template).

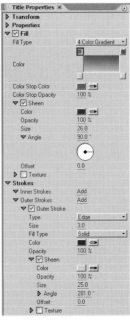

9 Open the Fill Type drop-down list and click on each option in turn to see what they do. When done, return to 4 Color Gradient.

10 Double-click on one or two of the four color-stop boxes around the 4 Color Gradient display to open the Color Picker. Select new colors.

Note: Each color is slightly different than the other three and the colors at the top are slightly darker than the bottom colors. This gives this rectangle extra depth.

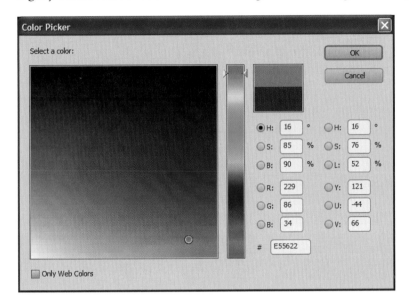

Lift a color from your video

Instead of using the Color Picker window to change the color stop color, use the Eyedropper tool to select a color from your video. Click the Show Video checkbox at the top of the Titler window, move to a frame you want to use by dragging the timecode left or right, drag the Eyedropper tool into your video scene, and click on a color that suits your needs.

11 Change the Color Stop Opacities by clicking each Color Stop box, and changing the opacity setting.

Note: You can change the opacity (transparency) of any color applied to any object or text, be it fill, sheen, or stroke. You can give a geometric shape or text a solid color stroke border and convert its fill color to 0% opacity to display only its edges.

12 Click the Sheen color box and change its color, opacity, size, angle, and offset.

Note: Sheen is a soft-edged color that typically runs horizontally through shapes or text. In this case it's the brown, horizontal line that runs through the entire rectangle.

13 Twirl down the two Outer Stroke disclosure triangles.

Strokes are outer or inner borders on text or graphic objects. They have the same collection of properties available for text and other Titler objects. In this case both strokes are 3 points wide and they fall adjacent to one another.

14 Change the size of the two Outer Strokes to 25 points each. As shown in the next figure, that more clearly displays the sheen applied to these borders.

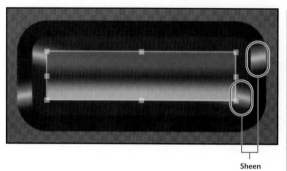 

Sheen

💡 **Sheen artistry**

Take a look at the Sheen properties for both Outer Strokes. Note that the angles are 281 degrees and 81 degrees (270 and 90 degrees are horizontal). That is, each sheen appears just a bit above the center line on one side and a bit below the center line on the other. If the sheens were to run through the entire box, they'd form an X. This is a clever bit of visual artistry. Before you expanded the rectangle, the sheens were on the top and bottom edges. In this taller mode, they are along the sides. To see how that works, drag the rectangle's bounding box top edge up and down and watch the sheens move along the edges.

15 Click Add next to Inner Strokes. That opens the Inner Stroke property.

16 Check the Inner Stroke box to turn on its parameters and experiment with this new Stroke by changing its Size, Fill Type, Color and Opacity.

Note: *Adding a sheen or a shadow to an object is just as easy. Merely select the object in the Titler screen, check the appropriate properties box and adjust the parameters.*

17 Click the *Title One* text to select it.

18 Open its Shadow properties.

Title One doesn't have an obvious shadow because the shadow size is only 2 points. It's more like an Outer Stroke.

19 Change all the characteristics to see how the Shadow feature works.

Take a look at my example in the next figure. Everything is self-explanatory, with the exception of Spread. Increasing the Spread value softens the shadow.

20 Select the black rectangle and take a look at its 4 Color Gradient.

All the Color Stops are black. This template's designer set an Opacity of 0% (completely transparent) to the Color Stops on the left side and 100% (opaque) to the stops on the right side. In that way the black rectangle's opacity gradually changes to give text appearing on it a more dramatic look.

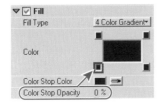

Experiment with effects

I encourage you to open a new title, select a Style, and draw an object. Do that for several distinctly different Styles. Then open the Fill, Strokes and Shadow properties and make lots of changes to each object.

Create new Outer and Inner Strokes. Add Sheens. Check a Texture box and add any graphic image or Photoshop file to add some real pizzazz to your text and object.

The more you play with the Titler the more you'll come to appreciate its depth and creative possibilities.

Review

Review questions

1. What are the differences between Point and Area (or Paragraph) Text?

2. Why display the Safe Title Margin?

3. What's the difference between a Style and a Template when it comes to using the Titler?

4. Describe two ways to change a font.

5. How do you create a circle in a square?

6. How do you apply a stroke or a sheen?

Review answers

1. You create Point Text with the Type tool. Its bounding box expands as you type. Changing the box shape changes the text size and shape accordingly. When you use the Area text tool, you define a bounding box and the characters remain within its confines. Changing the box's shape displays more or fewer characters.

2. NTSC TV sets cut off the edges of the TV signal. The amount lost varies from set to set. Displaying the Safe Title Margin and keeping your text within its borders ensures that viewers will see all of your text.

3. A Style can be applied to characters or objects you create in Titler. Templates give you a starting point to create your own full-featured graphic or text backgrounds.

4. With the text object selected, either click the Font drop-down list and select a new font or click the Font Browser button and view the fonts before choosing.

5. Hold down the Shift key as you draw using the Rectangle tool. Then hold down Alt+Shift when using the Ellipse or Rounded Rectangle tool and click in the center of the square to place the center of the circle there (you could drag it there later but this is more elegant).

6. Select the text or object to edit and check its Stroke (Outer or Inner) or Sheen boxes. Then start adjusting parameters and they will show up on the object.

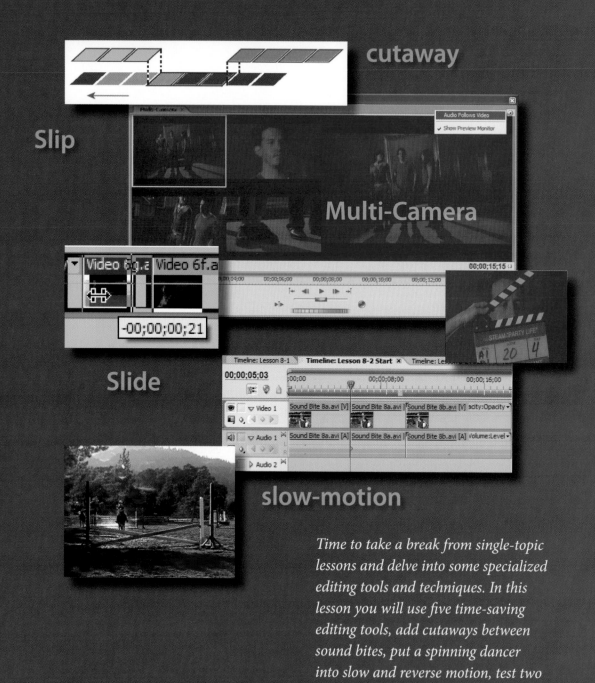

cutaway

Slip

Multi-Camera

Slide

slow-motion

Time to take a break from single-topic lessons and delve into some specialized editing tools and techniques. In this lesson you will use five time-saving editing tools, add cutaways between sound bites, put a spinning dancer into slow and reverse motion, test two specialized transitions and switch a four-camera production.

8 Applying Specialized Editing Tools

Topics covered in this lesson:

- Using five time-saving editing tools.
- Adding a TV news-style cutaway.
- Changing clip speed and direction.
- Using graphics with two transitions.
- Switching a four-camera production.
- Multi-camera and event shooting tips from Cinemagic Studios.

Getting started

In this lesson you try out three specialized editing tools—Rolling, Slip, and Slide, and two Program Monitor tools: Lift and Extract. All can simplify certain tasks. Adding cutaways is a frequent editing task. I show you how to use the Source Monitor to save time and a few editing steps. Two transitions require the use of graphics, and I explain them in this lesson. Premiere Pro makes it easy to apply slow, fast, and reverse motion to clip segments so you can gradually change speeds within a longer clip.

New to Premiere Pro 2.0 is a tremendously useful Multi-Camera feature that lets you edit as if you were switching among up to four cameras in a live production. Supplementing that is a collection of event shooting tips from a production company owner who specializes in multi-camera remotes.

Using five timesaving editing tools: Lesson 8-1

You use the first three tools—Rolling, Slide, and Slip—for a variety of situations including when you want to preserve the overall length of your program. They come in handy for precisely-timed projects such as 30-second advertisements. You've seen the Rolling Edit tool in action in the Trim panel.

You've worked with the remaining two—Extract and Lift—using the drag and drop method. In this mini-lesson you'll use the Program Monitor's Extract and Lift feature to remove selected groups of frames—even when they're spread out over one or more clips.

In some cases, it can be easier to make individual edits and forgo these specialized tools but it's good for any video editor to know how to use all five of them:

- **Rolling edit**—Rolls the cut point between two adjacent clips, shortening one and lengthening the other (thereby retaining the overall length of the project).

- **Slide edit**—Slides the entire clip *over* two adjacent clips, shortening and lengthening those adjacent clips without changing the selected clip's length or in- and out-points.

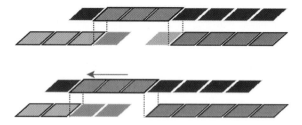

The Slide edit changes the in- and out-points of adjacent clips while retaining the original clip's edit points.

- **Slip edit**—Slips a clip *under* two adjacent clips. Slip changes a clip's starting and ending frames without changing its duration or affecting adjacent clips.

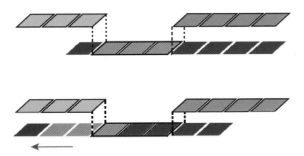

The Slip edit changes the in- and out-points of the selected clip while retaining the adjacent clip's edit points.

Note: *Two points: Though Slip and Slide tools are typically employed on the center clip of three adjacent clips, each tool functions normally even if the clip is adjacent to a clip on one side and a blank space on the other. And for Rolling, Slip, and Slide to work as expected, there need to be sufficient unused head or tail frames to make the edit changes.*

- **Extract edit**—Removes a selected range of frames and closes the gap by moving the following clips to the left.

- **Lift edit**—Removes a selected range of frames and leaves a gap.

Making Rolling, Slide, and Slip edits

1 Play the Lesson 8 intro video.

2 Open Premiere Pro to the Lesson 8 project.

3 Open the Lesson 8-1 sequence on the Timeline.

It has two sets of clips with enough head and tail frames to allow these edits.

4   Convert the Program Monitor to a floating window (Ctrl+drag its Drag Handle) and expand it to get a better view of the split screen as you make a Rolling Edit.

5   Select the Rolling Edit tool (keyboard shortcut N) from the Tools panel.

6   Drag the edit point between the first two clips on the Timeline, using the Program Monitor split-screen to find a better matching edit.

I suggest Rolling the edit point to the right 1;02 (1 second and 2 frames). You can use the Program Monitor timecode or the pop-up time code (both shown in the next figure) in the Timeline to find that edit.

Note: To facilitate making a precise, frame-specific edit, expand the view of the Timeline by pressing the equal sign key (=).

The Rolling Edit tool changes the out- and in-points of adjacent clips.

7   Select the Slide Edit tool (U) and place it over the middle clip (Clip B) of the second set of clips in the Lesson 8 Practice sequence.

8   Drag Clip B left or right.

This is just to demonstrate the edit. You don't need to find a specific edit point.

9   Take a look at the Program Monitor as you perform the Slide edit.

The two top images are the in- and out-points of Clip B. They do not change. The two larger images are the out- and in-points of the adjacent clips—Clip A and Clip C respectively. These edit points change as you slide the selected clip *over* those adjacent clips.

Note: As you move the clip, you will eventually run out of head or tail frames and the timecodes will stop changing in the Program Monitor.

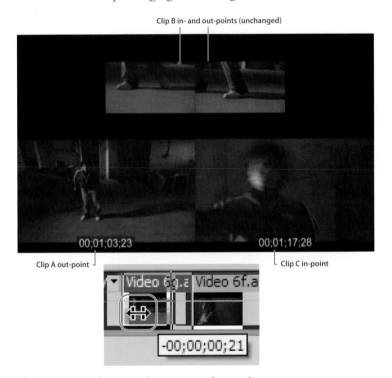

The Slide Edit tool moves a clip over two adjacent clips.

10   Select the Slip Edit tool (Y) and drag Clip B left and right.

11 Take a look at the Program Monitor as you perform the Slip edit.

The two top images are the out-point and in-point of Clips A and C, respectively. They do not change. The two larger images are the in-point and out-point of Clip B. These edit points change as you slip Clip B *under* Clips A and C.

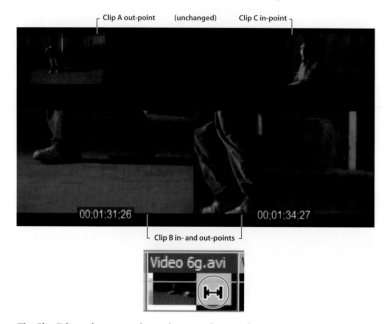

The Slip Edit tool moves a clip under two adjacent clips.

Note: *Try both the Slide and Slip Edit tools on Clips A and C. Both editing tools work on the first or last clips in a sequence.*

Using the Program Monitor's Lift and Extract functions

1 Click the History tab and click New/Open to undo all the Rolling, Slide and Slip edits you just did.

2   Move the Timeline CTI to Clip B of the second collection of clips.

3   Drag a Viewing Area Bar handle (highlighted in the next figure) in the Program Monitor so its CTI is roughly centered. This is simply to make it easier to set in- and out-points.

4   Drag the Program Monitor CTI within Clip A to where the dancer's left foot hits the floor—at about 16;18.

5   Press the Set In Point button (I).

6   Drag the Program Monitor CTI within Clip B to find a matching edit—at about 20;25.

7   Press the Set Out Point button (O).

As shown in the next figure, your Timeline now has a light blue highlighted zone between the in- and out-points, and a gray area in the Time Ruler with in- and out-point brackets at each end.

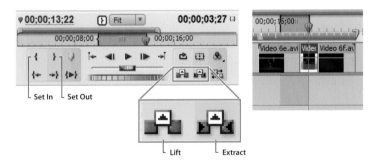

Note: The Lift and Extract buttons look the same until you get really close to the screen. As shown in the previous figure, Extract has tiny triangles indicating that adjacent clips will fill the gap left by the edit.

8   Click the Lift button.

That deletes those selected frames and leaves a gap.

9   Press Ctrl+Z to undo that edit.

10   Press the Extract button.

That performs the equivalent of a Ripple delete. Play this edit to see how, by clicking only one button, you made a matching edit.

Adding a TV news-style cutaway: Lesson 8-2

You use cutaways to cover jump-cuts and avoid viewer disconnects. For example, when you "butt" together two sound bites from the same interviewee, put a cutaway over their edit point—a hand shot, a reverse cutaway of the interviewer, or something the interviewee is talking about. Instead of putting two wide shots of a football game together, use a cutaway of a crowd shot, a parent shouting encouragement, or the scoreboard to cover their edit.

When adding cutaways you choose whether to add audio from the cutaway. For instance, if you use a reverse cutaway of an interviewer during a sound bite, you don't want to hear whatever sound is on that cutaway clip. But in the case of a parent shouting encouragement, you want to mix that shout with the wide shot's audio.

1   Click the Lesson 8-2 Finish tab in the Timeline and play the first set of clips. That is how your project should look and sound by the end of this mini-lesson.

Note: You can look at the second set of clips too. At the end of this mini-lesson I suggest you use it as a model for some extra credit work.

2   Open the Lesson 8 Practice sequence.

3   Select Sound Bite 8a and Sound Bite 8b (Ctrl+click in that order) in the Project panel and drag them to the Video 1 track.

You will trim the beginning and end of the first clip as well as cut out a portion to remove a pause. Then you will add a cutaway to cover that removed section and cover up the original edit point.

4   Use the Ripple Edit tool (B) to trim the beginning of the first clip to just before the horse rider says "Stay focused." That's at about 24 frames.

Note: You can position the CTI at 00;24 and use the Snap feature to make a frame-accurate trim.

5   Use Ripple Edit to trim the end of the first clip to just after the rider says "important stuff," about 11;06.

The next clip does not need trimming.

6   Listen to the middle of the first clip and use the Program Monitor to set an in-point right after she says "at other horses"—about 5;02.

You will do an Extract in a moment.

7   Set the out-point in the Program Monitor right before she says "keeping your heels"—about 6;20.

8   Target the Video 1 and Audio 1 tracks by clicking their headers (where the track names are listed—highlighted in the next figure).

9   Click the Extract button in the Program Monitor.

That performs the equivalent of a Ripple delete to remove that pause. Your sequence should be 18;09 long (more or less) and look like the next figure.

10   Listen to and watch the sequence. Notice how the rider's face makes little jumps at the two edit points.

You will cover up those two jump-cuts with a single cutaway.

11   Double-click Cutaway 8a in the Project panel to load it in the Source Monitor.

Note that it is 5;02 (five seconds and two frames) long.

12   Click the center clip in the Timeline to select it and click the Info panel's tab.

Note that this clip is 4;16 long. The cutaway is sufficiently long to cover this clip.

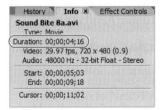

13   Put the Timeline CTI at the edit point between the first and second clip.

You will use the Source Monitor Overlay feature to place the clip there.

💡 **Placing cutaways**

Cutaways should either start or end at the edit point. If they start there, then the action ends or the interviewee finishes a comment while still on-screen. If a cutaway ends at the edit point, that lets the action or comment begin on-screen. Positioning a cutaway so it covers the end and the beginning of the two clips is generally awkward.

13 Click the Audio 2 track header to target it.

You will use this cutaway's audio. The Video 1 track header is already highlighted and therefore targeted. The audio and video from the cutaway will go to the targeted tracks.

14 Use the Set In and Out Points buttons to mark the beginning and end of the entire Cutaway 8a clip.

15 Check that the Toggle Take Audio and Video icon in the Source Monitor is set to Audio and Video(🖭).

Your set-up should look like the next figure.

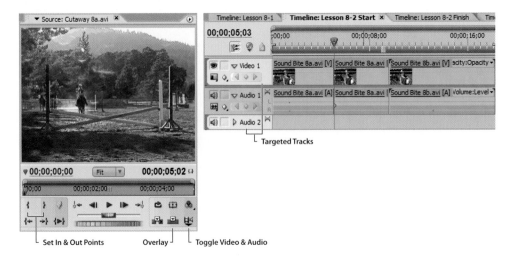

16 Click the Overlay button. (🖳).

That overlays the video on the Video 1 track, covering the sound bite video clip and its two jump-cuts, and places the audio on the Audio 2 track.

Note: If you want to reduce the volume of the cutaway audio clip, click it to select it, twirl down the Volume disclosure triangle in the Effect Controls panel, and reduce the volume level to about –6 dB.

17 Drag a Cross Dissolve from Effects > Video Transitions > Dissolve to the edit point between the second and third sound bite clips.

Since the third clip has no head frames, the transition will end at the edit point. But the dissolve makes this scene change work nicely.

Cutaway editing—extra credit

If you want to take cutaways to next level, you can use the second group of clips in the Lesson 8-2 Finish sequence as a model. It has an opening scene, the audio fades out as the rider begins speaking, and the sequence closes with a different shot that starts before the rider finishes her last comment.

Take note of a couple video editing techniques. I place the opening clip so the horse and rider move off-screen before putting the interview on-screen. And for the closing shot, I start with the horse and rider off-screen. Both techniques make for more comfortable edits—to ease viewers into and out of sound bites. In addition, I gradually fade the cutaway audio up and down to ensure those edits are not jarring to the viewers' ears. To do that means adjusting keyframes—a concept I explain in several lessons later in the book.

Changing clip speed and direction: Lesson 8-3

Playing clips in reverse presents all sorts of possibilities: kids diving out of a pond, a pitcher retrieving his fastball, and an explosive cloud of dust suddenly becoming an intact building. Create even more fun or drama by adding slow or fast motion.

In this mini-lesson you will make a spinning dancer gradually slow down, stop, and then rewind.

1 Click the Lesson 8-3 Finish tab in the Timeline and play that brief sequence.

The dancer starts spinning, gradually slows down, stops, and then spins backward, gradually accelerating until he freezes at the end.

2 Click the Lesson 8 Practice tab in the Timeline and delete the clips you worked on in Lesson 8-2.

3 Drag Video 8e to the beginning of the Video 1 track on the sequence.

Press the backslash (\) key to expand the view of that clip.

4   Select the Razor Edit tool and make three cuts at 1;00, 2;00, and 3;00, turning one clip into four. Your sequence should look like the next figure.

5   Right-click on the last clip and select Copy.

6   Move the CTI to the end of the sequence (use the Page Down shortcut key) and press Ctrl+V (Edit > Paste).

7   Move the CTI to the end of that newly placed clip and press Ctrl+V again.

8   Right-click on the third clip and Copy/Paste it to the end of the sequence.

Note: You'll need to use the backslash or minus key to shrink the view as you build this sequence.

9   Right-click on the second clip and Copy/Paste it to the end of the sequence.

10   Copy/Paste the first clip to the end of the sequence twice. Your sequence should look like the next figure, with ten clips in all.

11   Marquee select the final eight clips.

12   Click on any of those eight clips and drag the whole lot of them to the right, past the 18-second mark, to make room for the slow-motion clips.

The first two clips should remain in place at the beginning of the sequence.

Note: If you cut a clip's speed in half, that doubles its length. If the clip has a clip to its right, it will not double in length and push that adjacent clip to the right. Rather, it will play the first half of the clip in slow motion and discard the second half.

13   Right-click on the second clip and select Speed/Duration (or select Clip > Speed/Duration).

That opens the Clip Speed/Duration dialog box. You have a few options:

- **Speed**—As a percentage. Double time is 200% and half speed is 50%.

- **Link/Unlink button**—If linked (default setting), changing the speed changes the length accordingly. If unlinked, the length remains the same.

Note: Speeding up the clip shortens it. If you want to maintain duration, Premiere Pro will use all available head or tail frames to fill the space left from the speed change. If there aren't enough extra frames, it speeds up the clip only to the point that it uses all the available frames to fill the original space on the sequence. If there are no head or tail frames, it shrinks the clip.

- **Reverse Speed**—Plays the clip video and audio backwards at whatever speed you set. You can also disassociate the audio and have it play normally. I cover that unlinking technique later in the book.

- **Maintain Audio Pitch**—This is a very clever feature. When audio speeds up, it normally sounds like Alvin and the Chipmunks. When it slows down, it's basso profundo. Maintaining the audio's pitch means that the audio changes speed, but keeps the original pitch.

- **Duration**—Instead of a percentage, you can select a specific time. This is a great tool if you want to fill a gap and your clip is not quite long enough. You could simply use the Rate Stretch tool but that wouldn't give you the option to Maintain Audio Pitch.

💡 **Rapid fire narrations**

The Maintain Audio Pitch feature is great if you want to speed up an announcer's voice to fit his copy, like that end-of-commercial disclaimer common to car financing commercials.

14 Put 75% in the Speed text box and click OK.

15 Drag the third clip up next to the second, right-click, select Speed/Duration, type 50% and click OK.

16 Follow the same process for the fourth clip, giving it a 25% speed.

17 Drag the fifth clip over, right-click on it, select Frame Hold, select Hold On > Out Point, and click OK.

Note: Since the fifth clip is a copy of the fourth clip, putting a frame hold on its last frame will match the final frame of the fourth clip.

18 Play those first five clips. The dancer should gradually slow down and then freeze.

19 Drag over the sixth clip, right-click on it, select Speed/Duration, select 25%, click Reverse Speed and click OK.

20 Follow that same process for the seventh, eighth and ninth clips giving them 50% and 75% and 100% speeds and checking Reverse each time.

21 Drag the tenth clip over and put a frame hold on its In Point (that means it'll match the previous clip's out-point because it's playing in reverse).

22 Play your sequence. It should match the Lesson 8-3 Finish sequence.

> ### Getting that slow-mo music video look
>
> *Creating slow-motion music videos takes some preparation. How, you might ask, can the singer lip-synch while loping in slow motion on a beach?*
>
> *Here's how: Create a faster version of the music and then play that while shooting the video. The singer lip-synchs at a faster rhythm, and the video editor slows down the video to match the beat of the original tune.*
>
> *It takes some math to get the numbers right. Basically you slow the video down by the inverse of the speed increase. Here's one example: If you speed the music up to 150% of its original speed, you'll need to slow the video down to 67% to get the video to synchronize to the original tune. The inverse of 150% (1.5 times the original speed) is .67 (1 divided by 1.5).*

Using graphics with two transitions: Lesson 8-4

In Lesson 6 I skipped two transitions that require the use of graphic files: Image Mask and Gradient Wipe.

- **Image Mask**—This so-called transition (it's more like a video effect) has a narrow purpose—using a graphic or image to define how a portion of one clip will display on another. Premiere Pro converts the graphic image to grayscale, then converts pixels containing 50% or more gray to black and pixels containing less than 50% gray to white. Clip A displays in black areas and Clip B displays in white areas. Image Mask and its video effect twin are static, which limits their value. Later in the book I show you how to use a Track Matte that works similarly but also can change size and move to follow action.

- **Gradient Wipe**—This is a true transition. It lets parts of Clip A and Clip B display together using a custom mask and gradually moves from one scene to the next using a smooth animation. It's like other Wipe transitions, but in this case you control the shape of the edges. In a reversal of the Image Mask transition, Clip B shows through the black area, whereas Clip A shows through the white area (you can check Reverse in Effect Controls to swap that function). Also, in this case, Premiere Pro does see things as gray. As the transition progresses, the gray areas darken and more of Clip B shows through until at the end of the transition only lip B is onscreen.

1 Click the Lesson 8 Practice tab in the Timeline and delete the sequence you just completed.

2 Click New Item—the button at the bottom of in the Project panel (highlighted in the next figure)—and select Color Matte.

Note: You will use two color mattes—solid color, screen-size graphics—to get a better feel for how these transitions work.

3   Move the Select-a-Color slider up or down to a color you like, click in the screen to pick a shade, and click OK.

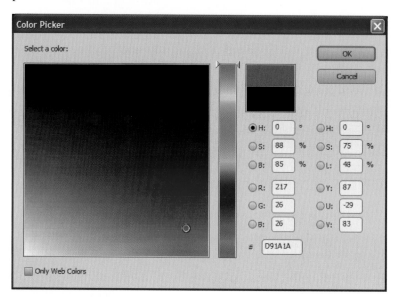

4   Give it a descriptive name and click OK.

5   Follow that process again to make another matte with an obviously different color.

💡 **Color mattes are useful objects**

Now that you know how to make color mattes, consider using them in your projects. For instance, use them if you want a simple color background for text or for pictures-in-pictures. You can tint videos by laying a color matte over a clip and reducing its opacity. I cover that kind of compositing later in the book.

6   Drag both Color Mattes to the Lesson 8 Practice sequence on the Timeline and press the backslash key to expand your view.

7   Apply the Image Mask transition (from Effects > Video Transitions > Special Effect) to their edit point.

That pops up the Image Mask Settings box.

8   Click Select Image (the Lesson 8 folder should open by default), and double-click Image Mask-1.jpg. That returns you to Image Mask Settings where you can see that this graphic is a blue oval.

Note: Premiere Pro will "see" the blue oval as black and let Clip A show through it while having Clip B display on the white area.

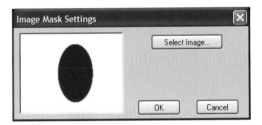

9   Click OK and move the CTI to the edit point to take a look at the transition in the Program Monitor.

10   Click the transition rectangle and view its parameters in the Effect Controls panel. Increase its Duration, change the border width, and give it a color.

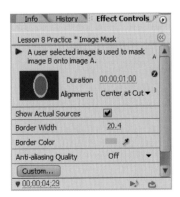

11 Click Custom and double-click Image Mask-2.jpg.

It consists of two gradients and a solid color object.

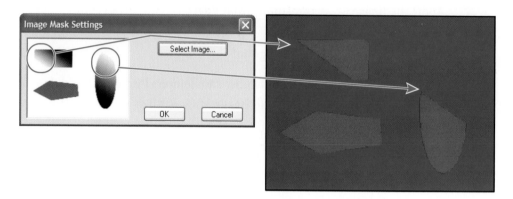

12 Click OK and note how Image Mask treats gradients.

Image Mask will see portions of the gradients as only black or white—transparent or opaque (highlighted in the previous figure).

13 Drag Gradient Wipe (from the Wipe transition bin) to the edit point, replacing Image Mask.

Note: *The Gradient Wipe Settings box should appear. If not, click on the transition rectangle in the Timeline to view its parameters in the Effect Controls panel and click Custom.*

14 Click Select Image, double-click Gradient Wipe-1.jpg, and note that it is a simple diagonal gradient.

15 Adjust the softness of the transition's edges by dragging the Softness slider, then click OK.

16 Drag the CTI through the transition and note that Clip B increasingly shows through Clip A.

17 Click Reverse in the Effects Panel and see how that transition works.

18 Click Custom and try the Gradient Wipe-2.jpg. As shown in the next figure (on the right), it uses multiple gradients.

Note: Gradient Wipe can use very elaborate wipes. All you need is basic graphics creation software. I used Photoshop CS to make the graphics used in this lesson because it's so easy to create gradients with it.

Two Gradient Wipe transitions.

Switching a four-camera production: Lesson 8-5

The Multi-Camera feature simulates live camera switching for up to four cameras. Your work takes place within a monitor that shows the four sources and the final output.

The workflow is as follows:

1 Place clips from multiple cameras on separate tracks—one above the other—in a sequence.

2 Synchronize the clips within that sequence.

3 Nest that multi-cam sequence in another sequence.

4 Enable the Multi-Camera feature.

5 Open the Multi-Camera Monitor.

6 View the clips and switch among the cameras.

7 Fine-tune the edits and apply effects and transitions on the sequence.

In this lesson you will work with four clips, shot with four cameras at the same time from different angles. The production crew used a clapper slate, shown in the next figure, for use later during editing to synch the four cameras. The clapper slate gives both a visual and an aural indication to set synch points.

However, we will forgo the clapper slate in this mini-lesson for two reasons:

- I needed to conserve space on the DVD. It can hold only about 21 minutes of DV files. This is not to be confused with MPEG-2 video, which is the standard, compressed video format used for feature films on DVD. Single-sided DVDs can hold about two hours of MPEG-2 video.

- There was too much dead space between the marker and "action."

Note: You can use any type of media in a multi-camera editing session, including footage from various cameras and from still images. You can add more than one clip to a track to accommodate the use of multiple tapes in a camera.

Few video producers have the luxury of working with a full crew, so they end up using other cues to synch up their multi-cam shoots. So this mini-lesson has a real-world feel to it. In addition I purposely trimmed the clips and changed the timecodes so the synch point timecodes would all be different.

This is a substantial lesson, so I've broken it into a three processes: setup, multi-camera switching and finalizing.

Creating the initial multi-camera sequence

1 Open the Lesson 8 Practice sequence and delete all the clips.

2 Double-click Video 8a to put it in the Source Monitor.

3 Move the Source Monitor CTI to where the dancer slams his foot to the floor. I selected 01;02.

You will use this as your clapper slate to set the synch point on all four clips.

4 Right-click in the Source Monitor Time Ruler and select Set Clip Marker > Next Available Numbered.

This adds a little *marker* triangle behind the Source Monitor CTI (you'll need to drag the CTI out of the way to see that marker).

Note: *You can put markers on clips or sequences. You use markers for a variety of purposes, most frequently to mark DVD Chapter points in sequences. In this case, you will have Premiere Pro move the four clips so the markers you place on their synch points all line up vertically.*

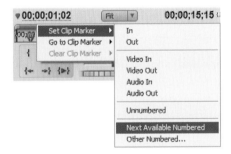

5 Check that the Video 1 and Audio 1 track headers are targeted (highlighted). If not, click on one or both as needed to target those tracks and move the CTI to the beginning of the sequence.

6 Click the Overlay button (Insert will work in this case too) on the Source Monitor to drop Video 8a on Video 1 and its audio on the Audio 1 track in the sequence.

Note: *You are placing this clip on Audio 1 because the Audio 1 track is the master audio source for the Multi-Camera edit and this clip has the best audio of the four angles.*

7 Repeat the synch point location process, including adding the clip marker, for Video 8b. I selected 01;12 as the synch point.

8   Click the Video 2 and Audio 2 headers to target those tracks, move the CTI to the beginning of the sequence and click the Overlay button in the Source Monitor.

Your sequence should look like the next figure. Note the marker icons (⬧) in the clips. You will line up those markers in a few steps.

Note: If you clicked the Insert button instead of Overlay, that would have moved the clips on Video 1 to the right. And if you did not target the Audio 2 track, the audio for Video 8b would replace the Video 8a audio on the Audio 1 track.

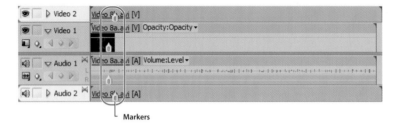

Markers

9   Repeat that process for Video 8c, targeting the Video 3 and Audio 3 tracks and moving the Timeline CTI to the beginning before clicking the Overlay button.

10   Right-click on the Video 1, 2 or 3 header, select Add Tracks, and click OK in the Add Tracks Dialog box.

The default setting is to add one video and one audio track, which is what you want to do in this case.

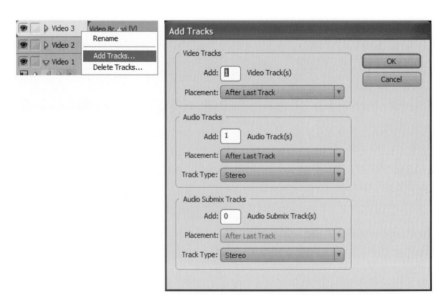

11 Repeat the marker setting and overlay process for Video 8d, targeting the newly added Video 4 and Audio 4 tracks.

Your sequence should look like the next figure.

Note: Video and audio clips placed above track 4 will not be available for multi-camera editing.

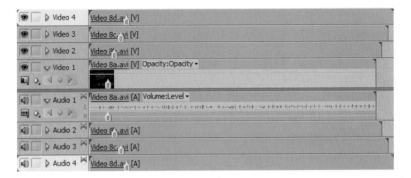

12 Marquee select the four clips.

13 Check whether the Video 1 track is targeted (highlighted). If not, click its header to target it (it's not necessary, in this case, to target an audio track).

14 Select Clip > Synchronize, Numbered Clip Marker (Marker 0 is the only choice), and click OK. The clips align to the Marker on the clip on Video 1.

15 Take a look at the Lesson 8 Practice sequence.

All the markers are lined up vertically. The beginning of the clips above Video 1 were trimmed because they all had more video before the synch point than the clip on Video 1. If you had targeted the Video 4 track, those extra frames would have remained intact. Either way works fine but this saves a trim step later.

Note: There are other synching options. If I had not changed the timecode from the original footage, you could have foregone creating all the Markers and selected Timecode.

Switching Multiple Cameras

Now you will nest that synched and trimmed sequence in another sequence, switch on the Multi-Camera function and edit this four-camera shoot.

1   Select File > New > Sequence and name it *Multi-cam*.

2   Drag the Lesson 8 Practice sequence from the Project panel to the beginning of the Video 1 track on the Multi-cam sequence.

3   Click on the Video 1 track header to target it, click on the nested sequence video clip to select it, and then select Clip > Multi-Camera > Enable.

Note: The command Multi-Camera > Enable will be unavailable unless you have the video track selected.

4   Open the Program Monitor Fly-out Menu and click Multi-Camera Monitor. That opens the five screen Multi-Camera Monitor.

5   Open the Multi-Camera Monitor Fly-out Menu and make sure that Audio Follows Video is deselected.

This means you will use audio only from the Audio 1 track from the Lesson 8 Practice sequence regardless of which camera is active. Otherwise the audio characteristics would change with each edit due to varying microphone placements.

6   Click the Play button and watch this video to get a feel for when to make your edits.

Note: After making your edits, you can go back and change them in the Multi-Camera Monitor or on the Timeline.

7   Move the CTI back to the beginning, click Play and start clicking any of the four screens on the left side to switch among those cameras.

I suggest you switch camera angles to match the rhythm. A red box will appear around the selected camera each time you make an edit.

Note: You can also press the number keys 1-4 to switch among the four cameras.

8   Use the playback controls to review your edited sequence.

Note that at each edit point a yellow box appears on that camera shot.

9   Close the Multi-Camera Monitor.

You can always return to it by selecting it from the Program Monitor Fly-out Menu.

10 Take a look at the sequence in the Timeline.

As shown in the next figure, it will have multiple cut edits. Each clip's label will start with [MC #]. The number represents the video track used for that edit.

Finalizing multi-camera editing

To change an edit in the Multi-Camera Monitor:

1 Open the Multi-Camera Monitor using the Program Monitor Fly-out Menu.

2 Click the Go to Previous (or Next) Edit Point buttons or use the Page Up or Down keys to move to an edit.

3 Click on a different camera to change that edit.

To change an edit in the Timeline:

1 Right-click on the clip you want to change.

2 Select Multi-Camera and then click on the camera number.

Note: Since you are editing on the Timeline, its rules apply. In this case, by doing what amounts to an overlay edit, you also replace the audio with the replacement clip's audio. If it's not the video that was on the Video 1 track, the audio will sound different. To retain the old audio, first ALT+click to select the clip. Using the Alt keyboard modifier unlinks the audio from the video. Then right-click, select Multi-Camera and change to a different camera. That will change only the video portion of the clip.

Joe Walsh, Cinemagic Studios, CEO.

EVENT AND MULTI-CAMERA SHOOTING TIPS FROM CINEMAGIC STUDIOS

Joe Walsh and his team at Cinemagic Studios (www.cinemagicstudios.com) in Portland, Oregon were my "go-to" guys when I worked as an independent video producer. This 25-year-old firm offers a full range of film, video, animation, and multimedia services. Their work has garnered 34 Telly Awards.

One of Cinemagic's fortes is shooting events—concerts, sports, roundtable discussions—using multiple cameras and switching them live, a process fraught with complexities and possible snafus. Here is Joe's event shooting checklist:

- Have a clear understanding of your client's expectations and budget.

- Do a site check and rehearsal to determine the best camera locations. Place the cameras on risers so that you can shoot over people's heads. Position the cameras so they don't break the plane and shoot toward each other.

- Cinemagic's multi-camera setup includes a digital switcher, intercom system, audio mixer, studio recorder, and monitors for each camera crew, plus preview and program feed monitors.

- Give yourself enough time to setup and have a pre-production meeting with your crew to discuss the project and assign their responsibilities.

- Make sure that all the cables are tucked away or taped down.

- After the setup, do a test record and playback check.

- *Jam sync*—set the timecode to match on all recorders—before starting to record.

- Have the cameras record separate tapes. That lets you fix snafus in post-production.

- Ensure that your location is well lit.

- Audio is crucial. Make sure you have enough mics in enough locations.

- When using wireless mics, select UHF instead of VHF to avoid frequency conflicts with other sources.

- Always keep fresh batteries on hand. As the batteries grow weak, reception problems occur.

Review

1 What's the basic difference between a Slide and a Slip edit?

2 What's going on when you use Rolling, Slip, or Slide Edit tools and the clip frames stop moving in the Program Monitor and you can't move the edit point any farther?

3 When you use the Source Monitor to Overlay a cutaway, how do you avoid covering up the original audio clips?

4 You create a freeze frame by selecting Frame Hold and checking Hold On the Out Point. Then you trim that clip's end and the freeze frame image changes. What's going on?

5 You apply a 50% speed to a clip between two other clips in a sequence. Will you see the entire clip in slow-mo?

6 What are the principal differences between the Image Mask and Gradient Mask transitions?

7 Describe four ways to set synch points for Multi-Camera clips.

▶ **Review answers**

1 You Slide a clip over adjacent clips, retaining the selected clip's original in- and out-points. You Slip a clip under adjacent clips, changing the selected clip's in- and out-points.

2 You've reached the end of the line—the beginning or end of the original clip. There are no additional head or tail frames to enable you to move the edit any farther.

3 Click the header of an audio track that has no audio in it at the CTI location to target it before making the Overlay.

4 Since you trimmed the clip's out-point, you changed the Hold On frame. Either use the Ripple Edit tool to trim it from the left (its in-point) or change the Hold On to the In Point.

5   No. You'll see half of the clip. Slow motion increases the number of frames but will not do the equivalent of an Insert edit. It will not shove adjacent clips farther into the sequence to make room for its longer length.

6   Image Mask sees everything in black or white and is merely a means to sandwich two clips together. Gradient Mask is a true transition that converts your graphic to grayscale and gradually moves from one clip to another.

7   Clip start, clip end, Timecode, and Markers. You used Markers in Lesson 8-5. If you had access to the original session videotapes you could have used Timecode or their clapper slate.

video effects

interpolation

keyframes

velocity

Premiere Pro 2.0 features more than 140 video effects—a mind-boggling collection of fantastic visual effects like lightning, spotlights and strobe lights. You can use video effects to change color attributes, adjust brightness and contrast, and simulate lens flare. Most effects come with an array of parameters, all of which you can animate—have change over time— using precise keyframe controls. New to Premiere Pro 2.0 is the ability to control the velocity and acceleration of those changing parameters to give them a more realistic feel. The possibilities are endless.

9 | Adding Video Effects

Topics covered in this lesson:

- Sampling some basic video effects.
- Manipulating keyframes and effect parameters.
- Adding keyframe interpolation and velocity.
- Taking some fantastic effects for a test drive.

Getting started

Video effects let you add visual flair or repair technical issues. Video effects can alter the exposure or color of footage, distort images, or add artistic style. You can also use effects to rotate and animate a clip or adjust its size and position within the frame.

Adding video effects is easy: drag-and-drop to a clip or select the clip and drag the effect to the Effect Controls panel. You can combine as many effects as you like on a single clip, which can produce surprising results. And you can use a nested sequence to add the same effects to a collection of clips.

Virtually all the video effect parameters are accessible within the Effect Controls panel, making it easy to set the behaviors and the intensity of those effects. You can apply keyframes independently to every attribute listed in the Effect Controls panel to make those behaviors change over time. And you can use Bezier curves to adjust the velocity and acceleration of those changes.

To try to fully explain the more than 140 video effects that ship with Premiere Pro 2.0 would be impractical. Rather, I will present a representative sample of what's available and explain how to use the various types of parameters you'll encounter. To really get a feel for Premiere Pro's possibilities, you'll need to do some experimenting.

Sampling some basic video effects: Lesson 9-1

In this lesson you will work with several effects, each offering something new in terms of its parameters or settings. Before diving into this lesson, take a look at the Lesson 9 Intro video.

> ### Adobe Certified Expert exam objective
>
> Describe the options and process required when working with clip-based effects by using the Effect Controls panel.

1   Open Premiere Pro 2.0 to the Lesson 9 project and switch to the Effects workspace—Window > Workspace > Effects.

2   Drag the top of the Effects panel frame to make it as tall as possible.

3   Open the Video Effects folder.

Note: There are 18 Video Effects categories. Some effects are difficult to categorize and could reside in multiple categories or in categories by themselves. But this taxonomy works reasonably well.

4   Click the Effects panel's Fly-out Menu and select New Custom Bin.

That bin/folder appears in the Effects panel below Video Transitions.

5   Highlight it and change its name to something like *My Favorite Effects*.

6   Open any Video Effects folder and drag a few effects into your custom bin.

Note: *The effects remain in their original folder and also appear in yours. You can use custom folders to build effect categories that match your work style.*

7   Drag the Black & White video effect (from the Image Control folder) to the clip on the Timeline.

That immediately converts your full-color footage to black and white—or more accurately, grayscale. It also puts that effect in the Effect Controls panel.

Note: *There are two other effects in the Effect Controls panel: Motion and Opacity. These are fixed effects. Premiere Pro automatically makes them available for all video clips. If this clip had audio, you'd see the Volume fixed effect. I cover Motion briefly in this lesson and in more depth in Lesson 10. Opacity and Volume are covered later in the book.*

8   Toggle the Black & White effect off and on, using the button (◉) in the Effect Controls panel.

Toggling an effect on and off is a good way to see how an effect works with other effects. This Toggle switch is the only parameter available with the Black & White effect. The effect is either on or off.

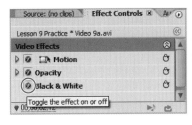

💡 **Resolve jarring shifts to grayscale**

Moving between full-color and black-and-white clips can be jarring. So here's a fix: Use a Cross Dissolve between clips or within the grayscale clip. To put one within the clip in this lesson, select the Razor Edit tool (C), cut the clip in two places, drag the Cross Dissolve transition to those edit points, select the first and third clip segments in turn, and switch off the Black & White effect on both. Now your sequence shifts gradually from color to black and white and back to color. Undo those edits by clicking the History tab and clicking Apply Filter.

9 Check that the clip is selected so its parameters are displayed in the Effect Controls panel, then click on Black & White to select it and press Delete.

10 Drag Camera Blur (Blur & Sharpen folder) into the Effect Controls panel.

This is the other way to apply a video effect—select the clip in the Timeline to switch on its display in the Effect Controls panel, and drag the effect to the Effect Controls panel.

💡 **Finding effects**

With so many video effects folders, it's sometimes tricky to locate an effect. If you know part or all of an effect's name, start typing it in the Contains text box at the top of the Effects panel. Premiere Pro immediately displays all effects and transitions that contain that letter combination, narrowing the search as you type.

11 Twirl down Camera Blur's disclosure triangles and note there are three items the Black & White effect did not have: a Setup button (⇥▤), a Percent Blur slider, and a stopwatch (the latter is to set keyframes, which I cover in Lesson 9-2).

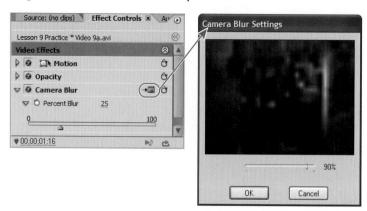

12 Click the Setup button, drag the slider to the right to increase the blur—you get a real time display in the Camera Blur Setting screen—and click OK.

Note: Most video effects do not have a Setup option. For those that do, you generally can access the Setup parameters in the Effect Controls panel as well.

13 Move the Percent Blur slider in the Effect Controls panel.

As you change that setting it shows up in real time in the Program Monitor.

14 Open the Effects Fly-out Menu and select Delete All Effects from Clip (you can not delete Motion and Opacity).

This is an easy way to start fresh.

15 Drag Spherize (Distort folder) to the Effect Controls panel and twirl down its disclosure triangles.

Like the Motion fixed effect above it in the Effect Controls panel, Spherize has a Transform button (⌷↖) that lets you directly control its location in the Program Monitor.

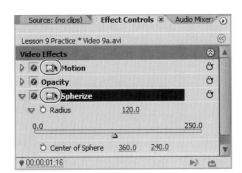

16 Move the Radius slider to about 120 so you can see the effect in the Program Monitor.

17 Click "Spherize" (on its name in the Effect Controls panel) to switch on its Transform control crosshairs in the Program Monitor (highlighted in the next figure) and drag the bulbous-looking effect around inside that screen.

Note: The Center of Sphere parameters in the Effect Controls panel change as you do this.

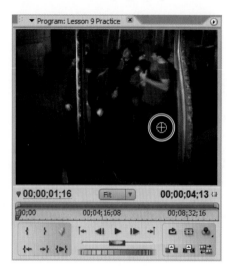

18 Delete Spherize and drag Wave Warp (Distort folder) to the Effect Controls panel and open its six disclosure triangles to display its eight parameters.

Note: Wave Warp has three drop-down lists. These are specific effect conditions that do not have numeric values associated with them. But even these are keyframeable. That is, you can switch from one discrete condition to another at any time in the clip's duration.

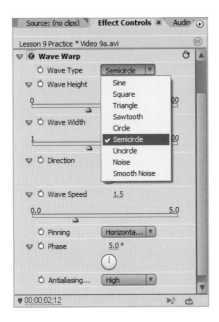

19 Make various selections from each of the three drop-down lists and adjust some of the other parameters.

Note: Eight parameters might seem like a lot. But that's about average for the video effects in Premiere Pro. I will show you two effects with 25 parameters each, later in this lesson.

20 Play this clip.

This is one of the animated effects you'll find in Premiere Pro. While virtually all Premiere Pro video effects let you animate them over time using keyframes, Wave Warp and a few others have built-in animations that operate independently of keyframes.

21 Reset the Wave Warp back to its starting point by clicking the Reset button in its upper right corner.

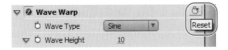

Manipulating keyframes and effect parameters: Lesson 9-2

Virtually all parameters for all video effects are keyframeable. That is, you can change the effect's behavior over time in myriad ways. For example, you can have an effect gradually *rack* out of focus, change color, warp into a funhouse mirror, or lengthen its shadow.

1   Expand the display of the Effect Controls panel until its view is wide enough for the Show/Hide Timeline View chevron (⊛) to become active and click that button to open the timeline (depending on your screen size, you might want to put the Effect Controls panel into a floating window—Ctrl+drag the drag handle).

2   Delete the Wave Warp effect and drag Fast Blur In from Presets > Blurs to the Effect Controls panel.

3   Play the clip to see how this preset works. The clip starts at the maximum blur value and sharpens at the one-second point.

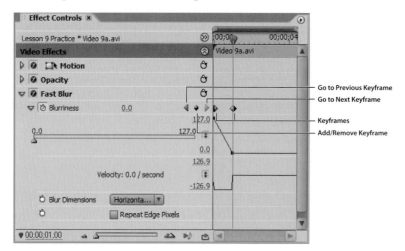

4   Drag the effect's second keyframe to the right and play the clip now.

It takes longer for the blurred image to sharpen into focus. Keyframes are not permanently affixed. You can change their position without changing their value.

5   Delete the Fast Blur effect, drag Replicate (Stylize folder) to the Effect Controls panel and twirl down its single disclosure triangle.

Note: Replicate has a Setup dialog box, but like other video effect setup dialog boxes, there are no keyframe controls within it. So for this exercise, work within the Effect Controls panel.

6 Put the CTI at the beginning of the clip (with the Effect Controls panel active, press Home or Page Up).

7 Click the Toggle Animation stopwatch (Ö) highlighted in the next figure.

That does three things:

• Switches on Keyframes.

• Adds a keyframe at the CTI location and gives it Replicate's default starting value of two (a 2x2 grid of replicated clips).

• Displays two thin black lines in the Effect Controls timeline: the Value Graph and the Velocity Graph. I cover Velocity in Lesson 9-3.

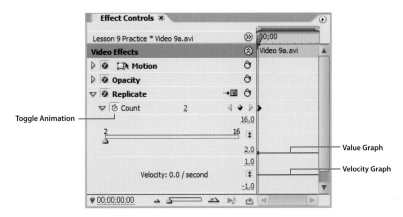

8 Drag the CTI to about the 1-second point.

Locate the 1-second point by looking in the Program Monitor or the Timeline Time Ruler. It's generally not easy to see an exact time in the Effect Controls timeline unless you really widen its viewing area.

9 Change the Replicate effect's Count parameter to 9 (mid-way between this effect's minimum and maximum values).

Note: That automatically adds another keyframe at that point, since changing a parameter at a location without a keyframe automatically adds a new keyframe.

10 Drag the CTI to about the 3-second point.

11 Click the Add/Remove Keyframe Button (between the two keyframe navigation buttons).

That adds a keyframe with the same value as the previous keyframe. In this way, the effect will not change from the 1-second to the 3-second position.

12 Go to the end of the clip (press Page Down and then press the Left Arrow key) to display the last frame of the clip.

Note: Pressing Page Down takes you to the frame following the last frame in a selected clip. That is by design. When you use the keyboard shortcut Page Down you want to go to the start of the next clip, not the final frame of the current clip.

13 Change the Count value to 16.

Your Effect Controls panel should look like the next figure.

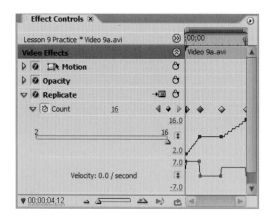

14 Play the clip and note how the effect builds to a 9 x 9 grid, holds for two seconds and changes to a 16 x 16 grid at the end.

Now you'll use two methods to change two keyframe values.

15 Click the Go to Previous Keyframe button twice to move to the second keyframe.

16 Use the Count slider to change its value to 2. That's one simple way to change a keyframe's value.

17 Click the Go to Next Keyframe button to move to the third (of four) keyframes.

18 Hover the cursor over that keyframe's Value Graph button (highlighted in the next figure). When it changes to this tiny Pen Tool cursor ($\mathsf{R}_\circ$), drag the button as high as it will go to change its value to 16.

This is the other way to change a keyframe's value.

Note: You can drag the Value Graph button only up or down. It will not allow you to move it left or right, to avoid inadvertently changing the keyframe's time position within the clip.

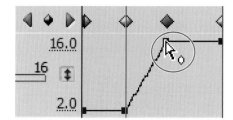

19 Drag Lesson 9 Text from the Project panel to the sequence after the video clip, position the CTI on it and click on it to display its parameters in the Effect Controls panel.

Note: If you don't move the CTI to the clip you're applying an effect to, you won't see that clip or its effect in the Program Monitor. Selecting a clip does not move the CTI to that clip.

20 Drag Radial Blur to that clip or to the Effect Controls panel and apply the following keyframes (use the next figure as a reference):

- Beginning of clip: Amount=30, Center X=0
- Center of clip: Amount=30, Center X=128
- Three-fourths into clip: Amount=1, Center X =64

21 Play this clip.

Note: Effects are great ways to animate or move a graphic or text over a video clip.

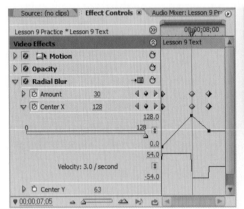 

Extra credit: Following action and combining multiple effects

I prepared four effect presets for you to deconstruct. One is a single effect that follows action. The others are three effects that work together. I suggest you check them out. Feel free to change the parameters as much as you want. You can always delete your work and start over by dragging the presets back into the Effect Controls panel.

💡 Creating an effect preset

If you plan to reuse an effect with keyframes, save it as a preset. To do that, set your keyframes, parameters, and interpolation controls (I cover interpolation in Lesson 9-3), click the effect name in the Effect Controls panel, open the Fly-out Menu, select Save Preset, give it a name, note whether to scale it to the clip length or anchor it to the clip In- or Out-Point, then click OK. It'll show up in the Presets folder.

1   Open the Effects panel's Fly-out Menu, select Import Preset and import the four Lesson 9 presets one at a time.

2   Drag Lesson 9 Radial Blur to the Effect Controls panel and twirl down all its disclosure triangles. The Effect Controls panel should look like the following figure.

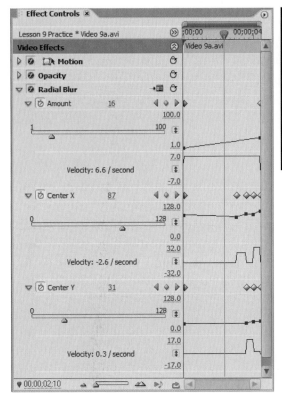
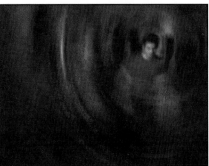

3   Play that effect and note how the radial blur changes and stays centered on the main dancer's face (see previous figure).

4   Move through the keyframes and check out how I set those keyframes to follow his movement through the frame and off camera.

5   Delete Lesson 9 Radial Blur and drag the three other Lesson 9 Presets (in this order)—Motion, Camera View, and Lens Flare—to the Effect Controls panel.

💡 Effect order counts

Clip-based (non-fixed) Video Effects work from bottom to top in the Effect Controls panel with the newest applied effect appearing at the bottom of the effect list. For example, if you apply the Tint effect and then apply Black & White, the clip will display as grayscale. Black & White trumps Tint because it appears below Tint in the Effect Controls panel effect list. If you apply Black & White first then apply Tint, the clip will have the color you select in the Tint effect. Opacity and Motion, which are fixed effects, are always the final two effects applied—even when, in this case, you used a Motion preset and applied it first. If you want Motion to be applied in a different order then use a clip-based motion effect like Camera View, Transform or Basic 3D. You can drag effects up and down within the Effect Controls panel to change their order.

6   Twirl down all the disclosure triangles that have the Toggle Animation stopwatch turned on (including Position in the Motion fixed effect).

If you see a sweep hand in the stopwatch, keyframes have been switched on. There are too many keyframed parameters in this combination of effects to see them all in a single screen without scrolling through them, but the middle of your Effect Controls panel should look like the following figure (I sliced it in two to fit better on this page).

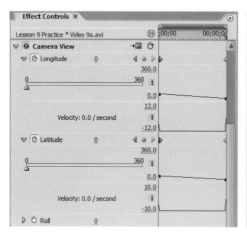
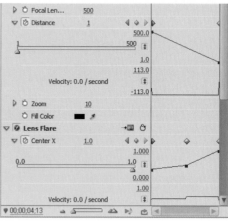

7 Play this effect-combo.

My goal when I put together these effects was to move the clip through 3-D space and move a lens flare across it. For a Lens Flare to look realistic, there needs to be movement (either camera movement or clip motion).

8 Make as many changes as you want. Experiment, deconstruct, delete and start all over. The purpose is to become comfortable with adding, moving, changing, and deleting keyframes.

9 Delete all the effects, either one at a time or click the Effect Controls panel's Fly-out Menu and select Delete All Effects from Clip.

That does not delete Motion nor change its parameters.

10 Click the Motion > Position Toggle Animation button to remove all keyframes and click Motion's Reset button to return the Motion parameters to their default values.

Adding keyframe interpolation and velocity: Lesson 9-3

Keyframe interpolation changes the behavior of an effect parameter as it moves toward or away from a keyframe. The default behavior that you've seen so far is linear—constant velocity between keyframes. What generally works better is something that mirrors your experience or exaggerates it—gradual acceleration or deceleration or super-fast changes.

Premiere Pro 2.0 offers two ways to control those changes: Keyframe interpolation and the Velocity Graph. Keyframe interpolation is the easiest—basically two clicks—while tweaking the Velocity Graph can become a full-time occupation. To get a handle on this feature will take some time and practice on your part.

The effect I use for this lesson is the Motion fixed effect. Its Position, Scale and Rotation parameters all lend themselves to speed changes. To make those parameter adjustments more obvious, I created a simple arrow graphic in Photoshop CS. It has a transparent background. If it had a solid color background, the motion would display that rectangular background as well, making for a disconcerting effect.

To start this lesson, simply continue where you left off in Lesson 9-2.

1   Replace the video and text clips on the Timeline with Graphic 9.psd from the Project panel.

2   Lengthen that arrow graphic clip in the Timeline by dragging its right edge to about the 10-second mark.

3   Stretch the Effect Controls panel as wide as practical. If you put it in a floating window, leave room to view the Program Monitor.

4   Open the Effect Controls panel's timeline (click the Show/Hide Timeline View chevron button).

5   Add Rotation keyframes in four places: the first and last frame plus two more in between.

To do that, position the CTI at the beginning of the clip, click Rotation's Toggle Animation button (that places a keyframe at the beginning of the clip with the default parameter value of zero), drag the CTI to the three other positions and press the Add/Remove Keyframe button in each spot. Your Effect Controls panel should look like the following figure.

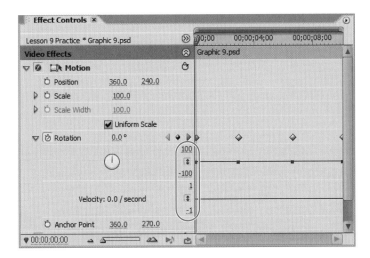

6   Look at the numbers highlighted in the previous figure.

•   100 and –100—Default values for the highest and lowest Rotation parameter settings. They will change to accommodate the actual high and low Rotation parameters once you change the keyframe settings.

•   1 and –1—Default relative velocity values. Since you have not changed any parameters, the velocity is a straight line with the value of zero.

7   Change the Rotation value for the second, third and fourth keyframes using three methods (navigate to the keyframes using the Go To Next/Previous Keyframe buttons).

• 2nd keyframe—click the Rotation number and type in 2x (two full clockwise rotations).

• 3rd keyframe—drag the Rotation wheel left until the value displayed is –2x0.0° (it's difficult to get that exact figure—if you end up at something like –2x2.0° that's OK).

• 4th keyframe—drag the Value Graph button to –1x0.0°.

Once completed, your keyframes and graphs should look like the next figure:

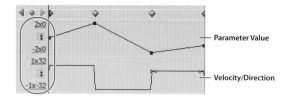

8   Drag the CTI through the clip and look at the Value and Velocity Graphs and the numbers to the left of the graphs (shown in the previous figure):

• The top and bottom Value numbers have changed to 2x0 and –2x0 (two full rotations in both directions) to show the actual maximum and minimum parameter values. They remain unchanged as you move the CTI.

• The Value Graph shows the parameters' values at any given time.

• The top and bottom Velocity numbers on the left side of the graph note the spread of the parameters' velocity in degrees per second. The numbers shown in the previous figure—1x32 and –1x32— mean 392° (360+32) clockwise and counterclockwise. Those values don't necessarily equal the actual high and low velocities but simply define what amount to the current maximum and minimum values on the Y-axis of an X/Y graph.

• The Velocity graph shows the velocity between keyframes. The sudden drops or jumps represent sudden changes in acceleration—*jerks* in physics parlance. Points on the graph above the middle of the Velocity Graph area represent positive (clockwise) speeds and points below the center represent negative (counter-clockwise) speeds. The farther the point or line is from the center, the greater the velocity (and you thought high school algebra was a waste of time).

9   Play that clip.

The arrow will spin clockwise twice, spin faster going counterclockwise four times, and spin slower going clockwise once.

10 Right-click on the first keyframe and select Ease Out.

That does several things:

- Changes the keyframe icon to an hourglass.

- The Value Graph button now has a Pen Tool handle and the graph has a slight curve.

- The Velocity Graph button has a similar Pen Tool handle and a more obvious curve. That curve shows the velocity change over time—its acceleration.

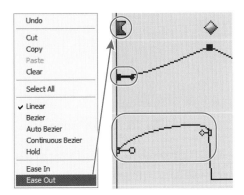

11 Play that portion of the clip. The effect looks more realistic.

12 Right-click on the next three keyframes and give them (in this order) Bezier, Auto-Bezier and Ease In. Here's a rundown on the Premiere Pro Keyframe Interpolation methods:

- **Linear**—The default behavior. A uniform rate of change between keyframes.

- **Bezier**—Lets you manually adjust the shape of the graph on either side of a keyframe. This allows for sudden acceleration changes into or out of a keyframe.

- **Continuous Bezier**—Creates a smooth rate of change *through* a keyframe. Unlike Bezier, if you adjust one handle, the handle on the other side of the keyframe moves in a complementary fashion to ensure a smooth transition through the keyframe.

- **Auto Bezier**—Creates a smooth rate of change through a keyframe even if you change the keyframe parameter value. If you choose to manually adjust its handles, it changes to Continuous Bezier point, retaining the smooth transition through the keyframe.

- **Hold**—Changes a property value without a gradual transition (sudden effect change). The graph following a keyframe with the Hold interpolation applied appears as a horizontal straight line.

- **Ease In**—Slows down the value changes entering a keyframe.

- **Ease Out**—Gradually accelerates the value changes leaving a keyframe.

Your Effect Controls timeline should look like the following figure (the value and velocity graph limit numbers might differ depending on the size of your Effect Controls panel).

Note: By adding these smooth curves, the parameter values change over the course of the effect such that they sometimes might be greater than the highest keyframe parameter value or less than the lowest keyframe parameter you set.

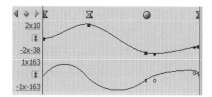

13   Play the entire clip and marvel (really) at how slick it looks.

Simply by adding Keyframe Interpolation, your Motion effect looks much more realistic.

14   Select the second keyframe—the Bezier hourglass—to activate it. Pen Tool handles appear on that keyframe's Value and Velocity Graph button as well as on the two adjacent sets of buttons. That's because changing one keyframe's interpolation handles can change the behavior of the keyframes next to it.

15   Drag the Velocity Graph handle, highlighted in the next figure, to the left.

That creates a steep velocity curve, meaning the arrow will accelerate quickly, then decelerate quickly but will still spin only twice between the first and second keyframe. You changed the velocity without changing the value.

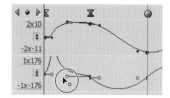

16   Select the third keyframe—the Auto Bezier circle icon—to activate it.

17   Drag the handle highlighted in the next figure and note that the circular keyframe icon immediately switches to an hourglass, because manually adjusting an Auto Bezier keyframe makes it a Continuous Bezier keyframe.

Note: As you drag the left handle, the right handle moves in concert with it to keep the Value Graph curve smooth through the keyframe.

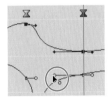

18 Click the Toggle Automatic Range Rescaling button (highlighted in the next figure) to un-constrain the curves.

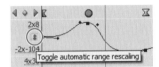

19 Adjust one or two handles and note that the curves can extend beyond the boundaries of the Value and Velocity Graphs rectangles.

By activating Automatic Range Rescaling, you always constrain the graph limits within the boundaries allotted in the Effect Controls panel. That's why the values to the left keep changing to let you know what the new upper and lower limits are.

Note: If you add another keyframe it'll have Keyframe Interpolation already applied to it. When you first add keyframes, you can grab their Value and Velocity Graph handles and adjust the curves manually. Making any such adjustment will change the keyframe icon to the Bezier Keyframe Interpolation hourglass.

One additional Velocity/Interpolation issue

When working with Position-related parameters, right-clicking a keyframe will offer two types of interpolation options: Spatial (related to location) and Temporal (related to time). You can make Spatial adjustments in the Program Monitor as well as the Effect Controls panel. You can make Temporal adjustments on the clip in the Timeline and in the Effect Controls panel.

I cover those motion-related topics in Lesson 10.

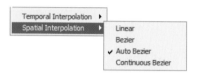

Taking some fantastic effects for a test drive: Lesson 9-4

This lesson combines hands-on, step-by-step tasks with experimentation. The purpose is to introduce you to three high-level effects and encourage you to explore further.

1　Select Help > Adobe Premiere Pro Help.

2　Open Contents > Effects: Reference > Gallery of Effects.

There you will see examples of about a third of the video effects that come with Premiere Pro.

Note: The other headings under Effects: Reference match the Effects panel's bin names.

A portion of the Premiere Pro Help file's Gallery of Effects.

3　Open Effects: Reference > Render effects > Lightning.

This gives you an explanation of each parameter—25 in all!—in the Lightning effect. Every Premiere Pro video and audio effect has such a listing in the Help file.

4　Close Help, return to the Premiere Pro workspace, and replace the Graphic 9.psd clip in the Timeline with the Video 9 clip.

5   Drag Page Curl (GPU Effects) to the clip and open its parameters in the Effect Controls panel (in the figure I put the clip over a gray matte to better display the Page Curl effect).

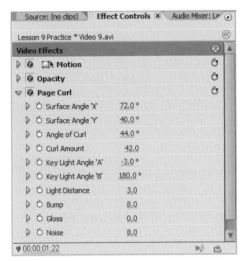

6   Change the Angle of Curl number to see that you can start the curl from any edge or corner of the clip.

To animate the curl, you need to apply keyframes to Curl Amount. You can have the page partially curl and then have it uncurl.

Note: This works like the Page Curl GPU Transition but offers many more options. In this case, you have total control over the animation, including adjusting the angle of the curl, the angle and distance of two light sources, the bump (the texture) of the surface, and how glossy or noisy the surface appears. It can work like a transition in that you can apply it to a clip above another clip on the Timeline to reveal the clip below it.

7   Delete Page Curl and drag Lighting Effects (Adjust folder) to the clip or Effect Controls panel.

8   Drag Texture 9.psd to the Video 2 track directly above the Video 9 clip in the Video 1 track.

9 Right-click on the clip in Video 2 and click Enable to de-select that.

Turning off Enable turns off the display of that graphic clip so it won't cover the clip below it in the sequence. You will use this graphic to add texture to a spotlight.

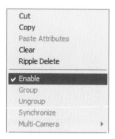

10 Select the Video 9 clip to display its parameters in the Effect Controls panel.

11 Change the Bump Layer to Video 2.

As with Page Curl, *bump* means texture. For this effect, you provide the texture by putting a graphic, image or video clip on a video track above the clip you apply Lighting Effects to.

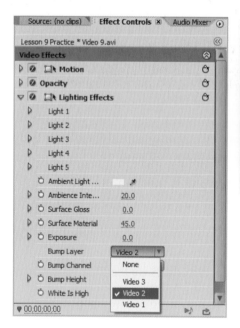

12   Change Bump Channel to G (Green) or B (Blue).

The spotlight now will have a texture.

13   Experiment with the spotlight placement, angle, intensity, color and the like.

Note: Lighting Effects has a Transform button, which, in this case, lets you drag each of the five lights to different positions on the screen in the Program Monitor.

14   Delete Lighting Effects and drag Lightning (Render folder) to the Effect Controls panel.

15   Click the Transform button (or the word "Lightning") to switch on the two crosshair targets in the Program Monitor.

They designate where the lightning will start and end.

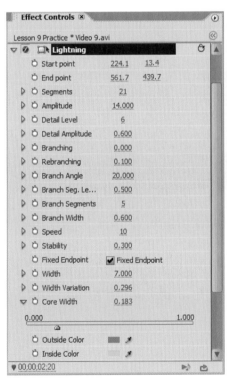

16 Drag the start and end points for the lightning to place them at opposite corners of the picture frame in the video.

17 Adjust some of the two-dozen other parameters including the outer and inner colors.

18 Drag another instance of Lightning to the Effect Controls panel (in some cases you can apply the same effect more than once to a clip) and give it the same start point but a different end point.

Third party plug-in providers

Now that you've got your feet wet, I think you have begun to see what Premiere Pro is capable of. What might surprise you is that the dozens of effects that come with Premiere Pro only begin to tap its potential. There are hundreds of effects and transitions available online—some for free, most for retail purchase—from a broad spectrum of third-party providers.

To get a taste of all that is out there, visit www.adobe.com, go to the Premiere Pro page and click Third-party Plug-ins. There you will see a list of effect packages, several of which contain dozens of effects. Most of those effects are deeply detailed and offer exciting possibilities. Check around a bit. Some third-party plug-in providers offer free trial packages or have demos of the effects online.

Review

▶ **Review questions**

1   What are the two ways to apply an effect to a clip?

2   List three ways to add a keyframe.

3   How do you make an effect start within a clip rather than at the beginning?

4   Dragging an effect to a clip turns on its parameters in the Effect Controls panel but you don't see the effect in the Program Monitor. Why not?

5   Describe two ways to change a keyframe's parameter setting.

6   How do you apply Keyframe Interpolation and adjust its settings?

▶ **Review answers**

1   Drag the effect to the clip or select the clip and drag the effect to the Effect Controls panel.

2   Move the Effect Controls panel's CTI to where you want a keyframe and switch on keyframes by clicking the Toggle Animation button, move the CTI and click the Add/Remove Keyframe button, and with keyframes on, move the CTI to a position and change a parameter.

3   One of two ways, depending on the effect. Some effects, such as Fast Blur, have a zero setting where they do not change the clip's appearance. In that case place a keyframe where you want the effect to start and set it to zero. Other effects are always "on" to some degree. In those cases, use the Razor Edit Tool to cut the clip where you want the effect to start and apply the effect to the segment to the right.

4   You need to move the Timeline CTI to the selected clip to see it in the Program Monitor. Simply selecting a clip does not move the CTI to that clip.

5   Use the Go to Next/Previous Keyframe buttons and change the parameter value directly next to the parameter descriptor, or drag that keyframe's Value Graph button up or down.

6   Apply Keyframe Interpolation by right-clicking on a keyframe and selecting one of the keyframe interpolation methods such as Bezier or Ease In. Change those default settings by dragging the Bezier curve handles.

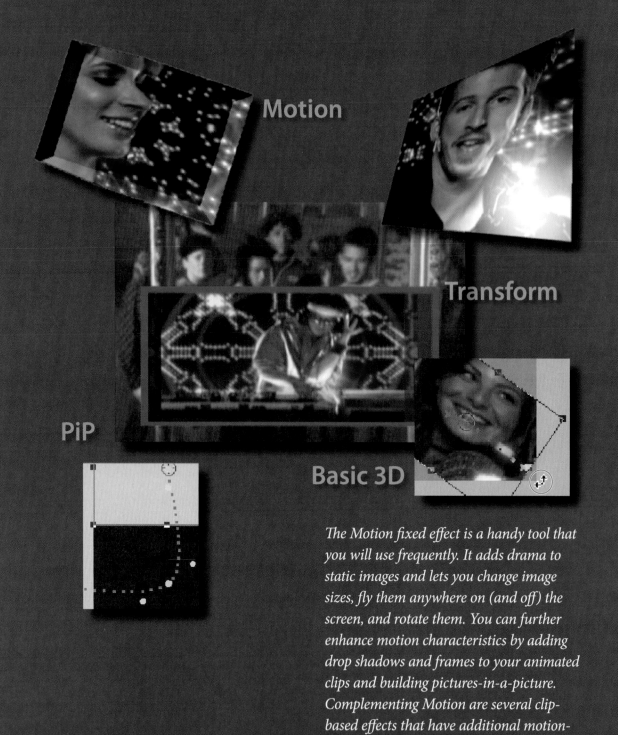

Motion

Transform

PiP

Basic 3D

The Motion fixed effect is a handy tool that you will use frequently. It adds drama to static images and lets you change image sizes, fly them anywhere on (and off) the screen, and rotate them. You can further enhance motion characteristics by adding drop shadows and frames to your animated clips and building pictures-in-a-picture. Complementing Motion are several clip-based effects that have additional motion-oriented features such as skewing images and adding reflective glints.

10 | Putting Clips in Motion

Topics covered in this lesson:

- Applying the Motion effect to clips.

- Changing clip size and adding rotation.

- Working with keyframe interpolation.

- Putting pictures-in-a-picture.

- Enhancing motion with shadows and beveled edges.

- Other motion effects: Transform, Basic 3D and Camera View.

Getting started

You've seen the Motion effect in action already in this book. You used its Rotation feature to test Keyframe Interpolation and you've seen how it can zoom and pan still images.

As you watch TV advertisements, you're bound to see videos with clips flying over other images or clips that rotate onscreen—starting as small dots and expanding to full-screen size. You can create those effects using the Motion fixed effect or several clip-based effects with motion settings.

You use the Motion effect to position, rotate, or scale a clip within the video frame. You can make those adjustments directly in the Program Monitor by dragging to change its position, or by dragging or rotating its handles to change its size, shape or orientation.

You can also adjust Motion parameters in the Effect Controls panel and animate clips using keyframes and Bezier controls.

Applying the Motion effect to clips: Lesson 10-1

You adjust Motion effect parameters in the Program Monitor and the Effect Controls panel. Before you start the lesson, view the Lesson 10 Intro video for a quick run-through of what's to come.

> ### Adobe Certified Expert exam objective
>
> Describe the options and process required when working with fixed effects. Author's note: You worked with clip-based effects in Lesson 9. Fixed Effects are Motion, Opacity and Volume. Motion and Opacity are automatically available for all clips including still images and graphics. Volume is available for all clips with audio. I cover Opacity and Volume later in the book.

1 Open Premiere Pro 2.0 to the Lesson 10 project and open the Lesson 10 Practice sequence.

2 Switch to the Effects workspace (Window > Workspace > Effects).

3 Click the Program Monitor, View Zoom Level drop-down list (highlighted in the next figure) and change the Program Monitor zoom level to 25%.

This is to help you see and work with the Motion effect's bounding box.

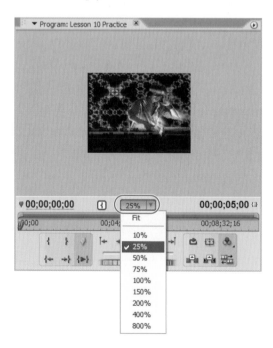

4 Expand the Program Monitor frame (if necessary) so there are no scroll bars in the screen. Your Program Monitor should look like the previous figure.

5 Import this Lesson's effect presets. To do that open the Effects panel's Fly-out Menu, select and open each Lesson 10 preset in turn (there are five in all).

6 Drag the Lesson 10-1 Preset from Effects > Presets to the clip on the Lesson 10 Practice sequence and play that clip.

This is how the Motion effect you'll work on should look by the end of this mini-lesson.

Note: I used the Rate Stretch Tool to lengthen this one-second clip to five seconds.

7 Twirl down the Motion disclosure triangle in the Effect Controls panel.

8 Click the Position Toggle Animation stopwatch to turn off its keyframes.

9 Click OK when prompted that the action will delete all keyframes.

10 Click the Reset button (to the right of Motion in the Effect Controls panel).

These two actions return Motion to its default settings.

Examining motion characteristics

1 Drag the CTI anywhere in the clip so you can see the video in the Program Monitor.

2 Click inside the Program Monitor screen.

That puts a bounding box with a crosshair and handles around the clip (as shown in the next figure) and activates the Motion Effect in the Effect Controls panel. Clicking on Motion or its Transform button (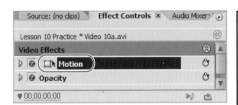) in the Effect Controls panel will also activate the clip bounding box in the Program Monitor.

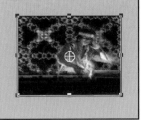

3 Click anywhere in the clip bounding box in the Program Monitor, drag this clip around and note how the Position values in the Effect Controls panel change.

4   Drag the clip so its center is directly over the upper left corner of the screen and note the Position values in the Effect Controls panel are 0, 0 (or close to that depending on where you placed the center of the clip).

The lower right corner of the screen is 720, 480, the standard NTSC DV screen size.

Note: Premiere Pro uses something like an upside-down X/Y axis for screen location. That coordinate system is based on a methodology used in Windows for so long that to change it now would create numerous programming headaches. The upper left corner of the screen is 0, 0. X and Y values to the left and above that point respectively are negative. X and Y values to the right and below that point respectively are positive.

6   Drag the clip completely off the screen to the left as shown in the next figure.

7   Fine-tune that adjustment by changing the Position values in the Effect Controls panel to -360, 240.

Since 360 is half of 720, this puts the right edge of the clip at the left edge of the screen frame.

8   Put the CTI at the beginning of the clip (press Page Up or Home) and apply a Position keyframe there by clicking Position's Toggle Animation stopwatch.

9   Drag the CTI to the center of the clip and change the Position values to 360, 240 (the center of the screen).

Changing the Position parameters adds a keyframe there.

10   Put the CTI at the end of the clip (press Page Down, then the left arrow key).

11   Change the Position values to 360, -240.

That puts the clip completely above the screen and adds a keyframe.

12   Play the clip.

It moves smoothly on-screen, then slides off the top. You have created a path (if you don't see the path, click on *Motion* in the Effect Controls panel to switch on its display). Make note of a few things (highlighted in different colors in the next figure):

- It's a curved path. Premiere Pro automatically uses Bezier curves for motion.

- The little dots describe both the path and velocity. Dots close together represent a slower speed, dots more spread out represent a faster speed.

- The little four-point stars are keyframes.

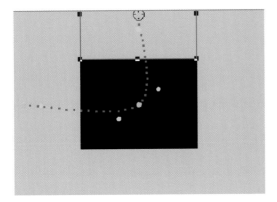

A Clip Motion Path (color added for emphasis): Red dots represent the Path (their spacing indicates relative Velocity), cyan dots are keyframes, yellow dots are Bezier handles and the magenta lines are the clip's bounding box.

13 Drag the center keyframe in the Program Monitor (the four-point star/square) down and to the left.

Notice that the dots get closer together to the left of the keyframe and farther apart to the right.

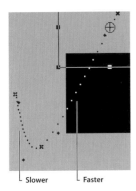

Slower   Faster

14   Play the clip and note that it moves slowly until the first keyframe then speeds up.

Note: By moving the center keyframe you changed its location and thereby the distance the clip traveled between it and its adjacent keyframes. But you did not change the time between keyframes. So the clip moves faster between keyframes that are farther apart and slower for those nearer to each other.

15   Drag the center keyframe again, this time down and to the right (use the next figure as a reference).

That creates a parabola with evenly spaced dots on both sides, meaning the velocity will be the same on both arms of the parabola.

16   Drag the center keyframe in the Effect Controls timeline first to the left, and then most of the way to the right.

Note: Now you are changing the time between keyframes but not changing their physical location in the screen. The little path/velocity dots in the Program Monitor will spread out or slide closer together but the keyframes will not change locations.

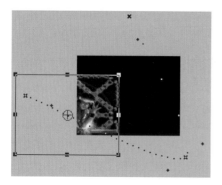

17   Play this clip and note how much slower it goes at the beginning and how much faster at the end.

It should behave the same way it did when you applied the Lesson 10-1 preset.

Changing clip size and adding rotation: Lesson 10-2

Simply sliding a clip around only begins to exploit the Motion effect possibilities. What makes the Motion effect so useful is the capability to shrink or expand the clip and to spin it.

For example, you can start a clip full-screen (or zoom in even farther) and then shrink it to reveal another clip. You can spin a clip onto the screen by having it start as a small dot and then spinning it off the screen, having it grow as it moves away. And you can layer multiple clips, creating several pictures-in-a-picture.

Before you dive into this mini-lesson, look at Motion's six keyframeable options:

- **Position**—The screen location of the clip's anchor point (its center unless you change the anchor point).

- **Scale** (Scale Height with Uniform Scale unchecked)—The relative size of the clip. The slider has a range from 0% to 100%, but you can use the numerical representation to increase the clip size to 600% of its original size.

Note: The percent refers to clip border perimeter, not clip area. So 50% is equal to 25% in terms of area and 25% is equal to 6.25% in area.

- **Scale Width**—You need to uncheck Uniform Scale to make Scale Width active. Doing so enables you to change the clip's width and height independently.

- **Rotation**—You worked with this in Lesson 9-3. You can input degrees or number of rotations. For example 450° or 1x90. A positive number is clockwise and a negative number is counterclockwise. The maximum number of rotations allowed in either direction is 90, meaning that you can apply up to 180(!) full rotations to a clip.

- **Anchor Point**—The center of the rotation, as opposed to the center of the clip. You can set the clip to rotate around any point in the screen including one of the clip's corners or around a point outside the clip like a ball at the end of a rope.

- **Anti-flicker Filter**—This feature is useful for images that contain high-frequency detail such as fine lines, hard edges, parallel lines (moiré problems), or rotation. Those characteristics can cause flickering during motion. The default setting (0.00) adds no blurring and has no effect on flicker. To add some blurring and eliminate flicker, use 1.00.

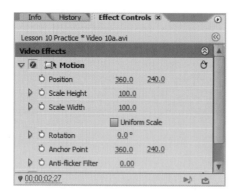

1 Drag the Lesson 10-2 preset (Effects > Presets) to the Effect Controls panel. That replaces the previous Motion settings.

2 Play this animation.

This is how the Motion effect will look by the end of this mini-lesson.

3 Click the Position and Scale Toggle Animation stopwatches to remove their keyframes and click the Reset button to return Motion to its default setting.

4 Place the CTI at the beginning of the clip, click the Position Toggle Animation stopwatch to switch on keyframes, and move the center of the clip to the upper-left corner (position 0,0).

5 Click the Scale Toggle Animation stopwatch and drag the slider to zero.

That sets the size to zero for the beginning of the clip.

6 Drag the CTI about a third of the way into the clip and press Reset. That creates two keyframes using Motion's default settings: the clip at full size and centered in the screen.

7 Drag the CTI about two-thirds of the way into the clip and click the Add/Remove Keyframes button for both Position and Scale.

Doing that causes the clip to remain centered and at full screen for the time between the two keyframes (you could also have clicked Reset again to use those default parameters).

8 Move the CTI to the end of the clip (Page Down, then left arrow) and change the Position parameters to 720, 480 (lower-right corner).

9 Drag a bounding box corner handle (in the Program Monitor) to shrink the clip all the way down to the center crosshairs. That sets Scale back to zero.

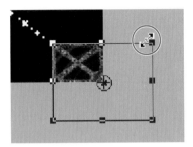

💡 **Changing clip size—like working with text**

As you did in the Titler, you can change clip size using the bounding box. Uncheck Uniform Scale, then to scale freely, drag a corner handle; to scale one dimension only, drag a side (not a corner) handle; and to scale proportionally, Shift+drag any handle.

10 Take a look at your Effect Controls timeline. It should look like the next figure.

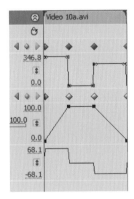

11 Play this clip.

The clip should grow from a tiny dot in the upper left, move to full-screen in the center, hold there for a while, and then shrink to a dot while moving to the lower-right corner.

Adding rotation and changing the anchor point

1 Move the CTI to the beginning of the clip (Page Up or Home) and click the Rotation Toggle Animation stopwatch.

That sets a keyframe for Rotation with 0.0° as the starting point.

2 Move the CTI to the second keyframe (click the Go To Next Keyframe button next to either Position or Scale).

3 Hover the cursor just outside a handle of the bounding box in the Program Monitor until it turns to a curved double-arrow cursor (↖) and drag the bounding box clockwise two full circles (see the next figure).

Note: You can fine-tune this move in the Effect Controls panel by setting Rotation to 2x0.0°.

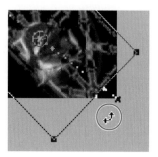

4 Move the CTI to the third keyframe and click Rotation's Add/Remove Keyframe button. That adds a keyframe with the same value as the preceding keyframe.

5 Move the CTI to the end of the clip.

6 Drag the Rotation circle (open the Rotation disclosure triangle) counterclockwise twice (you can't use the Program Monitor bounding box because the clip has been shrunk to a point).

That will return Rotation to its default setting of 0.0°. Your settings will look like the next figure. Play this clip. It will rotate clockwise twice, hold, and then rotate counterclockwise.

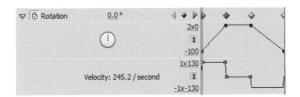

7 Return the CTI to the beginning of the clip.

8 Click the Anchor Point's Toggle Animation stopwatch, and set the numeric values to 0,0.

Note: This will make the clip spin around its upper-left vertex. The anchor point location uses the same coordinates used for Motion's Position parameter: 0, 0 is the upper left corner of the screen and 720, 480 is the lower right. These anchor point coordinates are independent of the clip Scale. You can set anchor points outside the clip to have the clip rotate around a point. Try –360 and 240 for example.

9 Move to the second keyframe and change the Anchor Point's values to 360, 240 (putting clip's rotation vertex in the center of the clip—its default location).

Note: You can adjust the Anchor Point parameters only in the Effect Controls panel. There is no crosshair target for the Anchor Point in the Program Monitor. Transform, the clip-based effect upon which Motion is based, displays crosshair targets for both the clip center and the anchor point in the Program Monitor.

10 Go to the third keyframe and click the Anchor Point Add/Remove Keyframe button to add a keyframe there using the previous keyframe's values.

11 Move to the fourth keyframe and change the Anchor Point to 720, 480 (setting the clip's rotation vertex to its lower-right corner of the screen). Your Anchor Point Velocity Graph should look like the next figure.

12 Play this effect. It should look like the Lesson 10-2 preset.

Working with keyframe interpolation: Lesson 10-3

The Motion effect moves clips through the screen over a period of time. Premiere Pro offers Keyframe Interpolation methods that suit both aspects of that motion: Spatial and Temporal.

Spatial Interpolation refers to the motion path—where the clip will appear on screen. Temporal Interpolation refers to changes in velocity.

When you worked with non-motion effects—Fast Blur, Wave Warp, and Replicate, for example—you worked with Temporal Interpolation in the Velocity and Value Graphs in the Effect Controls timeline. The effects you've worked with generally haven't had screen location parameters so Spatial Interpolation has not been an option (Lightning is one exception—its start and end points can have spatial and temporal interpolation).

The focus for this lesson is Motion's Position parameter. It has a Spatial Interpolation option that you will likely use time and again. You won't find it in the Effect Controls panel. It's in the Program Monitor.

1   Expand the View Zoom Level in the Program Monitor back to the default—Fit—and expand the Program Monitor's frame to get a better look at the keyframes.

2   Drag the Lesson 10-3 Preset to the clip.

3   Drag any keyframe handle in the Program Monitor. That will change the motion curve—the Spatial Interpolation—but will not convert the keyframes in the Effect Controls timeline into Bezier curves (their icons remain diamonds).

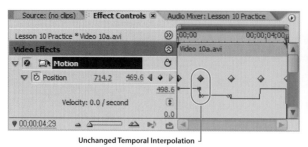 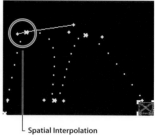

Unchanged Temporal Interpolation   Spatial Interpolation

4 Right-click on any keyframe in the Program Monitor and select Spatial Interpolation > Linear.

That changes the motion lines at that keyframe into straight lines and sharp angles (they'll start curving as they approach a keyframe with Bezier Spatial Interpolation).

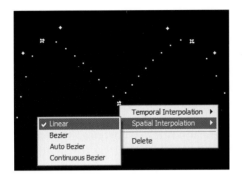

5 Right-click on any keyframe in the Program Monitor and select Temporal Interpolation > Auto Bezier (or any other Bezier Interpolation method).

That changes the Temporal Interpolation keyframe in the Effect Controls panel into a Bezier curve.

Note: *The keyframe in the Program Monitor does not switch to a Temporal Interpolation keyframe. It remains Spatial. To change the temporal characteristics of the keyframe selected in the Program Monitor, you need to drag its handles in the Effect Controls Velocity Graph.*

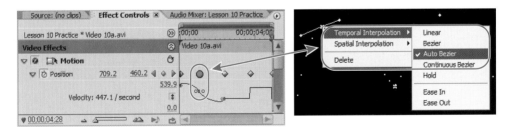

Putting pictures-in-a-picture: Lesson 10-4

The picture-in-picture—PiP—technique is one of the top uses of the Motion effect. And it's one of the easiest ways to see how you can composite—layer—clips. You will begin formal work on compositing later in the book. This mini-lesson will give you a taste.

To simplify things, I've set up a sequence with three layered clips in it, all ready to go. In Lesson 10-5 you will add drop shadows and beveled edges to the PiPs.

1   Open Lesson 10-5 Finish and play that sequence to get an idea of what you can do. It's five PiPs, each with a drop shadow and beveled edge.

2   Open the Lesson 10-4 Start sequence.

If you play this you will see only the clip on the top track. It covers all the clips below it in the sequence.

3   Twirl down Effects > Presets > PiPs > 25% PiPs > 25% UL.

Note the following:

•   All the PiP presets display clips at 1/16th their normal area (reminder: 25% refers to clip perimeter, not area).

•   LL, LR, UL and UR refer to screen locations: Lower Left, Lower Right, Upper Left and Upper Right.

•   Each PiP set offers different types of PiP moves.

•   Typically, you select a style and then adapt it to your needs. For example, you might change the start or end locations or the size.

Note: There is no 25% Center preset. You use one of the presets to create one. Simply change the start and end Position keyframes to 360, 240.

4   Drag PiP 25% UL Slide In Right from the 25% UL bin to the clip on the Video 3 track. Look at the Effect Controls timeline and play the sequence. It slides in from off the right edge of the screen and displays in the upper left corner of the screen.

5   Drag PiP 25% LR Spin In from the 25% LR bin to the clip on the Video 2 track. Look at the Effect Controls timeline and play the sequence. It spins in from infinity and displays in the lower right corner of the screen.

6 You can add the other three video clips to the sequence and apply PiP presets to them. The fourth and fifth clip will go on the Video 4 and Video 5 tracks. Drag the sixth clip above the Video 5 track and Premiere Pro will automatically add a new video track for that clip.

Note: The video clips are only one second long. Use the Rate Stretch Tool to lengthen them to match the length of the other stretched clips.

Enhancing motion with shadows and beveled edges: Lesson 10-5

PiPs have a much more realistic feel when their shrunken clips have drop shadows, beveled edges or some other kind of border.

1 Open the Lesson 10-5 Start sequence.

It has six layered clips (you might need to use the Timeline scroll bar to see them all). The top five all have 25% motion presets applied. I adjusted a Spin In preset for the top clip to change its location to the center of the screen. The clip on the bottom of the sequence in the Video 1 track will serve as the PiP background.

2 Drag the CTI past the 1-second point to display the five PiPs.

3 Drag Bevel Edges Thin (Presets > Bevel Edges) to the top clip in the sequence.

4 Zoom the Program Monitor view in to 150% to get a better look at this effect.

It'll show up in the center of the Monitor. The next figure shows how it'll look after you adjust the Bevel Edges parameters.

5 Open the Bevel Edges disclosure triangles in the Effect Controls panel and change its parameters as follows (use the next figure as a guide):

• Increase the Edge Thickness slightly.

• Change the Light Angle to about 140° to illuminate the dark beveled edge at the bottom of the clip.

• Change the Light Color by dragging the Eyedropper Tool to a purple area of the clip in the Program Monitor.

• Increase the Light Intensity to about .5 to emphasize the beveled edges.

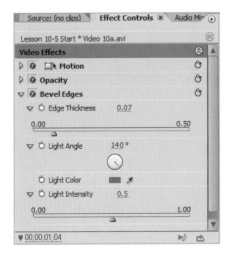

6   Click on Bevel Edges in the Effect Controls panel to select the effect so you can create a preset with the parameters you just applied.

7   Open the Effect Controls panel's Fly-out Menu, select Save Preset, Type in *Lesson 10 Bevel Edges*, give it a description if you want to, and click OK. This new Preset shows up immediately in the Presets folder.

Note: If you had used Keyframes with this effect, selecting one of the three Types—Scale or Anchor to In or Out Point—would have been of some value. The Presets I created for the lessons so far are all Anchored to the In Point to ensure they play at the speed I want— in contrast to the Scale setting, which adjusts Preset keyframe locations depending on the length of the clip.

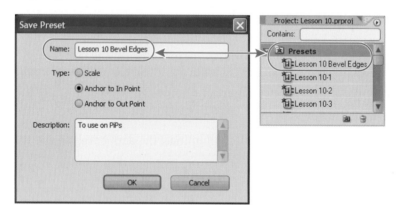

Saving presets for other projects

If you want to use this preset in other projects, export it. To do that, select the preset in the Effects > Presets folder, open the Effects Fly-out Menu, select Export Preset, navigate to an appropriate file folder, give your preset a name (it doesn't have to be the same as its name in the Presets folder) and click Save.

8   Drag Lesson 10 Bevel Edges from the Presets bin to the each clip on video tracks 2-5 (not to the clip on Video 1—that's the full-screen video you'll use as a background for the PiP).

9   Play this sequence (return the Program Monitor View Zoom Level to Fit). All five PiPs will have the same beveled-edge look.

Adding a drop shadow

1   Drag Drop Shadow (Video Effects > Perspective) on the top clip.

2   Change Drop Shadow parameters in the Effect Controls window as follows (use the next figure as a guide):

• Change Direction to about 320° or -40°.

Note: You want the shadow to fall away *from any perceived light source. In this mini-lesson you set the light direction for Bevel Edges to about 140°. To make shadows fall away from a light source add or subtract 180° from the light source direction to get the correct direction for the shadow to fall.*

• Increase the distance so you can see the shadow (you might need to adjust the View Zoom Level of the Program Monitor to see how this works).

• Give your shadow some Softness to make it more realistic. Generally, the greater the Distance parameter, the more Softness you should apply.

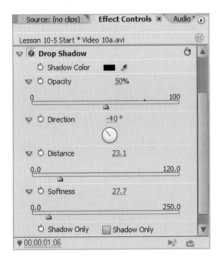

3   Apply these same values to the other four PiPs either one at a time or by saving and using a Preset.

4   Play this sequence. It should look like the Lesson 10-5 Finish sequence.

Other motion effects: Transform, Basic 3D, and Camera View: Lesson 10-6

If you use the Motion effect to apply rotation to your shadow and clip, the shadow will rotate with the clip as a single unit. That's unrealistic. It should always fall away from the rotating clip in the same direction. To get a realistic drop shadow with rotation applied to a clip, you can use the Transform, Basic 3D or Camera View video effects.

To skew your clips—tilt them to give them a 3D look—use Basic 3D or Camera View.

1   Open the Lesson 10 Practice sequence.

2   Drag the video clip from the Video 1 track straight up to the Video 2 track above it.

3   Drag Gray Matte from the Project panel to the Video 1 track directly below the clip on the Video 2 track.

The matte will let you see the clip's shadow.

4   Drag the Lesson 10-6 Motion preset (Presets folder) to the clip.

5   Drag Drop Shadow to the clip and change the Distance parameter to the slider's maximum value of 120 (you can exceed that by changing the numeric value).

6   Play the clip and note how the shadow sticks to the clip.

Note: The Drop Shadow behaves as if its light source were attached to the clip. That's because the Motion effect is the last effect applied to a clip. Drop Shadow becomes part of the clip and Motion rotates the clip and its shadow as a unit.

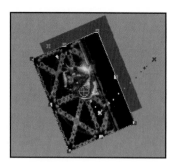

7   Turn off all Motion's keyframes and click the Reset button.

8　Drag the Lesson 10-6 Transform preset (Presets folder) to the Effect Controls panel above Drop Shadow. Placing it above Drop Shadow means you first Transform the clip, then apply a Drop Shadow.

Note: This is the clip-based effect the developers of Premiere Pro used as the foundation for the Motion fixed effect. It has Motion's parameters plus a few others: Skew, Skew Axis, Opacity and Shutter Angle.

9　Play this and note how the drop shadow looks more realistic because it always falls in the same direction.

10　Change the Skew and Skew Axis settings to distort the shape of the clip.

The drop shadow will change accordingly.

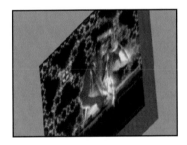

11　Change the Anchor Point and the Position settings to display both crosshair targets in the Program Monitor.

Note: Having both crosshair targets display makes it easier to make adjustments. But it takes some extra effort to differentiate between the two targets. Motion is easier to work with but Transform gives you all of Motion's parameters along with a visual reference to the Anchor Point.

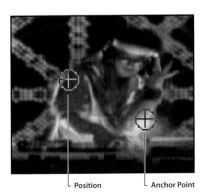

Position　　　Anchor Point

Get a glint with Basic 3D

Basic 3D can swivel and tilt your clip to give the impression it's moving through 3D space. What makes it even more fun is its Specular Highlight—a glint on the surface of the image that moves as you animate the clip.

1   Delete Transform or click its Toggle the Effect On or Off button (⊘) to switch it off.

2   Drag Basic 3D (Perspective folder) to the Effect Controls panel *above* Drop Shadow.

3   Click the Show Specular Highlight box.

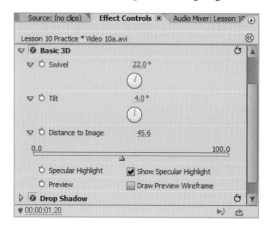

4   Adjust Swivel and Tilt until you see the highlight moving across the clip.

As you move the clip around, the shadow follows suit. But the farther out of kilter you go, the more likely the shadow will stop looking realistic.

Note: The highlight gets very bright when centered on the clip. When using Basic 3D, it's best to swivel and tilt the clip such that the specular highlight moves along the edge of the clip.

Camera View—extra features

Camera View warrants special mention. This effect gives the impression of a camera looking at your clip from different angles. It works a lot like the Basic 3D effect in that it rotates, flips, and zooms a clip. What makes it stand out from Basic 3D is that it gives immediate feedback in its Settings dialog box.

The Camera View effect also lets viewers see the clips below it on the sequence. Instead of offering only a solid color for the screen areas exposed when it's moved from full screen, you can click its Setup button in the Effect Controls panel and uncheck Fill Alpha Channel, making that space transparent. I cover other effects with transparent alpha channels in the compositing lessons.

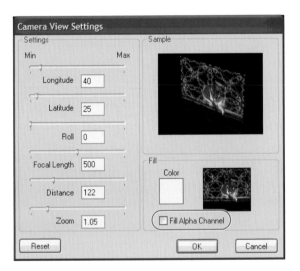

Review

▶ **Review questions**

1   What Motion Position parameter would you use to position a clip so it's centered and just off the right edge of the screen?

2   You start Rotation at its default setting, move the CTI and add a Rotation keyframe with a value of 2x, and then give a value of –2x to the next keyframe. Describe what will happen.

3   You want a clip to appear full screen for a few seconds and then spin away. How do you make the Motion effect's Rotation feature start within a clip rather than at the beginning?

4   How do you select the Motion Position Spatial Interpolation type and change it?

5   If you want to add a drop shadow to a spinning clip, why do you need to use some other motion effect besides the Motion fixed effect?

6   One way to apply the same customized effect to multiple clips is to use a preset. How do you make one?

▶ **Review answers**

1   1080, 240. Here's why: 1080=720 (full clip width) + 360 (half the width to put the clip's left edge on the right edge of the screen). The vertical center point is 240.

2   It will spin clockwise twice as it approaches the first keyframe. Then will spin counterclockwise *four times* as it moves to the next keyframe. The number of spins equals the difference between two keyframe rotation values. Set the Rotation value back to 0 (zero) to have it spin counterclockwise twice.

3   Position the CTI where you want the Rotation to begin and click the Add/Remove Keyframe button. Then move to where you want to spinning to end, change the Rotation parameter and another keyframe will appear.

4   Remember that Spatial Interpolation refers to a clip's location on screen. You set Spatial Interpolation in the Program Monitor screen by right-clicking the Position keyframe, selecting Spatial Interpolation and selecting the interpolation method. You adjust Spatial Interpolation in the Program Monitor by dragging the keyframe's Bezier handles.

5   The Motion fixed effect is the last effect applied to a clip. Motion takes whatever effects you apply before it (including Drop Shadow) and spins the entire assemblage as a single unit. To create a realistic drop shadow on a spinning object, use Transform, Basic 3D or Camera View and then place Drop Shadow below one of those effects in the Effect Controls panel.

6   Adjust the effect parameters to your liking, click on the effect name in the Effect Controls panel to select it, open the Effect Controls Fly-out Menu, select Save Preset, give the preset a name, select one of the three parameters, and click OK.

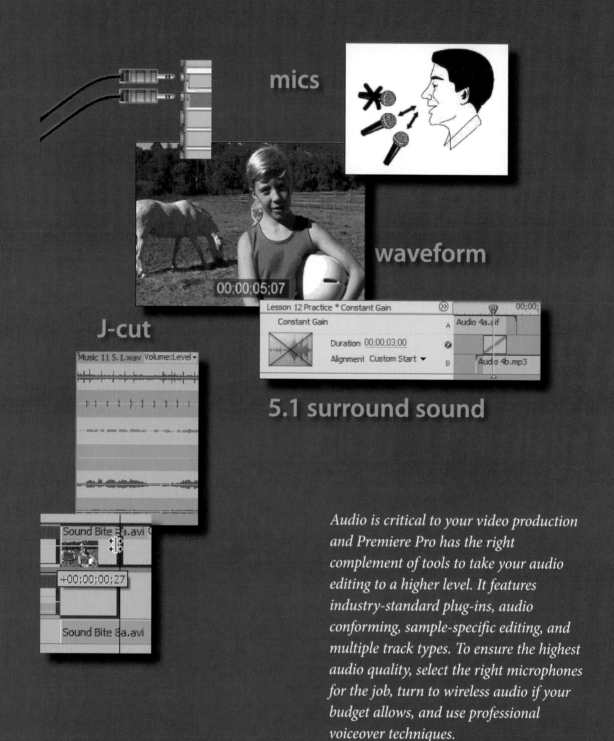

mics

waveform

J-cut

00:00:05;07

Lesson 12 Practice * Constant Gain

Constant Gain

Duration 00;00;03;00

Alignment Custom Start ▾

A Audio 4a.aif

B Audio 4b.mp3

00;00;

Music 11 5.1.wav Volume:Level ▾

5.1 surround sound

Sound Bite 8a.avi

+00;00;00;27

Sound Bite 8a.avi

Audio is critical to your video production and Premiere Pro has the right complement of tools to take your audio editing to a higher level. It features industry-standard plug-ins, audio conforming, sample-specific editing, and multiple track types. To ensure the highest audio quality, select the right microphones for the job, turn to wireless audio if your budget allows, and use professional voiceover techniques.

11 | Acquiring and Editing Audio

Topics covered in this lesson:

- Selecting the right mic for the job.
- Connecting mics to your camcorder or PC.
- Setting up a basic voice recording area.
- Voicing professional narrations.
- Premiere Pro—a high-quality aural experience.
- Examining audio characteristics.
- Adjusting audio volume.
- Adding J- and L-cuts.

Getting started

Audio typically takes a back seat to video but it's crucial to your projects. The best images lose their impact if their audio is mediocre. Your first goal is to acquire high-quality audio at the get-go, both in the field and when recording a narration. That means using the right microphones and using them correctly.

Premiere Pro gives video producers and audiophiles all they need to add top-notch aural quality to their productions. The program has a built-in audio mixer that rivals hardware found in production studios. The mixer lets you edit in mono, stereo or 5.1 surround sound, has a built-in instrument and vocal recording feature, and offers several ways to mix selected tracks.

You can perform industry-standard edits like J- and L-cuts on the Timeline, as well as adjust audio volume levels, keyframes and interpolation.

In addition, Premiere Pro's compliance with two audio industry standards: ASIO (Audio Stream In/Out) and VST (Virtual Studio Technology) ensure that it works smoothly with a wide range of audio cards and dozens of audio effect plug-ins. I cover those plug-ins, the full range of audio effects in Premiere Pro, and its Audio Mixer in Lesson 12.

Selecting the right mic for the job

Most likely you work with a camcorder that has an onboard mic. Onboard mics take the middle ground. They pick up sound from everywhere, including wind, the hum of overhead fluorescent lights, noises you make while handling the camcorder, as well as the the hum of the zoom lens motor.

What you need are external mics: specialized mics that serve narrower but useful functions. Here are the four basic types that suit most circumstances:

- Handheld
- Shotgun
- Lavaliere
- Surface mount

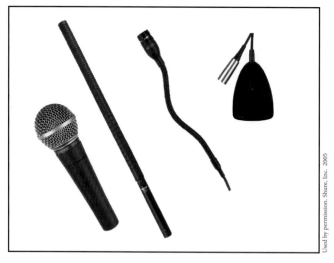

Used by permission. Shure, Inc. 2005

Four standard-issue mics: handheld, shotgun, lavaliere, and surface mount

Handheld mic

Handheld mics are the workhorses of the audio industry. Since they are built with internal shock mounts to reduce handling noise, you'll use these mics for interviews, place them on podiums to record speeches, and voice narrations with them.

Many handheld mics are omnidirectional, meaning that they pick up sound from all directions. They'll pick up ambient room noise as well as close-up audio. To minimize that unwanted noise, keep the mic as close to your subject as practical—usually about a foot from the speaker's mouth.

Basic handhelds start at about $25. Top-of-the-line, durable handhelds start at $150.

Position handheld mics 12 inches from the speaker's mouth at an angle of about 45°. That cuts down on pops made by your breath when you pronounce Ps and Ts.

Shotgun mic

So-named because it resembles a shotgun barrel, the shotgun mic's unidirectional barrel (called an interference tube) narrows the focus of the audio field to about 30 degrees.

Shotgun mics don't zoom. Think of them as looking through a long tube. They narrow your "view" of the sound.

Note: The telephoto-lens equivalent in the microphone world is a parabolic dish. You've seen networks use them along the sidelines of NFL games to get those great crunching hits.

Shotgun mics are a great way to reduce ambient noise and work well during informal, impromptu interviews. Instead of shoving a handheld mic in a nervous interviewee's face, hold a shotgun mic farther away.

A good shotgun mic will set you back about $1,000.

Lavaliere mic

Lavalieres are perfect for formal, sit-down interviews. Their tiny size means that you can conceal them to minimize that "Oh, we're watching TV" disconnect. The downside is that most require batteries. You can buy a basic lav at an electronics store for $25. High-quality lavs start at $200.

Surface mount—boundary—mic

You'll use these specialized mics to pick up several speakers at a conference table or on a theater stage. They're built to be placed on a flat surface and pick up sound waves both in the air and from the hard surface. A basic omni-directional boundary mic costs $40. Higher quality boundary mics cost about $150.

Wireless systems and mics

Wireless mics open a whole new spectrum of possibilities, enabling you to record sound from a distance. After you've used one, you'll wonder how you got along without it.

Depending on the wireless system, you can either hook up standard mics—handheld, shotgun or lavaliere—to a wireless transmitter or use mics with built-in transmitters. Entry-level set-ups cost about $200. Top-of-the-line systems retail for $2,000.

Used by permission. Shure, Inc. 2005

> 💡 **Best single-mic solution**
>
> *If I had to choose a single-mic system solution, I'd go with a wireless shotgun mic. A shotgun mic is versatile and using a wireless transmitter gives you great mobility. You can get crystal clear audio even though the mic might be far from you on a podium, or in your producer's hands in the middle of a crowd. Interviews will be more spontaneous— the mic can be less obtrusive than a typical handheld mic and there is no awkward pause while plugging a cable into the camera.*

Connecting mics to your camcorder or PC

Professional camcorders use rugged, reliable, three-pronged XLR jacks, which match professional mics and cables.

Most consumer and higher-quality *prosumer* camcorders use mini-plug connectors and do not have enough amplification to "hear" standard handheld mics.

So try before you buy. Take your camcorder to the electronics store and test some mics. You might need to buy an XLR-to-Mini adapter or a phantom power amplifier to use certain mics. Both cost less than $100 each.

Making the PC connection

Premiere Pro lets you record a narration directly to your project using a mic connected to your PC's sound card. Most sound cards have only a 1/8" (3.5 mm) stereo minijack outlet. Mics built specifically for PC use typically cost less than $25. When you visit your local electronics store, you'll have two basic options:

• Dynamic mics—Headset or a long-neck version that sits on your desk.

• Condenser mics—These typically are lavalieres, offer slightly better voice-over quality and require a battery.

Plug the mic into the correct soundcard outlet (usually marked Mic or with a mic icon) and not the Line-in jack used with amplified devices such as CD players and sound mixers.

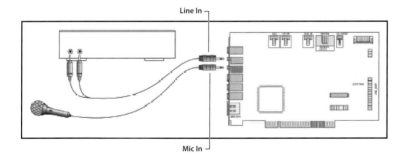

Whichever mic you choose, make sure that you also get a good headset—one that covers your ears to block out extraneous sound. Use that headset both when shooting your video and voicing a narration. It's important to hear how the mic hears you.

Setting up a basic voice-recording area

To create your voiceover narration, you'll need a quiet, sound-absorbing location. The easiest solution is to build a temporary recording area simply by hanging some thick blankets or fiberglass insulation on two joining corner walls. If you can create something like a four-sided, blanketed cubicle, so much the better.

It is an old audio myth that egg cartons, carpeting, and foam rubber work well. Avoid them.

If you drape the blankets only in one corner, point the mic *toward* that corner, place yourself between the mic and the corner, and speak *away* from the blankets. It seems counterintuitive, but the mic is sort of like a camera. It "sees" what's in front of it. In this case it *sees* your face and the hanging, sound-absorbing blankets.

Voicing professional narrations

Go over this checklist before recording your voiceover:

- **Practice reading your copy out loud**—Listen to your words. They should sound comfortable, conversational, even informal.

- **Avoid technical jargon**—That demands extra effort from your listeners, and you might lose them.

- **Short sentences work best**—If you find yourself stumbling over certain phrases, rewrite them.

- **Stress important words and phrases**—As you review your copy, underline important words. When you record your voiceover, you'll want to give those words extra emphasis—more volume and punch.

- **Mark pauses**—Mark logical breaks in narration with short parallel lines.

- **Avoid overly smooth and constant pacing**—That's characteristic of a scripted delivery. You don't want to remind viewers that this is TV. It's real life. It's conversational.

- **Punch up your voice**—Do not slip into a dull, monotone voice. Instead, add some zest and enthusiasm to your narration.

- **Practice**—Record a couple of narrations and listen. Most first-time narrators mumble or swallow words. Have you made yourself clear?

- **Don't pop your Ps and Ts**—As you say P- and T-words, you project a small blast of wind. Avoid speaking directly into the mic.

- **Wear a headset**—It'll help you avoid popping Ps or speaking with too much sibilance—an overemphasis on the S sound. And it'll help you minimize room noise and other extraneous sounds.

Premiere Pro—A high-quality aural experience

Premiere Pro offers professional-quality audio editing tools that rival many stand-alone audio mixing and editing products. For example:

- **Sample-specific edits**—Video typically has between 24 and 30 frames per second. Edits fall between frames at intervals of roughly 1/30 second. Audio typically has thousands of samples per second. CD audio is 44,100 samples per second (44.1kHz). Premiere Pro lets you edit between audio samples.

- **Three types of audio tracks**—Mono, Stereo and 5.1 (six channel surround). You can have any or all of these track types in a sequence.

- **Submix tracks**—You can assign selected audio tracks to a Submix track. That lets you apply one instance of audio and effect settings to several tracks at once.

- **Channel editing**—You can split out individual audio channels from stereo and 5.1 surround sound files and apply effects only to them. For example, you can select the two rear channels in a 5.1 track and add reverb to them.

- **Recording studio**—you can record any instrument or mic you can connect to an ASIO-compliant sound card. Record directly to a track on an existing sequence or to a new sequence.

- **Audio conforming**—Premiere Pro upconverts audio to match your project's audio settings. In addition it converts so-called fixed-point (integer) data to 32-bit floating point data. Floating point data allow for much more realistic audio effects and transitions.

Note: Floating point data have no fixed number of digits before and after the decimal point; that is, the decimal point can float. This leads to more accurate calculations.

> 💡 **Camcorder kHz and bit rate settings**

Many DV camcorders give you two audio quality options: 16-bit audio recorded at 48kHz (16-bits of data per sample at 48,000 samples per second) or lower quality 12-bit audio recorded at 32kHz. The latter option lays down two stereo tracks on your DV cassette: one with audio recorded by the on-camera mic and the other giving you an option to insert a narration or some other audio. If you recorded at 32kHz and set your project to 48kHz, that is not a problem. Premiere Pro will simply take a little longer to upconvert your audio during the conforming process.

Examining audio characteristics: Lesson 11-1

Audio editing is similar to video editing. It uses most of the same tools and you apply transitions and effects in much the same way.

But audio has some characteristics that are different than video and do effect the way you approach audio editing. In this and the remaining mini-lessons in this chapter I introduce you to audio editing. As I mentioned earlier, I cover more advanced audio editing topics in Lesson 12: the Audio Mixer, audio effects and Adobe's professional audio product, Audition 2.0.

1   Play the Lesson 11 Intro video.

2   Open Premiere Pro to the Lesson 11 project.

It has three music clips —mono, stereo and 5.1 surround sound—as well as a narration clip, audio clips from Lesson 4, and the sound bites and cutaways you worked with in Lesson 8.

3   Double-click Narration 11 Mono.wav to open it in the Source Monitor.

That displays a waveform. The peaks and valleys indicate volume levels.

Note: *As highlighted in the next figure, the Toggle Take Audio and Video button automatically switches to Audio-only when you add an audio-only clip to the Source Monitor.*

4   Open the Source Monitor Fly-out Menu and select Audio Units.

That switches the Time Ruler from the standard video-oriented time increments (seconds; frames) to audio samples.

5   Drag the left handle of the Viewing Area Bar to the right to zoom in on the Source Monitor timeline until the difference between numbered markers is 1,000 samples (use the following figure for a reference).

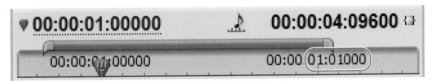

6   Type in 1:0 in the Current Time Display and press return.

7   Press the Left Arrow key once and note that the sample that precedes 1:0 is 0:47999. There are 48,000 audio samples per second in this clip (48kHz). Switching to Audio Units enables you to make sample-specific edits down to (in the case of this project's settings) 1/48,000 of a second. This might seem like splitting hairs, but there are times when cutting audio with this precision will come in handy.

Note: Audio units display with colons (:) versus semi-colons (;) for Video frame timecode.

8   Drag the center of the Viewing Area Bar to the left and right to take a closer look at the audio peaks and valleys.

Note: You can drag the right or left handle of the Viewing Area Bar to change the zoom level.

9   Double-click Music 11 Mono.wav in the Project panel and play it in the Source Monitor.

This is the Adobe Audition 2.0 theme song. Notice the tall thin line at 1:45:09620 (refer to the next figure). That is a drum hit. You can use the waveform display to find sounds like this, including clicks and pops that you might want to remove or edit around.

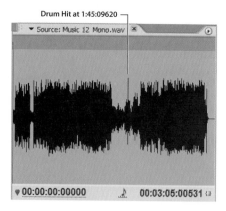

Drum Hit at 1:45:09620

10 Double-click Music Stereo.wav and take a look at it in the Source Monitor.

This is how a stereo signal looks. The display follows the industry standard: left channel on top, right on the bottom.

Note: The basic waveform follows what you saw in the monaural waveform with the exception of a segment of the right channel (highlighted in the following figure), where the guitar music (and a couple of other parts) assigned to the right channel had a rest.

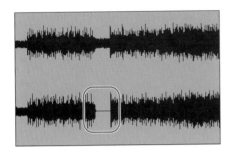

11 Select Edit > Preferences > Audio and make sure the 5.1 Mix Down Type is set to Front + Rear + LFE.

You need to use that setting to hear all six channels of the 5.1 clip in the next step.

11 Double-click Music 11 5.1.wav and take a look at it in the Source Monitor.

This is a 5.1 surround sound clip that I made using the Surround Sound Encoder in Audition 2.0. It has six channels: right, left, center, right-surround (rear), left-surround (rear) and LFE (low-frequency effects—the subwoofer channel).

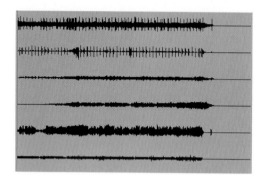

12 Click on Music 11 5.1 in the Project panel to select it and select Clip > Audio Options > Breakout to Mono.

That creates six links, one for each channel (it does not create six new audio files). Using Breakout to Mono lets you edit individual channels of a stereo or 5.1 clip. For example, you might want to give the LFE channel a bass boost. That does not change the original 5.1 clip. You can link this edited channel to the other 5.1 mono channels and create another 5.1 clip.

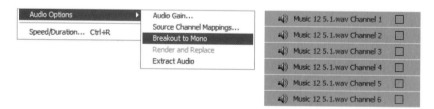

> ## 💡 Waveforms are immutable
>
> *Nothing that you do in Premiere Pro will affect the original audio or video clip or the visible audio waveform. If you change a clip's volume or apply audio effects to it, the waveform will always display the clip's original volume levels.*

13 Drag Music 11 5.1 to the Timeline and notice that Premiere Pro will not let you drop it in the Audio 1 track.

Audio 1 is a stereo track. When you drag an audio clip to a sequence that does not have a track that matches the clip's type, Premiere Pro automatically creates a new track to suit that clip type. Even though Premiere Pro appears to move the new clip below the Master Audio Track, the new track will appear above the Master Audio track once you release the mouse button.

14 Expand the view of the newly-added Audio 2 track by clicking its Collapse/Expand Timeline disclosure triangle (highlighted in the next figure) to open its waveform view, dragging the boundary between Video 1 and Audio 1 up the screen, and dragging the bottom of Audio 2 down.

Your sequence should look like the next figure. Note the labels for each of the six channels in this 5.1 surround sound clip.

15 Click the Source Monitor's drop-down list of clips added to the Source Monitor (highlighted in the next figure) and select Music 11 Mono.

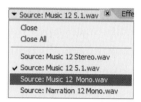

16 Move the Timeline CTI to the beginning of the sequence.

17 Click on the Audio 1 track header.

Note: You need to target an audio track for the Source Monitor Insert or Overlay feature to place an audio clip in the Timeline. Even if, as is true in this case, the track is for stereo clips only and the clip is mono. In this case Premiere Pro will automatically add the correct type of track. Were there no targeted audio track, clicking Insert of Overlay would have no effect.

18 Click the Source Monitor Overlay button and note that because there was no mono audio track in the sequence, Premiere Pro adds a mono audio track below the 5.1 track and inserts that clip there.

Note: You can tell the audio track type by its icon: Mono is a single speaker, Stereo is a double-speaker, and 5.1 says 5.1. The Master audio track is stereo by default. You can change that in the Project Settings > Default Sequence.

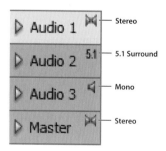

Adjusting audio volume: Lesson 11-2

You might want to decrease or increase the volume of an entire clip or parts of a clip. For example, you might want to bring the natural sound on a video clip down by half while you narrate, gradually fade up the audio at the start or end of a clip, or fade up an interview just as the narrator completes a segment. The latter is part of a J- or L-cut. I explain them in lesson 11-3.

1　Select Window > Workspace > P Pro 2.0 CIB Workspace (or any other workspace) to get your workspace back in order.

2　Delete the audio clips in the Timeline by marquee selecting them and pressing delete.

3　Delete all the added audio tracks by right-clicking an audio track header, selecting Delete Tracks, checking Delete Audio Track(s) in the Delete Tracks window (shown in the next figure), and clicking OK.

Your sequence now has only two audio tracks: Audio 1 and Master (both are stereo).

4   Drag Music 11 Stereo.wav from the Project panel to the Audio 1 track.

5   Expand the track view by clicking the Collapse/Expand Track disclosure button.

6   Click the Show Keyframes button (◢) and select Show Clip Keyframes.

This lets you edit a clip's volume in the Timeline rather than using the Volume effect in the Effect Controls panel.

7   Hover your cursor over the Volume Level Graph—the thin, horizontal yellow line between the left and right channels—until it turns into the Vertical Adjustment Tool (◥⁺) cursor and then drag that yellow line up and down.

Note: A dB (decibel) level readout gives you feedback on the volume change (0dB is the default starting point no matter the actual volume of the original clip). It's not easy to move to an exact setting. You use the Effect Controls panel Volume effect to do that.

8   Ctrl+click the Volume Level Graph in four places evenly spaced along the yellow line. That places four keyframes on the volume line.

9   Drag the first and last keyframes all the way to the left and right respectively to place those keyframes on the first and last frames of the clip.

10 Drag the second and third keyframes left and right respectively to about two seconds from the beginning and two seconds from the end.

11 Drag the start and end keyframes all the way to the bottom of the clip view to create a fade up and a fade out.

12 Play the beginning and end of the clip to see how this works.

Note: As you slide keyframes around in the clip you will invariably change their volume setting values. Adjusting keyframes on the Timeline is quick and easy. You'll want to use the Volume effect in the Effect Controls panel to fine-tune those keyframe parameters.

13 Right-click on the second and third keyframes and select Ease In and Ease Out respectively.

Note: As you can see, you can apply Keyframe Interpolation in the Timeline. However, selecting one of the Bezier curve options would create a more pronounced curve in the middle. So stick with Ease In and Ease Out for most audio keyframes.

Adjusting audio in the Effect Controls panel

The Audio fixed effect works like any other effect in that you can use keyframes to change audio over time. Also you can apply an audio transition (which changes audio volume levels over time) and adjust its settings in the Effect Controls panel.

1 Make sure the Music 11 Stereo clip is selected on the Audio 1 track and open the Effect Controls panel. Twirl down the Volume disclosure triangles and widen the Effect Controls panel so you can see its timeline.

If the timeline is not open, click the Show/Hide Timeline View chevron button. Make note of a few things:

• **Bypass**—This is something you haven't seen up to this point because only audio effects have this option. For the Volume effect, turning on Bypass at any point in the clip (Bypass is keyframeable) switches back to the clip's original volume level. You can use Bypass to switch any audio effect off and on any number of times within a clip.

- **Level**—The only adjustable parameter.

- **Keyframes**—All the keyframes and Keyframe Interpolation methods (hourglass icons) you applied to the clip in the Timeline show up in the Effect Controls timeline.

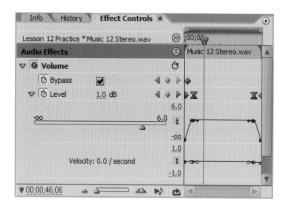

2   Adjust some keyframes and their parameters. Click Bypass and experiment with that.

3   Marquee select all the keyframes in the Effect Controls timeline and press Delete.

4   Drag the Constant Power audio transition (Audio Transitions > Crossfade) to the beginning of the clip on the Timeline.

5   Click the transition rectangle on the clip to select it and view its parameters in the Effect Controls panel.

6   Change the duration to three seconds.

That gives you a nice fade in.

7   Do the same for the end of the clip and you have a fade out.

Replace the clip on the sequence with Audio 4a.aif and Audio 4b.mp3.

8   Trim the end and beginning of the clips respectively to give them tail and head frames for a smooth transition.

9   Drag Constant Power to that edit point and listen to how that works.

10   Replace Constant Power with Constant Gain and listen to it.

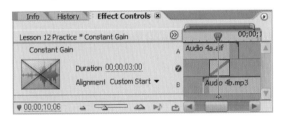

> **♀ Favor Constant Power**
>
> *Constant Gain changes audio at a constant rate in and out as it transitions between clips. This can sometimes sound abrupt. Constant Power creates a smooth, gradual transition, like a video cross dissolve. It decreases audio for the first clip slowly at first and then quickly falls off at the end of the transition. For the second clip, this audio crossfade increases audio quickly at first and then more slowly as it reaches the end of the transition. Constant Power is the default audio transition. Rely on it for most transitions. But your ears are the best judge. In this particular case, you might prefer Constant Gain.*

Adding J-cuts and L-cuts: Lesson 11-3

Frequently you'll want to start a video clip by having its sound play under the previous video clip and then transition to its associated video. This is a great way to let your audience know that someone is about to say something or that a transition is coming. This is called a J-cut, so named because it looks vaguely like a 'J' on the sequence.

Conversely, another slick editing technique is to let audio tail off under the next video clip. This is an L-cut.

To do either of these cuts requires that you unlink the audio and video portions of a linked A/V clip so you can edit them separately. After they've been unlinked, you can move that audio segment to another audio track and then extend or shorten the audio portion to make the J- or L-cut. There are two unlinking methods—a right-click context menu and a keyboard modifier. I'll show you both.

1   Open the Lesson 11-3 Finish sequence and play it.

This is how your J- and L-cuts will look and sound by the end of this mini-lesson. It has the sound bite and cutaway clips used in Lesson 8.

Note: In this case the cutaway clips aren't being used as cutaways. They're B-roll—basic video used to piece together a project.

The cutaway *video* plays over the first few words of the sound bite *audio* and then the cutaway *video* dissolves to the interview clip while the cutaway *audio* fades out—a J-cut. That process is reversed for the end of the sound bite—an L-cut.

2   Open the Lesson 11-3 Start sequence.

3   Right-click the second clip and select Unlink.

4   Complete the Unlink process by clicking outside that clip in the Timeline to deselect it.

Now when you click on either the audio or video portion of that clip, only that portion is selected. You'll re-link these clips, then use a keyboard modifier to temporarily unlink them.

5   Shift+click on both of those unlinked clips to select them (if one is already highlighted, there's no need to Shift+click on it).

6   Right-click on one of them and select Link.

Now you'll use the keyboard modifier unlinking method.

7   Alt+click on the audio portion of the second clip. That unlinks it and selects it.

8   Drag that unlinked audio portion of the second clip straight down to the Audio 2 track.

Note: As you move the audio portions of your clips in the sequence, take care that you don't slide them left or right when you drag them. Otherwise the audio and video will get out of synch. Premiere Pro gives you a visual cue to help you line up your clips: if you see a black line with a triangle, your clips are properly lined up. If that black line disappears, you have moved out of synch. In that case, move the clip around a bit until the black line reappears.

9   Using the Rolling Edit Tool (N) to move the edit between the first and second *video* clips (not the audio clips) to the right about one second, moving the horse and rider off camera before showing the interview clip.

Use the Program Monitor and the Timeline pop-up timecode displays to help make the edit. As I mentioned in Lesson 8, letting the interviewee get off screen before cutting to the interview video makes for a more comfortable shift.

10 Drag the left edge of the audio portion of the second clip to the left to give you some room to fade it up (it has a few header frames).

11 Apply four keyframes on the clips in the Timeline (use the following figure as a guide):

• **First audio clip**—You will fade the audio at the end of the clip down just before the rider in the second clip (Sound Bite 8a) starts talking. To do that, place a keyframe at that point (use the beginning of the waveform in the second clip to find that spot) and place another keyframe at the end of the clip. Drag the end keyframe all the way down to fade the cutaway audio out.

• **Second audio clip** –At the beginning of the clip and just as the rider starts talking. Drag the beginning keyframe all the way down to have that sound bite audio fade up.

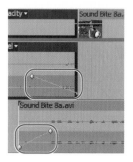

12 Play that J-cut. The cutaway's natural sound should fade as the rider begins speaking.

13 Drag a Cross Dissolve video transition to the edit point between the two video clips to make this work even more smoothly.

Adding an L-cut

Now that you've unlinked the center clip, adding an L-cut at the end of this segment will take only a few steps.

1 Move the Timeline CTI to just after the rider says "thumbs up"—about 12;21.

2   Drag the entire third clip (not the left side but the whole clip) to the left until the Snap feature causes its first frame to line up with the CTI.

This cutaway clip will cover up (overlay) the video portion of the rider's last few words but that final interview audio snippet will play along with the audio of the cutaway.

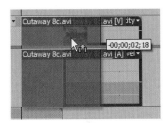

3   Add six keyframes as follows (use the next figure as a guide):

•   **Second audio clip**—Put one keyframe directly after the rider says "important stuff" and another one at the end of the clip. Drag the end keyframe all the way down to fade that sound bite audio under the cutaway.

•   **Third audio clip**—At the start, a half-second or so into the clip, a half-second or so before the rider says "important stuff" (on the other audio clip) and directly after the rider finishes talking. Drag the first keyframe all the way down, move the second and third to about –9 dB (to play the cutaway audio quietly *under* the sound bite), and the fourth to full volume or 0 dB (move the volume graph to the center of the clip (its default position), between the right and left channels).

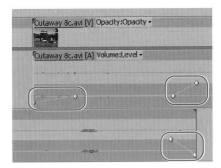

4   Add a video Cross Dissolve between the video portions of these two clips.

5   Play that L-cut.

The closing cutaway's natural sound should fade up quietly beneath the rider's closing comment, then climb to full volume at the end.

Review

1   Why should you use external mics?

2   When you set up a voice recording space in the corner of a room, which way do you face to voice the narration and why?

3   When I videotape indoors, my audio has a "tin-can" quality. What's going on?

4   You want to start your piece by fading up your audio. Explain three ways to do that.

5   Why use a J-cut or an L-cut?

6   You have a quiet video clip, but in the middle someone honks a car horn. How could you remove that sound and replace it with the original quiet background of the original clip?

▶ **Review answers**

1   Your camcorder's onboard mic picks up sound all around you, including noise you make when handling the camcorder. External mics capture sound at the source. Using external mics is invariably better and greatly improves the quality of your production.

2   As counterintuitive as it seems, you face *away* from the sound absorbing material. The mic picks up sound from the direction it's facing. The absorbing material minimizes the reflections the mic picks up.

3   The mic is probably too far from your subject and you're in a room with reflective surfaces such as flat walls and an uncarpeted floor.

4   Drag an Audio Crossfade transition (Constant Power or Constant Gain) to the beginning of the clip. Or use the Volume Graph in the Timeline clip display with two keyframes, dragging the first keyframe to the first frame and dragging that keyframe to the bottom of the clip. Or use the Volume audio effect and two keyframes to fade up the audio. Use interpolation controls to smooth what would otherwise be a straight-line fade-in.

5   To either ease into a clip such as a sound bite, or to let it fade out. A J-cut starts audio under the preceding video (which also has associated audio or a narration) and then fades up as you transition or cut to the video portion of that clip. An L-cut fades audio under the next clip as a way to ease out of that audio/ video clip.

6   Use keyframes to silence that portion of the audio. Then add part of the original audio to another audio track and fade that up to fill the audio gap you created in the original clip. Adobe Audition also has several tools to remove noises effectively. I cover that software in Lesson 12.

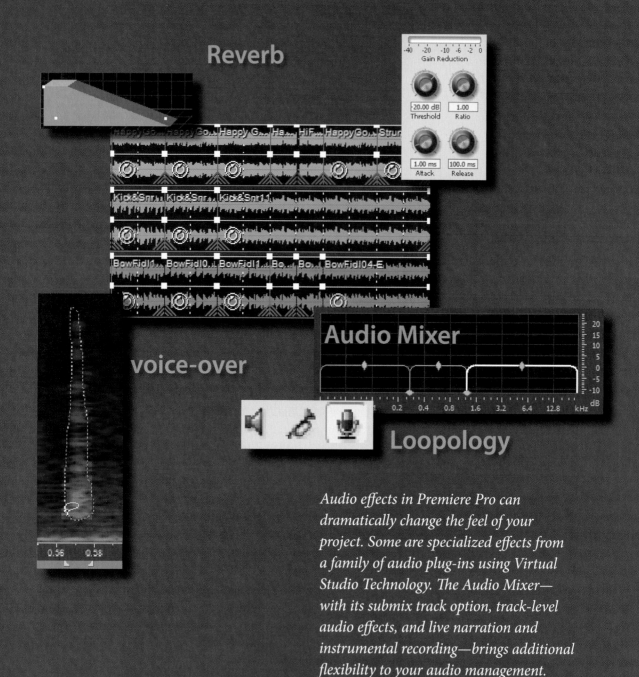

Reverb

Gain Reduction
-40 -20 -10 -6 -2 0

-20.00 dB
Threshold

1.00
Ratio

1.00 ms
Attack

100.0 ms
Release

HappyGo... HappyGo... Happy G... Ha... HiF... HappyGo... Strun

Kick&Snr... Kick&Snr... Kick&Snr11

BowFidl1... BowFidl0... BowFidl1... Bo... Bo... BowFidl04-E

voice-over

Audio Mixer

20
15
10
5
0
-5
-10

0.2 0.4 0.8 1.6 3.2 6.4 12.8 kHz
dB

Loopology

0.56   0.58

Audio effects in Premiere Pro can dramatically change the feel of your project. Some are specialized effects from a family of audio plug-ins using Virtual Studio Technology. The Audio Mixer— with its submix track option, track-level audio effects, and live narration and instrumental recording—brings additional flexibility to your audio management. To take your audio talents to a higher level, consider Adobe's professional audio product, Audition 2.0.

12 | Sweetening Your Sound and Mixing Audio

Topics covered in this lesson:

- Sweetening sound with audio effects.

- Trying out stereo and 5.1 surround sound effects.

- Working with the Audio Mixer.

- Outputting tracks to submixes.

- Recording voice-overs.

- Creating a 5.1 surround sound mix.

- Moving up to professional editing with Adobe Audition 2.0.

Getting started

Premiere Pro ships with more than 20 audio effects that can change pitch, create echoes, add reverb and remove tape hiss. As you did with video effects, you can set keyframeable audio effect parameters to adjust the effects over time.

The Audio Mixer lets you blend and adjust the sounds from all the audio tracks in your project. Using the Audio Mixer, you can combine tracks into single submixes and apply effects, panning or volume changes to those groups as well as to individual tracks.

Adobe Audition 2.0 takes audio editing to a higher level. It includes more than 5,000 music loops—snippets of music—that you can place on any number of tracks to create your own unique musical arrangements. In addition, you can add numerous audio effects, record your own audio (instruments and voice), and use Audition to remove vinyl record clicks, audience coughs, and ambient noise from live recordings.

Sweetening sound with audio effects: Lesson 12-1

For most projects you will probably be happy to use audio in its original, unaltered state. But at some point you might want to apply effects to it. If you use music from old cassette tapes, you can use the DeNoiser audio effect to automatically detect and remove tape hiss. If you record musicians or singers in a studio, you can make it sound like they were in an auditorium or a cathedral by adding Reverb. And you can use Delay to add an echo, DeEsser to remove sibilance, or Bass to deepen an announcer's voice.

You'll try a few audio effects in this mini-lesson. I encourage you to do some experimentation. Listen to the possibilities. Test some effects not covered here. Each effect is non-destructive—that is, it does not change the original audio clip. You can add any number of effects to a single clip, change parameters, and then delete them and start over.

View the Lesson 12 Intro video, then move on to this mini-lesson.

1   Open Premiere Pro to the Lesson 12 project.

2   Drag Ad Cliches 12 Mono.wav to the Audio 1 track (it's a mono track) of the Lesson 12 Practice sequence.

Feel free to play this little ditty.

3   Open the Audio Effects > Mono folder.

There are 19 Mono audio effects.

Note: All the Mono effects have the Mono single-speaker icon (◄). If you open the Stereo folder, they'll have a double speaker icon (◄◄), and the 5.1 group will have (◄).

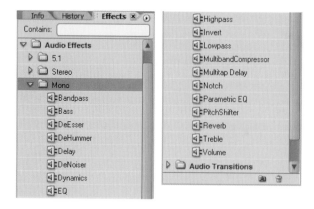

4 Drag Bass to the Ad Cliches clip, open the Effect Controls panel and twirl down its two disclosure triangles.

5 Play the clip and move the Bass Boost slider left and right. This increases or decreases bass.

6 Delete Bass from the Effect Controls panel and add Delay. Try out its three parameters:

- **Delay**—Time before the echo plays (0 to 2 seconds).

- **Feedback**—Percentage of echo added back to audio to create echoes of echoes.

- **Mix**—Relative loudness of echo.

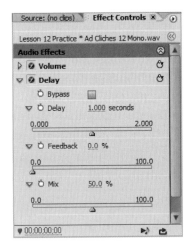

Note: I won't explain or list all the attributes of all the audio effects. To learn more about audio effect parameters, select Help > Adobe Premiere Pro Help, open the Adobe Help Center Contents tab, and open Effects: Reference > Audio Effects. You'll see a list of all the audio effects.

7   Play the clip and move the sliders to experiment with the effect.

Lower values are more palatable, even with this over-the-top audio clip.

Adobe Certified Expert exam objective

Describe the options and process required when working with clip-based effects by using the Effect Controls panel. Author's note: This is the same objective I listed in the video effect lessons. It applies to audio effects as well.

8   Delete Delay and add PitchShifter to the Effect Controls panel.

This has three nifty items: knobs, presets and a Reset button. You can tell an audio effect has presets by the tiny triangle next to what would normally be the Reset button (⟳ .) and the addition of a rectangular Reset button (both highlighted in the next figure).

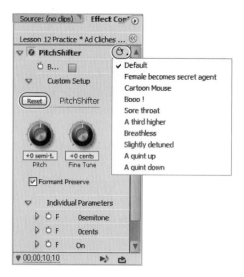

9   Try some of the Presets and note their values below the knobs in the Effect Controls panel.

10   Use the Individual Parameters sliders and apply keyframes at the beginning and end of a few phrases.

Use wildly different Pitch settings from –12 to + 12 semitone steps (2 steps equals a second in musical parlance—from C to D for example) and switch Formant Preserve on and off.

Note: Formant Preserve is not a misprint. Formant is the character, resonance, and phonetic quality of a particular voice. Formant Preserve attempts to retain those elements even with severe pitch changes. Unlike Bypass, which uses a checkbox connected to its keyframe feature, Formant Preserve's checkbox keyframe is connected to a slider. That can lead to an inaccurate placement of the moment when you switch Formant Preserve on or off. To help remedy that, move the slider only far enough to go from on to off or vice versa rather than using the checkbox.

11 Delete Ad Cliches from the sequence and replace it with Music 12 Mono (you can do that by dragging Music 12 Mono to the beginning of the sequence, on top of Ad Cliches, to do an Overlay edit).

Note: The three Music 12 audio clips were all made using Audition 2.0 loops. I'll demonstrate that process later in this lesson.

12 Drag Treble to that clip and increase its parameter.

This guitar clip lends itself to a treble boost.

Note: Treble is not simply Bass in reverse. Treble increases or decreases higher frequencies (4,000 Hz and above) while Bass changes low frequencies (200 Hz and less). The human audible frequency range is roughly 20 Hz to 20,000 Hz. Apply both Bass and Treble to a clip and switch between them by clicking their Toggle Effect On or Off buttons (◉).

13 Delete Treble, drag Reverb to the Effect Controls panel and open Reverb's Custom Setup.

14 Play the clip and drag the three white handles in the display to change the character of the reverb.

This is a fun effect that can give audio recorded in a "dead" room—a room like a recording studio with minimal reflective surfaces—some real life. As shown in the next figure, each of the three handles in the graphic control corresponds to a knob below it:

- **Pre Delay**—The apparent distance the sound travels to the reflecting walls and back.
- **Absorption**—How much of the sound is absorbed (not reflected).
- **Mix**—The amount of reverb.

Additional controls:

- **Size**—The apparent relative size of the room.

- **Density**—The density of the reverb "tail." The larger the Size, the greater the Density range (from 0-100%).

- **Lo Damp**—Dampens low frequencies to prevent the reverb from rumbling or sounding muddy.

- **Hi Damp**—Dampens high frequencies. A low Hi Damp setting makes the reverb sound softer.

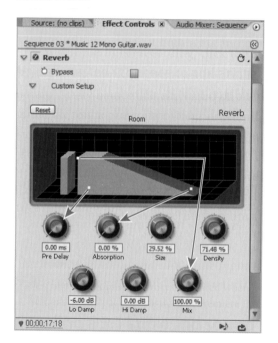

💡 A treasure trove of VST plug-ins

Reverb's rack of control knobs is a signal that this is a VST (Virtual Studio Technology) plug-in. These are custom-designed audio effects that adhere to a standard set by Steinberg audio. Invariably, those who create VST audio effect plug-ins want them to have a unique look and offer some very specialized audio effects. A wide variety of VST plug-ins is available on the Internet.

Trying out stereo and 5.1 surround sound effects: Lesson 12-2

The Mono Audio Effects collection is a subset of the Stereo and 5.1 Effects. Those multi-channel effect groups have additional effects that relate to their extra channels. Here's how they work:

1   Drag Music 12 Stereo to the sequence.

As shown in the next figure, since there is no stereo audio track in this sequence, Premiere Pro will automatically display your new clip below the Master Audio track, and then when you drop it there, will create a new stereo audio track *above* the Master Audio track, placing Music 12 Stereo there. This move will not overlay Music 12 Mono since the clips reside on separate tracks.

2   Play the sequence. Both clips play in unison.

3   Mute the Audio 1 track by clicking its Toggle Track Output button (highlighted in the next figure).

4   Attempt to drag any Mono audio effect to the Music 12 Stereo clip on its newly created stereo audio track.

You'll get one of the universal "No" symbols (⊘). You cannot apply a Mono effect to a stereo clip.

5   Drag Balance from Effects > Audio Effects > Stereo to the Music 12 Stereo clip.

6   Drag the Balance slider in the Effect Controls panel left and right while you play this clip.

I mixed this clip with the guitar panned all the way left and the honky tonk piano panned hard right. If you move the slider all the way to either end you will hear only one instrument.

Note: If you hear both instruments when panned one way or the other, it's because you did not mute the Audio 1 track.

7   Add two keyframes and have the audio pan from left to right.

8   Add two Bypass keyframes somewhere toward the middle of your clip.

The first one should have the Bypass box checked and the second should be unchecked (your Effect Controls panel timeline should look like the next figure).

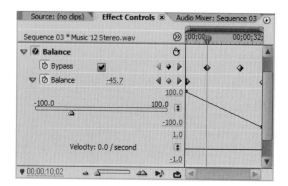

9   Play the clip.

The sound should begin to move from the left to the right, jump to the center at the first Bypass keyframe, hold there until the next Bypass keyframe, and then jump toward the right and finish its move to the right channel. Bypass tells Premiere Pro to ignore any effect settings.

10   Delete Balance and apply Fill Right or Fill Left.

The Fill effect duplicates the selected channel, places it in the other channel, and discards that other channel's original audio. So Fill Right will play the honky tonk piano in both left and right channels and will discard the guitar (the track in the left channel).

💡 **Use the same effect more than once**

You've probably seen an equalizer. Many car and home stereos have them. They enable you punch up or cut a number of pre-set frequency ranges. The Premiere Pro EQ effect fits that bill but offers only five frequency ranges. If you want more possibilities you can use Parametric EQ. It lets you select only one frequency range but you can use Parametric EQ multiple times and select multiple frequencies. In effect, you can build a full graphic equalizer within the Effect Controls panel.

11   Drag Music 12 5.1 to the sequence and Premiere Pro will add a 5.1 audio track to accommodate this new audio clip type.

12   Mute the Audio 2 track.

13   Drag Channel Volume from the Audio Effects > 5.1 folder to the Music 12 5.1 clip. Channel Volume lets you control the volume level for each of the six channels in a 5.1 surround sound clip and both channels of a stereo clip. The default setting for each channel is 0 dB, meaning no change from the original volume.

14   Play the clip and drag the sliders for each channel to experiment with this effect.

Note: If you don't hear all six channels it's because you need to change the 5.1 Mix Down setting. As you did in Lesson 11-1, select Edit > Preferences > Audio and change the 5.1 Mix Down Type to Front + Rear + LFE.

A Look at one more VST plug-in

Check out one more audio effect. This one is guaranteed to make your head spin. Drag MultibandCompressor to the Effect Controls panel. As the next figure shows, you'll need to dramatically expand the Effect Controls panel to see its parameters (I put the Effect Controls panel in a floating window).

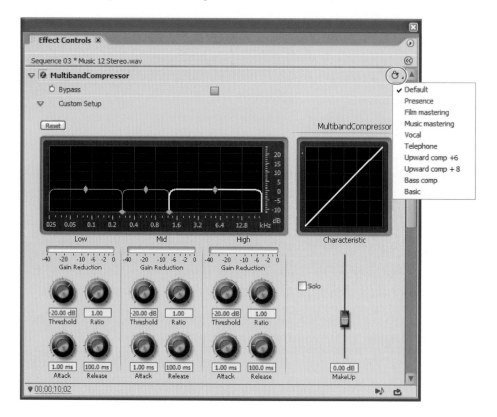

The MultibandCompressor's purpose is to narrow the dynamic range for up to three sets of frequency ranges. Explaining its parameters could take a full lesson (refer to Premiere Pro Help for parameter details). Instead, note that it offers a collection of presets accessed by clicking the button highlighted in the previous figure.

Editing keyframes using the clip effect menu

You might have noticed that tucked away along the top edge of all clips—audio and video—is a drop-down menu of all the effects applied to a selected clip. You can find it just to the right of the clip name.

You might not be able to see the clip effect menu in all instances. The audio or video track needs to be in its expanded view. To do that, click the disclosure triangle to the left of the track name. If that does not reveal it, the clip is not wide enough. Zoom in on the Timeline to expand the width of the clip and reveal the Clip Effect Menu.

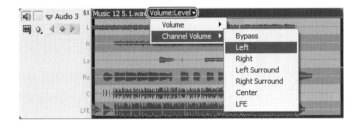

Adobe Certified Expert exam objectives

Explain how to set and use keyframes in the Timeline.

For Audio clips the header is always Volume: Level. For Video clips it's Opacity: Opacity (despite Motion residing on the top of that drop-down list). Every time you add an effect—video or audio—Premiere Pro adds that effect (along with a list of its parameters) to the bottom of that clip's effect drop-down list.

1   Open the Clip Effect Menu by clicking Volume: Level (highlighted in the previous figure).

2   Select Left Channel.

3   Drag the Volume Level Graph line up or down to change the left channel's volume.

4   Ctrl+click on the yellow line to add a couple of keyframes and adjust them by dragging them left or right along the graph line or up or down.

The advantages to clip-based effect and keyframe editing are that you can get a better overall view of the entire clip and if you want to change only one or two parameters, you can easily access them. Some disadvantages are that you can't change the parameters while the clip is playing, setting an exact parameter value is challenging, and changing more than a couple of parameters in the Timeline view gets tedious.

Working with the Audio Mixer: Lesson 12-3

There is a big difference in how Premiere Pro handles layered audio tracks and layered video tracks.

Clips in higher-numbered video tracks cover what's below them on the Timeline. You need to do something to those higher video track clips—adjust opacity, create PiPs, or use specialized keying effects (I cover them later in the book)—to let clips below them show through.

Clips in audio tracks all play together. If you have ten layered audio tracks loaded up with a variety of audio clips and do nothing to them in terms of adjusting volume levels and stereo panning, they'll all play as one grand symphony or cacophonous mess.

While you can adjust volume levels using each clip's volume graph in the Timeline or Volume effect in the Effect Controls panel, it's much easier to adjust volume levels and other characteristics for multiple audio tracks using the Audio Mixer.

Using a panel that looks a lot like production studio mixing hardware, you move track sliders to change volume, turn knobs to set left/right panning, add effects to entire tracks, and create submixes. Submixes let you direct multiple audio tracks to a single track so you can apply the same effects, volume and panning to a group of tracks without having to change each of the tracks individually.

In this mini-lesson you will mix a song recorded by a choir in a studio (see following sidebar for more information).

Adobe Certified Expert exam objectives

1. List and describe the basic process of mixing audio and the tools and options available to mix audio.
2. Given a scenario, mix and adjust audio by using the Audio Mixer.

"Sonoma" by the Occidental Community Choir

I have the good fortune to sing with the Occidental Community Choir (www.occidentalchoir.org). One thing that makes our group of 40 vocalists, musicians, composers, and arrangers unique is that choir members write most of the music we perform.

For this mini-lesson on audio mixing you will mix a studio recording of "Sonoma," an homage to our home county in California written by Randal Collen. It's a five-channel session: two mics on the choir, and one each on a clarinet, flute and double bass.

1 Double-click Music 12 Sonoma Stereo Mix and play it in the Source Monitor.

2 This is how your final mix should sound.

3 Open the Lesson 12-3 sequence on the Timeline.

4 Play the sequence and note that the instruments are way too loud compared to the choir.

Note: For this studio recording, the clarinet and flute players were in separate isolation booths. They wore headsets so they could hear each other and us. The recording engineer set their mic levels to full volume knowing we'd reduce those levels during mixing. The bass player was in a separate booth but his door was left ajar so the choir could hear him. We could have closed his door and all worn headsets, but connecting up 44 singers, musicians and a conductor would have been too much of a headache.

5 Select Window > Workspace > Audio and adjust the Audio Mixer so you can see all five tracks plus the Master track.

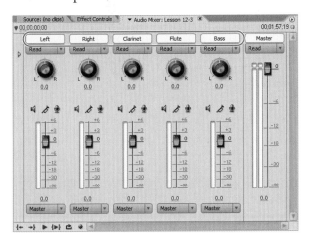

6 Change the track names along the top row of the Audio Mixer by highlighting each one and typing in a new name: *Left, Right, Clarinet, Flute,* and *Bass* (see previous figure). Those name changes will show up in the Audio Track Headers in the Timeline.

7 Play the sequence and adjust the sliders in the Audio Mixer to create a mix that you think works well.

I recommend setting Left to 4, Right to 2, and dropping the Clarinet, Flute and Bass to -17, -11 and −20 respectively.

8 Watch the Master track VU (volume unit) meter as you make your adjustments.

Little hash marks (highlighted in the next figure) indicate the loudest passages. They stay there a couple of seconds and then move as the music volume changes. They are a good way to see how balanced your left and right channels are. You want them to approximately line up most of the time.

Note: *You want to avoid setting the volume too high (the VU meter line will turn red). That leads to distortion.*

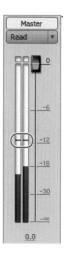

9   Adjust each channel's Left/Right Pan using the knobs at the top of each track (when completed, your parameters should match those in the next figure):

- Left—all the way left = -100

- Right—all the way right = +100

- Clarinet—left-center = -20

- Flute—right-center = +20

- Bass—centered = 0

Note: *It's best to pan a choir recorded with left and right mics all the way to the left and right to fill both channels. But there's no need to spread the instruments out that much. They should sound like an ensemble. And in general a bass should be centered because listeners do not perceive low frequencies as directional.*

10   Click the Show/Hide Effects and Sends button (highlighted in the next figure).

This opens a set of empty panels where you can add effects to entire tracks and assign tracks to submixes.

11   Click the Effect Selection button for the Left track and select Reverb from the drop-down list.

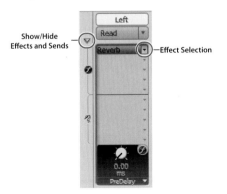

12 Isolate that track by clicking its Solo button (that mutes the rest of the channels).

You can click Solo buttons on more than one track to listen to a group of tracks. You can also click the Mute button to switch off audio playback for one or more tracks. You'll use the Enable Track for Recording button in the next mini-lesson.

Solo Track

Enable Track For Recording

Mute Track

> 💡 **Keep tabs on Mute and Solo settings**
>
> *After working in the audio mixer for a while, then returning to the Timeline, you might not hear anything. Audio Mixer Mute and Solo settings do not show up in the Timeline but still are in effect when you play a clip in the Timeline, even if the Audio Mixer is closed. So check those Mutes and Solos before shutting down the Audio Mixer.*

13 Click the Reverb effect drop-down list and make changes to each parameter. Play the clip to listen to your changes as you make them.

Note: *It's easier to apply effect parameters in the Effect Controls panel but you can only edit clips there, not audio or video tracks. In this case you could apply this effect to the clip instead of the track because there is only one clip on the track. But I want you to see how track-based effects work.*

14 Undo your settings by removing the Reverb effect. To do that, click the Effect Selection button and select None.

Automating changes in audio tracks

In Lesson 12-3 you set volume and panning values for entire tracks while listening to the audio. Premiere Pro also lets you apply volume and panning values that change over time, and you can apply them as you play your sequence.

To do that, use Automation modes accessed via drop-down menus at the top of each track in the Audio Mixer. Using one of the automation modes creates a series of track (as opposed to clip) keyframes for volume and panning, saving you from adding them one at a time.

Briefly, here's what each setting means (you can read more about this in Premiere Pro Help):

- **Off**—Ignores any changes you apply. Lets you test some adjustments without recording them.

- **Read**—Adjusting a track option (such as volume) affects the entire track uniformly. This is the default setting you used when setting the mix volume in step 7.

- **Write**—Records adjustments you make as you listen to a sequence.

- **Latch**—Works like Write but won't apply changes until you move the volume slider or panning knob. The initial property settings are from the previous adjustment.

- **Touch**—Works like Latch except when you stop adjusting a property, its option settings return to their previous state before the current automated changes were recorded.

Outputting tracks to submixes: Lesson 12-4

You place your audio clips into audio tracks on the Timeline. You can apply effects and set volume and panning on a clip-by-clip basis. Or you can use the Audio Mixer to apply volume, panning and effects to entire tracks. In either case, by default Premiere Pro sends audio from those clips and tracks to the Master track.

But sometimes you might want to route tracks to submix tracks before sending them on to the Master track.

The purpose of submix tracks is to save you steps and to ensure some consistency in how you apply effects, volume and panning. In the case of the "Sonoma" recording, you can apply Reverb with one set of parameters to the two choir tracks and Reverb with different parameters to the three instruments. The submix can then send the processed signal to the Master track, or it can route the signal to another submix.

1   Right-click on an audio track header in the Timeline and, using the next figure as a guide, select Add Tracks. Set the Video and Audio Tracks Add values to 0, Audio Submix Tracks Add to 2, Submix Track Type to Stereo and click OK.

That adds two submix tracks to the Timeline, two tracks to the Audio Mixer (they have a darker hue), and adds those submix track names (Submix 1 and Submix 2) to the drop-down lists at the bottom of the Audio Mixer.

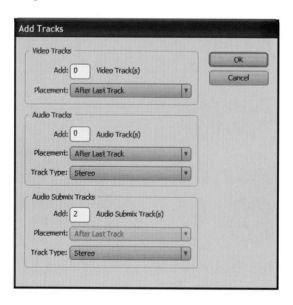

2   Click the Left track's Track Output Assignment drop-down list (at the bottom of the Audio Mixer) and select Submix 1.

3   Do the same for the Right track.

Now both the Left and Right tracks have been sent to Submix 1. Their individual characteristics—panning and volume—will not change.

4   Send the three instrument tracks into Submix 2.

5   Apply Reverb to the Submix 1 track, click its Solo button, play the audio and adjust the Reverb parameters to make it sound like the choir was singing in large auditorium (setting Size to about 60 is a good place to start).

6   Apply Reverb to the Submix 2 track, click its Solo button, switch off the Submix 1 Solo button (you can *solo* more than one track, but in this case you want to solo only Submix 2), play its audio and set its parameters to create a sound a bit less dramatic than the voices.

7   Check the Solo button on Submix 1 and listen to these two submixes as a single mix to see how they sound.

Feel free to tweak the Volume and Reverb settings.

Recording voice-overs: Lesson 12-5

The Premiere Pro Audio Mixer is also a basic recording studio. It can record anything you can connect to your soundcard. In this case, you'll use your PC's mic to do a voice recording.

1   Make sure that your PC's mic is plugged in to the Mic input on your sound card and if your mic has a switch, it's turned on.

2   Minimize Premiere Pro (click the little dash in the upper-right corner).

3   Select Start > Programs > Accessories > Entertainment > Volume Control.

Note: If you can't track down this little audio applet, look in C:\Windows\System32 and double-click sndvol32.exe.

4   Select Options > Properties.

5   Click the Recording radio button, make sure Microphone is checked, and click OK.

6   In the Recording Control window, make sure the Microphone is Selected, its volume is sufficiently high and then minimize or close the Recording Control window.

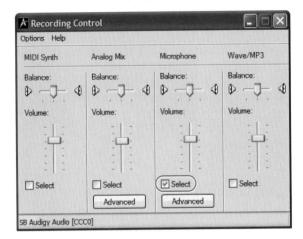

7   Maximize Premiere Pro (click its name in the Windows Task Bar).

8   Select Edit > Preferences > Audio Hardware and check that your Default Device is the hardware you have connected your mic to.

Note: Generally, selecting Adobe Default Windows Sound 1.5 or Premiere Pro Windows Sound will cover most circumstances. But if you have a higher-end audio card you should select it, refer to its product manual and make any needed changes to its ASIO settings.

9   Add a mono audio track to the Timeline (right-click on a track header and open the Add Tracks dialog box).

10   Click the Enable Track for Recording button (the microphone) at the top of that newly added audio track in the Audio Mixer.

You can enable as many tracks as you like but you can't record to the Master or a submix track.

11 Click the red Record button at the bottom of the audio mixer. It'll start blinking.

12 Move the CTI to where you want this narration to begin (it'll cover up any audio on the selected track at that location).

13 Click the Play button in the Audio Mixer and start your narration.

Note: If you chose to locate the CTI in the music, you'll hear the music as you record your voice. Being able to hear your sequence's audio as you narrate can be a big help. Laying down video clips then recording a narration is a workflow some editors follow.

14 When you finish recording, click the Stop button.

An audio clip appears on the selected audio track and in the Project panel. Premiere Pro automatically names that clip based on the Audio track number or name and adds that audio file to the project file folder on your hard drive.

 What About Feedback?

If you record audio and you have not taken steps to mute the output, you might get feedback—that lovely screeching noise that happens when a mic gets too close to a loudspeaker. There are several ways to deal with that: You can click the Mute button for the track, turn down your speakers (use headphones to hear yourself) or select Edit > Preferences > Audio and click Mute Input During Timeline Recording.

Creating a 5.1 surround sound mix

Premiere Pro lets you create a full, digital, 5.1 surround sound Mix. You can use 5.1 surround sound in two places: audio on a DVD or an audio file for playback on a PC with 5.1 surround sound speakers.

5.1 digital audio has six discrete channels: left front, front center, right front, right rear or surround, left rear or surround and the LFE (Low Frequency Effects) channel designated for a subwoofer.

If you have a 5.1 surround sound set-up on your PC, this will be a lot of fun and lead to much experimenting. If you don't have a six-speaker set-up this will at least give you a feel for how to add 5.1 surround to a DVD.

Here are the basic steps to follow:

1   Create a new sequence with seven mono tracks and a 5.1 Audio Master track.

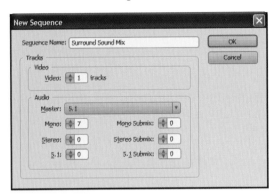

2   Marquee select the five clips from Lesson 12-3 and Copy/Paste them into tracks 1-5 of the new sequence (target its Audio 1 track to place them there).

3   Drag Music 12 - Sonoma-Left and -Right to tracks 6 and 7.

You'll put them in the rear speakers. Your sequence should look like the next figure.

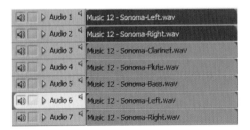

4   In the Audio Mixer, drag each track's 5.1 Panner *puck* to the proper location (use the next figure as a reference).

5   Set volume levels for tracks 1-5 that are similar to those you set for the stereo mix. For Audio 5, the bass, use the LFE volume knob and place its puck in the center. Set volume levels for tracks 6 and 7 (Left-rear and Right-rear) to 0 and –2 respectively.

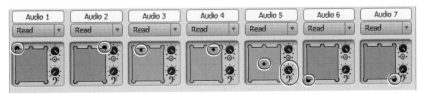

Now you have some options:

• You can move the clips on Audio 6 and 7 about a tenth of a second (3 frames) into the timeline, (causing them to play a little after the rest of the clips) to make it sound like they're coming from the back of the room. To do that, select each clip in turn, press the plus sign (+) on the numeric keypad, type 3 on the numeric keypad and press Enter.

• You can add a Reverb with a Size parameter a bit higher than what you choose to set for the front channels. You might find that you don't need to have as much reverb for the front channels when you work in 5.1 surround sound.

Moving up to professional editing with Adobe Audition 2.0

Adobe Audition 2.0 is a complete, professional, recording studio that offers advanced audio mixing, editing, and effects processing on an unlimited number of tracks. You'll want to use Adobe Audition 2.0 for music productions, radio broadcasts, or to enhance audio for your Premiere Pro videos.

Rather than give you a series of full-blown lessons on Audition, I will offer some brief demonstrations with a few step-by-step instructions. I will leave out some details but I think you'll get the gist of the added value Audition can bring to your video production.

If you have a copy of Audition, fire it up and follow along. If you don't have a copy, you can download a 30-day trial version from the Adobe website. Go to www.adobe.com, select Products > Video and Audio and click Tryouts.

Start in Premiere Pro. Select any of the Sonoma audio clips on the Timeline and select Edit > Edit in Audition. That opens Audition with that clip loaded in Audition's Edit mode, with the clip's waveform displayed.

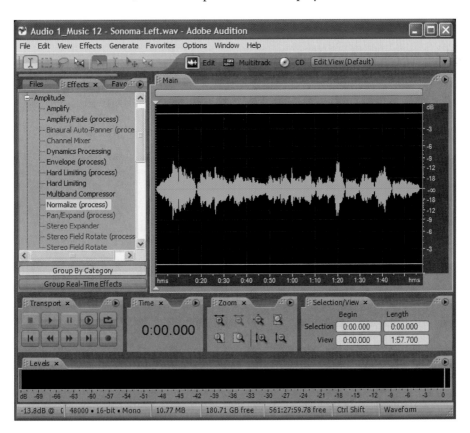

Audition's powerful and helpful effects

To quickly see how much more Audition has to offer, click the Effects tab, open the Delay Effects group, and double-click Studio Reverb. It offers many more options than Reverb in Premiere Pro. And there are a dozen presets. Great Hall works well for a choir.

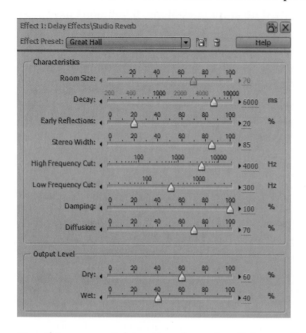

One thing you might notice about the clip's waveform is that its peaks do not reach all the way to the top or bottom. The clips used in the recording session mini-lesson all have relatively narrow dynamic ranges. Audition's Normalize effect can remedy that.

To apply it, open the Amplitude Effects group and double-click Normalize.

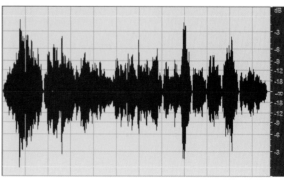

Normalize amplifies a clip's audio. The purpose is to set the audio to a standard level, particularly if you are creating a CD with multiple tracks recorded under varying conditions.

Normalize has several options. The easiest is to select a percentage of the full range up to 0 dB, when distortion kicks in. Since this is one of several choir tracks, it's best not to select 100%, because mixing multiple tracks (basically adding their loudness together) that have been *normalized* to 100% will lead to overly loud, distorted sound. In this case 65-75% will work well. You want the final mix's peak levels to climb to just below 0 dB.

You typically normalize after you've mixed all your tracks. Audition has a Group Normalize feature that lets you Normalize multiple clips in one pass.

After you make changes to your audio files you can save them in Audition and return to Premiere Pro. The changes will show up immediately there.

Frequency-Space Editing

One of the most useful of Audition's features is Frequency-Space Editing. Here you can *see* your clip's sound. Brighter colors in this view indicate louder volume. The location on the Y-axis indicates frequency.

As shown in the next figure, it's easy to spot and remove noises—coughs, page turns, or clicks on old vinyl records. Use the lasso tool to identify what you want to remove and click Repair Transient (in the Favorites tab). That removes the lassoed section and does something like a cross dissolve using the sound on both sides of that removed section.

The previous figure shows a click caused by the conductor's baton hitting his music stand. Listen to the before and after clips: Click Removal 12 Before and After in your Lesson 12 folder.

Mixer and Multitrack views

You've seen the Audio Mixer in Premiere Pro. Audition's mixer has several extra features that give you easier access to submixes and effects. The following figure shows about half of its options.

You create your mixes in the Multitrack view. I created an Audition 2.0 Session using the Sonoma audio files from this lesson. To access it, click the Multitrack button toward the top of the interface and select File > Open Session, navigate to the Lesson 12 folder and double-click on Lesson 12 Sonoma Audition.ses.

Loopology

Audition lets you create music from scratch using a technique Adobe calls Loopology. Audition ships with more than 5,000 music loops—snippets of music recorded by real musicians using real instruments (as opposed to MIDI files). Loops don't come with the trial version of Audition but I have provided some for your use in this lesson. Use them to experiment with Loopology and learn some of the basics.

1   Select File > Open Session, navigate to the Lesson 12 Audition Loop Session Example folder (in the Lesson 12 folder) and double-click Lesson 12 Audition 2.0 Loop Session.ses.

That opens the collection of clips shown in the next figure.

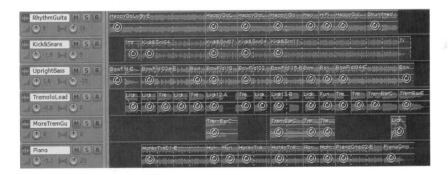

2   Click anywhere in the first audio track and press Alt+A to add a track directly below the first track.

3   Click on HappyGoLuckyE.cel in the Files panel, and click the Play button at the bottom of that panel.

This is an Audition loop: a guitar lick in the key of E.

4   Drag and drop that clip in that second track (labeled Track 7) and then left-click and drag it to the beginning of the track.

5   As shown in the next figure, drag its right edge to make three instances of this loop (three measures or bars). Note the dotted, vertical lines indicating the bar lines between measures.

 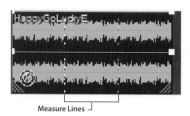

Measure Lines ⌐

6   Take a look at the other clips in the first track (labeled RhythmGuitar). Create a duplicate of the contents of that track in the empty track below it by dragging those clips, one at a time, from the file window to the second track, right-clicking and dragging them into position, and lengthening them (if necessary) by dragging their lower right-edge to match the clips in the RhythmGuitar track at the top of the Multitrack view.

7   Click the Solo (S) buttons on the top two tracks, click the Play button (in the bottom left corner of the workspace) and compare the loops on the two tracks.

The fifth loop in the second track (Track 7)—HappyGoLuckyB—won't match. It's been transposed up a step in the top track.

8   Right-click on your copy of HappyGoLuckyB in the second track, select Loop Properties, and change Transpose Pitch to 1 half-step (refer to next figure).

None of the remaining loops need transposing.

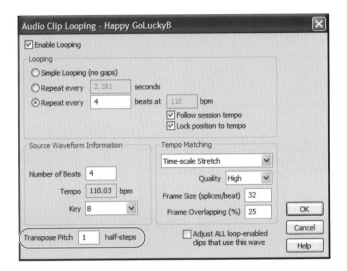

9   Feel free to take any of the loops used in this session and create your own custom music. Simply start fresh by selecting File > New Session.

Review

▶ **Review questions**

1   There are at least four ways to make audio move from the right channel to the left and back. What are they?

2   You are playing a 5.1 surround sound clip but can't hear all the channels. What's a possible cause?

3   What's the difference between Delay and Reverb?

4   You want to change an announcer's voice from normal to a high-pitched squeak and back again. How would you do that?

5   How do you apply the same audio effect with the same parameters to three audio tracks?

6   Audition's Frequency Space view facilitates click, pop and cough removal. Describe the process.

▶ **Review answers**

1   Balance adjusts the overall balance, left or right. Channel Volume enables you to adjust the volume of each channel individually. You can also use the Audio Mixer's Left/Right Pan knob. Or use clip or track keyframes on the Timeline.

2   Check Edit > Preferences > Audio and make sure the 5.1 Mixdown includes all channels.

3   Delay creates a distinct, single echo that can repeat and gradually fade. Reverb creates a mix of echoes to simulate a room. It has multiple parameters that take the hard edge off the echo that you hear in the Delay effect.

4   One way is to use PitchShifter, select its Cartoon Mouse preset, and apply Bypass keyframes to turn it on and off.

5   The easiest way is to create a submix track, assign those three tracks to that submix track and apply the effect to the submix.

6   Listen and watch as your audio plays. You'll spot coughs and clicks by their distinctive sharp peaks. Draw a lasso around the part you want to remove and double-click Repair Transient (from the Favorites folder).

compositing

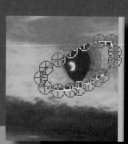

keying

alpha channel

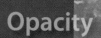

Opacity

One important feature of Premiere Pro is its ability to composite (or layer) any number of video clips, graphics and still images. You've already done some compositing: placing text and logos over videos and creating PiPs. Other compositing techniques involve changing opacity, using chroma keys, working with mattes, or applying Premiere Pro keying effects that combine multiple clips. Compositing will become a significant part of your video productions.

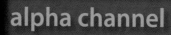

13 | Compositing Techniques

Topics covered in this lesson:

- Making compositing part of your projects.
- Working with the Opacity effect.
- Two multiple-track video effects: Blend and Texturize.
- Working with alpha channel transparencies.
- Applying chroma, color and luminance keying effects.
- Using matte keys.

Getting started

Premiere Pro and other nonlinear editors like it have a general operating practice: Clips in video tracks above Video 1 trump clips in tracks below them on the timeline. In other words, whatever appears on the highest track covers up whatever is below it.

However, the object isn't to use clips in tracks above Video 1 to obliterate what's beneath them. It's to use compositing to enhance what's down there. Premiere Pro gives you many ways to layer videos, graphics and images for best effect.

You use compositing techniques on clips so the clips below them on the Timeline can show through. There are four basic compositing methods:

- Reducing the opacity of an entire clip.
- Alpha channel transparencies in clips and effects.
- Chroma, color and luminance keying effects.
- Matte keying effects.

In the upcoming mini-lessons you will try all of these compositing methods and use different techniques with a few you've already tried. Once you see all the possibilities, you'll start to plan and shoot your projects with layered videos, graphics and images in mind.

Making compositing part of your projects

You see compositing when you watch a TV meteorologist standing in front of a map or other graphic. As shown in the following photos, most times they're standing in front of a green or blue wall. The technical director uses a keying effect to make that wall transparent, and then inserts a weather graphic. You can do the same thing in your video projects using a Premiere Pro video keying effect.

Matt Zaffino, Chief Meteorologist—KGW-TV, Portland, Oregon.

Most computer games with live actors, and many movies use compositing. "Green screen" studios enable game developers and film directors to place actors in science fiction and other settings created with 3D computer graphics. Such sets make it possible for actors to work in relative safety while the finished product shows them dangling from a skyscraper, hundreds of feet in the air.

Shooting videos with compositing in mind

Making keying effects work well takes some extra effort. Proper backdrop colors, lighting, and keying techniques all come into play. You need to consider which keying effect will work best for your circumstances.

Adobe Certified Expert exam objectives

1) Given a term related to transparency, describe the term and explain how it is used.

2) Describe how to composite clips and tracks.

Some keys use textures or graphics, so there is not a whole lot of planning you need to do. But most keying effects take some extra thought and work:

• High contrast scenes lend themselves to making either the dark or light portions transparent. Same holds true for shooting light objects against a dark background or vice versa.

• Solid color backgrounds are fairly easy to make transparent. Take care that the subjects you don't want to key out aren't wearing clothing with colors that match the background. I will present detailed tips for working with chroma key green and blue screens in Lesson 13-4.

• For most keying shots you need to use a tripod and lock down your camera. Bouncing keyed objects create viewer disconnects. There are exceptions to this rule. Typically, if you're keying in wild, animated backgrounds then camera movement will not be a problem.

• Most times you want your background (or the other images you'll insert in the transparent areas you create with keying effects) to match those keyed shots. If you're working with outdoor scenes, try to shoot the keyed shots outside or using lights balanced for daylight.

Examples of composited clips

Before you get started on this lesson, take a look at some composited clips I created for the upcoming mini-lessons. This is to give you an idea of some of the compositing techniques that you will work on.

1 Open Premiere Pro to Lesson 13. Its Project panel is loaded with a wide range of goodies: graphics, videos, still images, and mattes.

2   Open the Lesson 13 Finish sequence and take a look at the collection of composited clips there:

• Three views of the Duomo, the main cathedral in Sienna, Italy: superimposed over a sunset, with an added stained glass window, and with both a sunset and stained glass.

• A model shot in front of a green screen with an animated background inserted behind her.

• Leaves floating over a sunset created with the Luma key.

• A cat's eyes revealed in the sky using a garbage matte key.

• An image revealed in another image using the Track Matte Key and a blur effect.

• A traveling matte that highlights and moves with a horse and rider.

Working with the Opacity effect: Lesson 13-1

One easy way to see compositing at work is to place a video or graphic on a superimposing track and make it partially transparent—turn down its opacity—to let videos on lower tracks show through. You can accomplish this using the Opacity effect. Though it can be very useful, you'll discover in this mini-lesson that Opacity's blanket approach to compositing is not always effective. You may want to use some of Premiere Pro's other similar tools in certain circumstances.

Adobe Certified Expert exam objective

Describe the options and process required when working with fixed effects.
Author's note: Opacity is the third of Premiere Pro's three fixed effects. You've already worked with the other two: Motion and Volume.

In this mini-lesson you'll reduce opacity on several items. In subsequent mini-lessons I'll show you ways to achieve more effective results using some of the same clips.

1   Minimize Premiere Pro and view the Lesson 13 Intro video.

2   Re-open Premiere Pro.

3   Open the Lesson 13 Practice sequence.

4   Drag Photo 13b from the Project panel to the Video 1 track.

5   Drag Orange Matte to the Video 2 track directly above Photo 13b.

The matte completely covers the photo.

6   Click the Orange Matte clip to select it and twirl down Opacity in its Effect Controls panel.

Opacity has only one parameter: percent.

7   Use keyframes to set an Opacity of 100% (opaque) at the beginning of the clip and an opacity of 0% (completely transparent) at the end.

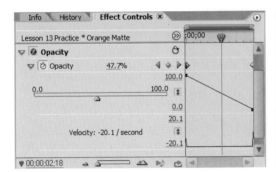 

8   Play the clip. The orange gradually becomes less opaque and more like a tint. Finally it disappears altogether.

9   Right-click on the Orange Matte and select Copy.

You'll paste the Opacity parameters on another clip to save a few steps.

10   Drag Gradient 13 on top of the Orange Matte clip on Video 2 to do an overlay edit.

11   Right-click on Gradient 13 and select Paste Attributes.

That applies the Opacity parameters with the keyframes you set for the Orange Matte to the Gradient.

💡 **Copy a clip and paste its attributes**

This is a tremendously useful tool. You can copy a clip and paste it somewhere else in any sequence. Or you can merely paste its attributes—any effects applied to it along with their parameters and keyframes—onto another clip. That latter feature is a great way to achieve consistent results. If you do PiPs, you can set a clip size, then apply that to all the clips in the PiP, changing only their screen location.

12 Play the composited clips.

I used the Titler to make this gradient. It's simply a rectangle with a 4 Color Gradient Fill. If you double-click Gradient 13 in the Project panel, that will open the Titler and you can change the characteristics of the gradient.

13 Drag Texture 13.psd on top of Gradient 13 in the Video 2 track to do an Overlay edit.

14 Right-click and select Paste Attributes.

Since you have not done any other copying, the previous Copy remains in effect and the texture clip will acquire the Opacity parameters and keyframes.

I made this texture graphic using a simple preset in Photoshop CS.

15 Play this composited clip and note how the texture shows up in the clip.

You'll use a much more effective means to add texture in Lesson 13-2.

16 Replace Texture 13 with Photo 13a, Paste Attributes to it and play it.

It adds a nice sunset glow to the clip. In Lesson 13-3 I'll show a *much* better way to composite the sunset with the cathedral.

Note: If you place the sunset photo on the lower track and the building above it, and apply a reduced opacity to the building, the effect will look the same.

17 Finally, replace Photo 13a with Photo13d, Paste Attributes to it and play it.

Using Opacity to composite a scene with another clip that has a bright object with a dark background is relatively effective. But later I'll show you ways to avoid the washed-out-look common to shots composited using Opacity.

Two multiple track video effects: Blend and Texturize: Lesson 13-2

Two video effects combine clips on two tracks:

- **Blend**—Works something like opacity but gives you extra options that can have some surprisingly colorful results.

- **Texturize**—Enables you to give a clip something akin to an embossed feel using a clip below it on the sequence.

1   Marquee select the clips in the Lesson 13 Practice sequence and press Delete.

2   Drag Photo 13b back to the Video 1 track.

3   Drag Photo 13a to the Video 2 track, directly above Photo 13b.

Note: To see this effect you need to switch off the display of the clip on Video 2. You could turn off the entire Video 2 track by clicking its Toggle Track Output eyeball, but then nothing on that entire track would be visible. Premiere Pro lets you switch off an individual clip.

4   Right-click on the clip on the Video 2 track and select Enable to uncheck it.

That switches off that clip's display and changes the clip color in the sequence to light blue.

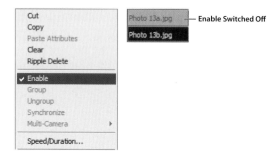

5   Apply the Blend video effect (Video Effects > Channel > Blend) to the clip on the Video 1 track.

6   Select Video 2 from the Blend With Layer drop-down list.

That list includes every video track in your sequence.

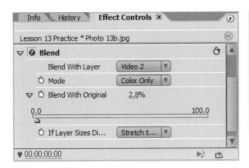

7   Work your way through the Blend modes and move the Blend With Original slider to see how this effect works.

Crossfade duplicates the Opacity effect while Color Only is the most colorful. The Mode parameter is keyframeable, so you can switch from mode to mode within a single clip.

8   Delete Blend from the Effect Controls panel and replace it with Texturize (Video Effects > Stylize folder).

9   Select Video 2 in the Texture Layer drop-down list.

Note: As with Blend, you need to un-Enable the Texture Layer clip to see this effect. Since you've already done it, there's no need to duplicate that step here.

10   Set the Texture Contrast to its highest value (2) and adjust the Light Direction for greatest effect.

Even in something as untextured as a sunset, you get an embossed feel (see the image on the left in the next figure).

11   Drag Texture 13.psd on top of Photo 13a in the Video 2 track to do an overlay edit.

12 Right-click and uncheck its Enable feature.

It'll look like the image on the right (you might need to move the Texturize Contrast slider slightly to see that).

Two examples of the Texture Effect

13 Replace Photo 13a on the sequence with Stained Glass 13a.psd, right-click and deselect Enable.

This is a 200x200 pixel graphic. Texturize can use small frame-sized clips like this to make a repeated texture pattern. Since DV is 720x480, there will be slightly more than three across and more than two down.

14 Change the Texture Placement to Tile Texture and that will distribute several instances of this circular graphic around the scene.

Note: Because you deselected Enable for the texture layer clip, you cannot apply motion or any other effect to it. But all is not lost. You can use a nested sequence to accomplish that. I set up such a sequence for the next step.

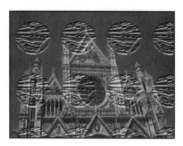

15 Drag Lesson 13 Nested Sequence 1 (it's a logo with Motion applied to it) on top of Texture 13 in the Video 2 track. This is a spinning logo.

16 Right-click and deselect Enable.

17 Play the clip and the spinning logo moves through the image, even though the nested sequence's clip is un-Enabled.

Working with alpha channel transparencies: Lesson 13-3

Many graphics and some of Premiere Pro's transitions have what are called alpha channels—portions of the clips or gaps in the transitions that Premiere Pro can make transparent, revealing what's below those clips and transitions on a sequence. You'll work with both in this mini-lesson. You continue where you left off in Lesson 13-2.

1 Drag Photo 13e to Video 1, past the clips you worked on in previous mini-lessons.

2 Place Logo 13 on Video 2 above that clip.

This is a Photoshop graphic with an alpha channel. By default, Premiere Pro makes the graphic opaque and its alpha channel transparent, allowing whatever is below the alpha channel on the sequence to show through. You can use the Alpha Adjust effect to *see* the alpha channel.

3   Apply Alpha Adjust (Video Effects > Keying folder) to Logo 13.

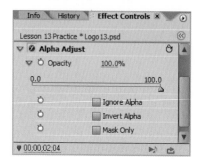

Alpha Adjust is the clip-based version of the Opacity Fixed Effect. As with the Transform effect's connection to Motion, you can use Alpha Adjust to apply Opacity at some other point in the effect chain, instead of second-to-last where it would occur if you were to use the Opacity fixed effect. Alpha Adjust has a few extra parameters in addition to Opacity:

- **Ignore Alpha**—Makes the alpha channel opaque, covering up the clip below it.

- **Invert Alpha**—Makes the graphic transparent and the alpha channel opaque.

- **Mask Only**—Converts the graphic to a white silhouette.

4   Check both Invert Alpha and Mask Only to create something like a spiral porthole.

5   Select Alpha Adjust in the Effect Controls panel and press Delete.

Video effects that work with graphic file alpha channels

Four video effects work well with graphic file alpha channels: Alpha Glow, Bevel Alpha, Channel Blur, and Drop Shadow. You've already seen Drop Shadow, so I'll highlight only the other three:

1 Apply Alpha Glow (Video Effects > Stylize folder) to the graphic on Video 2, open its Settings dialog box, and experiment with its settings.

The Start and End Color parameters set the colors of the glow.

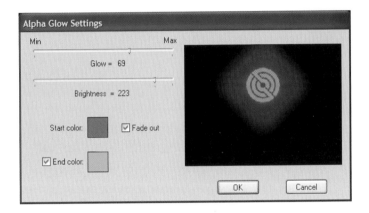

2 Delete Alpha Glow from the Effect Controls panel and drag Bevel Alpha (Video Effects > Perspective) in its place.

Give this graphic a 3D beveled feel by adjusting the effect's parameters.

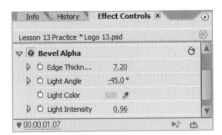

3 Add Channel Blur below Bevel Alpha in the Effect Controls panel.

This shifts individual color values—red/green/blue—as well as blurring the graphic into its alpha channel. As you make adjustments to its parameters consider that these color and blurring changes are all keyframeable—all these cool color shifts can happen over time.

Video effects with built-in alpha channels

Several Premiere Pro video effects have alpha channels. You've tried out four motion effects: Motion, Transform, Basic 3D and Camera View. When you use them to reduce the clip size or tilt it at an angle, they reveal what's below them in the sequence. I'll briefly show you Camera View because it has an option to turn off the alpha channel.

Two other effects have alpha channels: Lens Distortion and Strobe Light.

1 Put Video 6d on the Video 1 track and Video 6a on Video 2 (place them after the clips you worked on earlier).

2 Apply Camera View to the clip on Video 2, open its Settings dialog box, uncheck Fill Alpha Channel and click OK.

Leaving Fill Alpha Channel checked would put a solid color matte beneath this effect.

3   Adjust its parameters so you can see the clip on Video 1 beneath it (I also used Motion to slide the clip a bit to the right—something Camera View can't do).

Note: You could take the four Multi-Camera clips you used in Lesson 8, synch them up and use Camera View or any other motion effect to have them all play together in the same screen.

4   Delete Camera View and apply Lens Distortion to the clip on Video 2.

5   Open its Settings dialog box and uncheck Fill Alpha Channel.

6   Adjust its parameters to display it over the clip on Video 1 (again, I used Motion to slide it off to the right and enlarge it).

7   Delete Lens Distortion and drag Strobe Light to the Effect Controls panel.

This clip has several parameters (you can learn more about it in Premiere Pro Help). The only one applicable to this lesson is Strobe.

8   Open the Strobe drop-down list and select Makes Layer Transparent.

9   Play the sequence and watch how the Strobe Light effect quickly jumps back and forth between the clips on Video 1 and 2.

You can use Strobe Light to make flashes of any color and you can use keyframes to switch back and forth from that view to the view that shows the clip below it on the track.

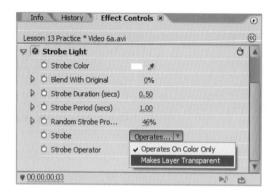

Applying chroma, color and luminance keying effects: Lesson 13-4

Using Opacity to combine two or more clips works well for some images but it's an inexact science. You can get more precise compositing results using keying effects.

Keying effects use various methods to make portions of a clip transparent. To get a quick overview, open Effects > Video Effects > Keying. There are 17 effects. With the exception of Alpha Adjust (the clip-based Opacity video effect) they fall into three basic camps:

- **Color/Chroma**—Blue Screen, Chroma, Color, Green Screen, Non-Red, and RGB Difference.

- **Luminance**—Luma, Multiply, and Screen.

- **Matte**—Difference, Garbage, Image, Remove, and Track.

You'll work with Color/Chroma and Luminance keys in this mini-lesson and Matte keys in Lesson 13-5.

Color keys and Chroma keys all work in basically the same way: you select a color for them to make transparent and apply a few other parameters (basically adjusting the width of that color selection).

Luminance keys look for dark or light areas in a clip and make them transparent (or opaque). In this mini-lesson I'll show you the Chroma, Green Screen and Luma keying effects.

Mattes typically do the equivalent of cutting a hole in a clip using a graphic or some other user-defined region.

1 Drag Photo 13a to Video 1 and Photo 13b to Video 2 (place them after the clips you worked on earlier).

This is the reverse order you used in lesson 13-1. You will *key out* the blue sky (make it transparent) to display the sunset clip below it in the sequence.

2 Apply Chroma Key to the clip on Video 2.

Take a look at its parameters in the Effect Controls panel.

- **Similarity**—The range of the target color that will be made transparent.

- **Blend**—How much of the clip that you are keying out blends with the underlying clip.

- **Threshold**—Shadow amounts of objects not keyed out that are retained in the keyed-out color.

- **Cutoff**—Darkens or lightens shadows. Dragging too far to the right—beyond the Threshold slider—effectively switches off the Chroma Key effect.

- **Smoothing**—The amount of anti-aliasing—edge softening—applied to the boundary between transparent and opaque regions.

- **Mask Only**—Displays a white silhouette of the opaque areas in the keyed clip. Use this to fine-tune the parameters to avoid creating transparent holes in areas you don't want to key out.

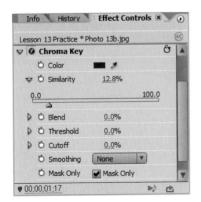

3   Drag the Color Eyedropper into the clip in the Program Monitor and click somewhere in the sky to select its blue color.

 Get an average color value to improve keying

The Eyedropper selects a color from a single pixel. Frequently that single pixel does not represent the average color of the region you want to key out, leading to keying results that are less than satisfactory. When using the Eyedropper to get a color sample for a key, Ctrl+click to get a subsample, a 5x5 pixel area.

4   Slide Similarity to the right to about 25% until all the blue disappears and some of the sunset starts showing through sections of the cathedral.

If you have not seen a chroma key at work before, that little parameter change is sure to get your attention. But you've keyed out too wide a selection of color. You'll fine-tune that in the next steps.

5   Click Mask Only.

Your keyed shot should look like the image on the left in the next figure.

6   Adjust the Similarity slider until there are no more holes in the silhouette—to about 13%.

Zoom in to adjust parameters

Use the View Zoom Level in the Program Monitor to zoom in on the image and get a closer look at the boundary between the silhouette and the sunset. That will help you fine-tune Similarity and other parameters. You'll note that it's darned hard to get rid of all the artifacts near the edges without cutting some small holes in the building. You need to find a reasonable compromise such that, at regular magnification, your viewers won't notice.

7 Uncheck Mask Only.

Your keyed shot should look like the next figure on the right. Because the sky is so uniformly blue (that's why I selected this shot), there's no real need for you to adjust the other parameters.

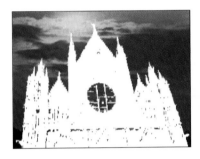 

8 Delete the sunset clip on Video 1, move the clip on Video 2 to Video 3, and place Stained Glass 13 on Video 4, above the cathedral photo on Video 3.

You placed the stained glass image above the cathedral clip to help position it (you'll move it to Video 2 in a moment) and you moved the cathedral clip up because you're going to put another instance of it below it on the timeline.

9 Drag and slightly expand the stained glass clip in the Program Monitor to position it so it completely covers the window (see next figure, left image).

10 Drag that stained glass clip from Video 4 to Video 2, below the clip on Video 3.

11 Select the clip on Video 3 to display its parameters in the Effect Controls panel (Chroma Key is still applied to it), drag the Eyedropper tool to the cathedral window and Ctrl+click there to get a 5 x 5 subsample or average color value.

12 Use Mask Only, Similarity and Blend to attempt to key out the window without keying out edges of the cathedral (refer to the next figure, center image).

You will not be able to do it. But, because this graphic has a transparent alpha channel, you can put another instance of the cathedral image below it on the sequence to fill the holes left by the chroma key, in effect creating a three-layer image sandwich.

13 Drag Photo 13b to Video 1.

14 Uncheck Mask Only for the clip on Video 2.

Your image should look like the image on the right in the next figure.

Using a nested sequence to add another chroma key

If you try to add the sunset to this three-clip composite, it won't work. You could drag the cathedral photo to Video 4 and place the sunset image on Video 3 but that would cover the stained glass graphic and the cathedral shot on tracks 2 and 1. The solution is to create a nested sequence.

1 Drag Photo 13a to Video 1 and Lesson 13 Nested Sequence 2 to Video 2 (place them after the clips already on your sequence).

That nested sequence is the same three-layer image sandwich you just created.

2 Apply Chroma Key to the Nested Sequence clip, select the sky color, and adjust Similarity. Your clip should look like the next figure.

Using the Blue and Green Screen keys

The Blue and Green Screen keys are your best bets for accurate, relatively-low-budget-but-professional-looking keying. To use these effects you need to shoot your video in front of so-called chroma key blue or green backdrops. These use very specific colors that the Blue and Green Screen keys can readily remove. But shooting video that will key cleanly is not guaranteed. See the following sidebar for some helpful advice.

Tips for effective chroma key shots

Chroma key video shoots don't always go smoothly. For the Blue and Green Screen keys to work effectively, you should follow these tips:

• Use flat lighting—two lights at 45° angles to the screen—to avoid creating hot spots. No need to overdo the lighting. Simply make it even.

• The actor's lighting does not have to be flat. Controlled spotlights or lights with "barn doors" work well.

• If you're going to key-in an outdoor background, use daylight-balanced blue gels over your lights to re-create outdoor lighting (or shoot your chroma key shots outdoors). If you're working with live actors, use a fan to blow their hair around to enhance the illusion.

• Avoid chroma key spill—keep actors at least four feet away from the backdrop to avoid picking up its reflected color. A back light on the actors minimizes spill.

• The tighter the shot, the more realistic the finished look will be.

• Fast-paced action is harder to key right to the edges of your subjects.

• Use a wide-open iris on your camcorder to limit the depth of field and to throw the green screen a bit out of focus, making it easier to key out.

• Chroma key fabric and paper costs about $8 a square yard and paint about $60 a gallon. You can find many dealers online.

• Which color to use? With chroma green, you have a reasonable assurance that no one will have clothing that matches it and therefore will key out. Chroma blue works well because it's complementary to skin tones.

• Consumer and prosumer camcorders do not key as well as professional camcorders because they record less color information. But, because they give more weight to green colors to correspond to the color sensitivity of human eyes, green screens key more cleanly than blue.

1   Drag Background 13 to Video 1 and Video 13 to Video 2 (place them after the clips already on the sequence).

2   Use the Rate Stretch tool to drag the end of Video 13 to make it as long as the clip below it (Background 13)—5 seconds.

Note: I made Background 13 using a third-party collection of customizable animated backgrounds. It's a looping video—meaning the last frame flows smoothly into the first frame such that I could string together several of these clips in a row and they would play seamlessly. Several companies make products like this (along with animated borders and lower and upper third backgrounds for supers), with varying levels of customizability and pricing. An Internet search on "animated video backgrounds" will give you an idea of what's out there.

3   Play the sequence and note a couple things:

• The production crew used a chroma key green screen.

• The green screen in this shot is not as brightly lit as most green screen shots. You will use the Brightness & Contrast video effect to add some sparkle to it.

• There is no camera movement, although on some other shots from this production there is movement because the crew knew the editors would use wildly animated backgrounds that lend themselves to that kind of action.

4   Apply the Green Screen Key (Video Effects > Keying) to the clip on Video 2.

You'll see an immediate change. Both the Green and Blue Screen Keys are pre-set to key out their respective colors. Nevertheless, some fine-tuning is in order.

5   In the Effect Controls panel, twirl down the Green Screen Key disclosure triangles and check Mask Only.

There will be kind of a white haze to the entire clip (see image on the left in the next figure).

6   Adjust Threshold and Cutoff to create a solid silhouette with a sharp contrast between the model and the background.

I recommend a Threshold of 43% and a Cutoff of 19%. Your screen should look something like the image on the right in the next figure.

7   Uncheck Mask Only and play the video.

I think the model could have a bit more illumination and contrast. You'll add that in the next step.

> 💡 **Blurring the background can be effective**
>
> *Sometimes blurring a keyed shot's background can give it a realistic look. Typically, you want to make the subject, which you've shot with a key in mind, the focal point of your composited clip. By using a background that's a bit out of focus, the subject stands out even more. To create that illusion, simply use the Fast Blur video effect on the background clip. You can try it on Background 13 but it's generally more effective when the background is a set as opposed to an animation.*

8   Check that the clip on Video 2 is selected and then drag the Brightness & Contrast effect (Video Effects > Adjust) to the Effect Controls panel *above* the Green Screen key.

9   Make some adjustments to suit your taste. I recommend 25 Brightness and 43 Contrast.

10 Drag Brightness & Contrast *below* the Green Screen Key in the Effect Controls panel to see how effect order counts.

As I mentioned in Lesson 9, clip-based effect order goes from top to bottom in the Effect Controls panel with the two fixed effects, Opacity and Motion, applied last.

As shown in the image on the left in the next figure, placing Brightness & Contrast below the Green Screen Key means it's applied *after* keying, so only the model becomes brighter. Placing it above the Green Screen Key (the image on the right in the next figure) means it's applied to the clip *before* keying, which brightens both the model and the green screen. That causes the animation inserted into the green screen to become brighter.

Green Screen Key composite with Brightness & Contrast added after applying the key (left) and before (right).

Using the Luma Key

Luminance keys—Luma, Multiply, and Screen—create transparencies using clip brightness values. Luma is the catch-all of this category. Multiply creates transparencies in bright areas of the clip and Screen creates transparencies in dark areas.

1 Drag Photo 13e to Video 1 and Photo 13f to Video 2 (place them after the clips you worked on in previous lessons).

2 Apply the Luma Key to the clip on Video 2 (the leaf).

3 Adjust its parameters in the Effect Controls panel to remove the dark background.

There is no Mask Only option in this effect so it's a little more difficult to find a happy medium. I suggest Threshold 48 and Cutoff 43.

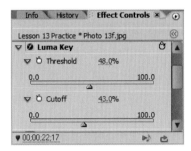

Extra credit tasks

Take this key a few steps further.

1 Use Motion to move the leaf to the lower left corner.

2 Apply Drop Shadow to it and adjust those parameters to have the shadow fall down to the right.

3 Drag another instance of Photo 13f from the Project panel to Video 3 above the clips on Video 1 and 2.

4 Right-click on the clip on Video 2, select Copy, right-click on the clip on Video 3, select Paste Attributes.

That applies the Luma Key, Motion and Drop Shadow to that clip.

5   Use Motion on it to move it the lower right, spin it 180 degrees and change the Drop Shadow Direction to have it fall at the correct angle (add 180 to whatever setting you chose for the first clip).

Your composited shot should look like the next figure.

Using matte keys: Lesson 13-5

Matte keys cut "holes" in one clip to allow portions of another clip to show through, or create something like cutout figures you can place on top of other clips.

The nomenclature can be confusing. Matte keys are not the same as color mattes like the orange matte you used earlier in this lesson. However matte keys generally use matte graphics that you create to define the areas you want to make transparent or opaque.

There are two basic types of matte keys:

• **Garbage**—Four-, eight- or 16-sided polygons, so named because you typically use them to remove something you don't want in the video. You move their vertices to define the outline of an area you want to display.

• **Graphic**—You create a shape that you want to key out or key in using a graphic or another clip. These include: Difference, Image, Remove, and Track.

In this mini-lesson you will work with the Sixteen-Point Garbage Matte Key and the Track Matte Key. I'll briefly explain Difference, Image and Remove. You'll start by trying to use the Luma Key. You'll see it has some limitations that a garbage matte can help you overcome.

1   Drag Photo 13e and Photo 13g to Video 1 and Video 2 (place them after the clips you worked on in previous lessons).

2   Apply Luma to the clip on Video 2 and adjust the parameters to attempt to show only the cat's eyes.

No matter what Threshold and Cutoff parameters you select, the white highlights on the cat's fur show through the sunset.

3   Toggle the Luma Key off by clicking the little (⊘) next to its name in the Effect Controls panel.

4   Drag Photo 13g from the Project panel to Video 3 above the other two clips.

You will use a garbage matte key on the clips on the Video 2 and 3 tracks to have only the cat's eyes display in the sky.

5   Drag the Sixteen-Point Garbage Matte Key to the clip on Video 3.

6   Click the effect's Transform button (▯▸) (to the left of the effect name) in the Effect Controls panel to highlight its 16 crosshair target handles in the Program Monitor.

7   Drag the 16 handles to make a rough outline of the cat's right eye (you'll fine-tune it later).

8   Click the clip in Video 2 to select it, drag the Sixteen-Point Garbage Matte Key to it and follow the same procedure to outline the cat's left eye.

Note: *When you select the second clip, the cat looks unchanged. In fact what you're seeing is the cat's right eye from the clip in Video 3 and the rest of the cat in the clip on Video 2 revealed when you created the garbage matte cut-out on Video 3. The reason you are applying this garbage matte to two instances of the same clip is because you can't apply this effect to the same clip twice. Once you create a cut-out, you can't create another one elsewhere in the same clip.*

9   Fine-tune the placement of the garbage matte's vertices using the View Zoom Level in the Program Monitor to zoom in on the cat's eyes. Try to remove the black areas around the edges of the eyes.

You've created something that looks too much like you cut holes in the sky. There are a few ways to remedy that. Here are four:

- Switch the Luma Key back on. That gives the eyes an orange cast that matches the sky.

- Apply a blur effect to the two cat clips.

- Apply the Tint effect and Map Black to the dark areas of the sky, and Map White to a light orange area of the sky.

- Use the Orange Matte with opacity in a five layer composite.

I took that latter approach in the example in the Lesson 13 Finish sequence. I also applied motion to the cat photos to have the eyes appear in the upper right corner, and I used the same garbage matte parameters (Copy/Paste Attributes) used on the cat photos on the Orange Mattes to have them fit exactly over the cat's eyes so they wouldn't add an extra orange hue to the sky. I finished the whole thing off by applying Cross Dissolves to gradually reveal the cat's eyes.

Create a split-screen effect

You can use garbage mattes to create split-screen effects. The most frequent application is simply to layer two clips, apply the Four-Point Garbage Matte Key to each, and move the vertices to create two side-by-side rectangles. You can also layer more clips and use the Eight- and Sixteen-Point Garbage Mattes to create all sorts of shapes.

The one little gotcha is that the garbage matte key reveals part of a clip. It does not shrink the clip to fit it in the borders of the garbage matte as happens when you use Motion to make PiPs. So plan your shots accordingly. If you want to put more of the scene within the garbage matte's borders, use Motion or some other effect to accomplish that.

A cool effect is to lock down your camcorder on a tripod, ensure the lighting, focus and exposure settings don't change for the duration of the shoot, and have an actor do a scene on one side of a set and then play another role in the other half of the set. You can use a garbage matte on one of the scenes to have the actor appear in both sides of the set at once.

This takes some planning. The actor shouldn't cross the line that divides the set in two (though you can keyframe the Garbage Matte box edges to accommodate some overlap) and there can't be any movement in the vicinity of the scene's dividing line.

Mattes that use graphics or other clips

There are four Keying effects that fall into this category. You'll work with the Track Matte because it's the most useful and works the best. Here's a quick rundown on the others:

- **Difference Matte**—A very difficult effect to get to work smoothly. In theory you use it to place multiple actors/animals/objects that could not all be in a scene at the same time in the same set. You have to shoot the various shots using the exact same lighting and camera angle and you need to work with high-end video to have a chance of making it work. It's best to stick with green/blue screens.

- **Image Matte**—Works just like the Image Mask Video Transition. You apply it, load up a graphic or still image, and the effect makes dark areas transparent and light areas opaque. It's a static effect with limited usability.

- **Remove Matte**—Specifically for graphics that when used in keyed shots have something akin to a thin halo around their edges. Apply this key to remove it.

Using a Track Matte key

A Track Matte key works like an Image Matte but has several advantages and one obvious difference. What makes it different is that you place the matte—a still image, graphic or something you created in the Titler—on a video track (thus its name) rather than apply it directly to the clip.

A Track Matte uses the clip on a separate track to define areas of transparency in the selected clip and reveal whatever is below it on a sequence. Its huge advantage is that you can animate the matte. For example, you can use Motion's Scale parameter to gradually reveal the matte or move it on the clip to follow action. The latter application of the Track Matte is called a traveling matte.

Just about every older movie involving "impossible" motion—spaceships, Superman in flight, or giant spiders—used traveling mattes.

You will do both types of Track Matte Keys.

1 Drag Photo 13c to Video 1, Photo 13a to Video 2 and Track Matte 13 to Video 3.

Note: When using the Track Matte Key effect, place the track matte clip on a video track that is above the clip you are applying Track Matte Key to.

2 Apply the Track Matte Key to the Video 2 clip.

Note: Unlike when you used the Texturize and Blend effects in Lesson 13-2, you do not have to un-Enable the clip you use in the Track Matte Key effect. When you select the Matte video track, Premiere Pro automatically disables only the portion of the track used in the Track Matte Key, meaning other clips in the track will be processed normally. This is a terrific feature that saves a bunch of steps and allows you to use the selected track for other clips elsewhere in the sequence.

3 Set Matte to Video 3, Composite Using to Matte Luma (this graphic does not have an alpha channel), and check the Reverse box (the rectangle is white, which the Track Matte sees as opaque, so Reverse makes the rectangle transparent).

Your composite will look like the next figure. Track Matte 13 is simply a white, rectangle on a black background that you could make in any graphics program.

4   Change the Motion effect settings on the Video 3 clip to move the graphic to the lower right corner, directly on the horizon line of the sunset photo.

5   Use the Motion Scale parameter and keyframes to start the matte at zero percent and grow to its full size by about a second into the clip.

6   Apply the Fast Blur Video Effect (Blur & Sharpen folder) to the Track Matte 13 clip using a Blurriness parameter of about 35 to soften the edges of the matte.

7   Click the Video 1 clip to select it, click its Motion effect to switch on its handles in the program monitor, and shrink and move it to fit in the full-size view of the track matte.

Your finished work should look like the next figure (you can refer to the Lesson 13 Finish sequence to check your work).

Making a traveling matte

You will use this effect time and time again. It's a great way to follow action. In this case you will tint the entire shot except for the cantering horse. You will use the Track Matte Key to highlight a portion of the untinted clip and have it display over the tinted clip below it in the Timeline. You can also reverse this and tint the highlighted action and have it play over the untinted clip. If necessary, refer to the example of this effect I created in the Lesson 13 Finish sequence.

1 Layer four clips: Cutaway 8a on Video 1, Orange Matte on Video 2, Cutaway 8a on Video 3, and Track Matte 13 on Video 4.

2 Select the Video 2 clip (the Orange Matte) and apply 35% Opacity to it.

That will put a tint over Cutaway 8a on Video 1.

3 Select the Video 3 clip (the other instance of Cutaway 8a) and apply the Track Matte Key to it.

4 Set Matte to Video 4 (the track with Track Matte 13 on it) and Composite Using to Matte Luma.

5 Select the Video 4 clip (the Track Matte 13 graphic) and apply Fast Blur to it using a Blurriness of about 25%.

6 Now for the tricky part—using the Motion effect on the Track Matte 13 clip. Set keyframes for Position, Scale Height and Scale Width (uncheck Uniform Scale) to have Track Matte 13 highlight the cantering horse.

You'll need to set about eight keyframes. Move the CTI to advance the video and drag the Track Matte 13 clip in the Program Monitor to adjust its location and change its size for each new position. If you run into problems, Copy/Paste Attributes from the clip in the Lesson 13 Finish sequence onto your copy of Track Matte 13.

7 Play the video. It should look like the next figure.

Review

▶ **Review questions**

1   List at least three ways to blend two full-screen clips.

2   How do you create a logo with beveled edges and a glow that grows and then shrinks?

3   You want to create a silhouette of a teapot in a video and you want to add a logo in that silhouette. Describe a way to do that.

4   In a color/chroma key, what do Similarity, Blend, Threshold and Cutoff do?

5   What's the value of the Mask Only parameter?

6   What's the difference between an Image Matte and a Track Matte?

▶ **Review answers**

1   Opacity (or its non-fixed twin: Alpha Adjust) and the Blend and Texturize video effects. You can also use Multiply and Screen. Screen works a lot like Opacity in that it combines both clips. Multiply tends to have more dramatic results.

2   Apply Bevel Alpha and Alpha Glow. Use keyframes on Alpha Glow to animate the size of the glow.

3   There are always multiple means to an end in Premiere Pro. Here's one approach. Shoot the teapot such that the background contrasts with the pot. Use the Luma Key on it to create the silhouette and use Motion to position the logo in the silhouette. A very slick extra effect is to use a white pot, have steaming hot water in it so the steam comes out of the spout, and shoot that over a black background. Then the steam will add some animation to the silhouette.

4   Similarity and Blend work together to set a width for the color range that will be keyed out of a superimposed clip and to blend the two clips smoothly together. Threshold and Cutoff deal with shadows. Threshold controls the amount of shadows from the superimposed clip that will display on the lower track's clip. Cutoff controls how dark or light those shadows are.

5   It's the best way to view your keyed effect critically. Switch it on before you fine-tune parameters like Similarity, Threshold and Cutoff.

6   You apply an Image Matte directly to a clip by clicking that clip's Image Matte Settings box and selecting the Image Matte graphic file. Track Matte is not as direct. For that you use a matte graphic that you place on a separate video track. Track Matte is much more useful in that you can animate and apply effects to its matte graphic.

Fast Color Corrector

Clip Sample   **Output Sample**

nested sequences

color wheel

shortcuts

Premiere Pro offers about a dozen video effects that can enhance or adjust colors. You will take a few of them for a test drive in this lesson including a new effect, the Fast Color Corrector. Premiere Pro's depth lends itself to specialized editing techniques. In this lesson I show you a few such editing tricks as well as some uses for nested sequences. The more you use Premiere Pro the more likely you'll rely on keyboard shortcuts. I present several that will speed up your editing.

14 | Enhancing Color, Editing Tips, & Shortcuts

Topics covered in this lesson:

- An overview of color-oriented effects.
- Adjusting and enhancing color.
- Using nested sequences.
- Three quick editing techniques.
- Recommended keyboard shortcuts.

Getting started

Most feature films are color corrected. The purpose is less to fix a shot gone bad and more to give the film a "look" that matches its mood or genre: from warm reds for landscapes and sepia tones for historic shots to cold blues for hard-edge films or a gritty look for urban dramas. Color correction—or color enhancing—is big business, and Premiere Pro has a full suite of professional color enhancing effects.

Those color-oriented effects offer more than color correction. You can select a color and change it, create a 3D look, convert a clip to grayscale with the exception of a single color, or remove all colors outside a specific color range. I'll give you a sample of some of these in this lesson.

In previous lessons, you've encountered a few uses for nested sequences. I review those uses in this lesson, show you a couple more and show you one little goodie: how to put more than one transition at an edit point.

Software as deep as Premiere Pro fosters plenty of functionality. In this lesson I show you three nifty editing techniques: obscuring someone's identity, creating a real mirror effect, and adding white flash transitions.

Premiere Pro's default keyboard shortcuts are too numerous to use, much less memorize. But there are several you will come to rely on. I list my favorites and show you how to customize keyboard commands to suit your editing style.

An overview of color-oriented effects

Premiere Pro has more than 20 video effects that adjust or enhance color. Some have narrow functionality while others are professional-level tools that take a lot of trial and error to gain some level of expertise. There are entire books on color correction and a good number of video editors who specialize in that field.

Premiere Pro offers a wide range of possibilities—more than enough to spark some ideas for your upcoming video projects.

To get an idea of what Premiere Pro has to offer in the color effect department, click the Effects tab and type *color* in the Contains text box. That displays 18 effects. There are several more that have to do with color.

I have grouped the color-oriented effects into four categories and listed them within those groups from simplest to most complex (more or less). This taxonomy is one example of why you might want to create and organize some custom effects bins. Here's a brief overview of the color effects (**—covered in this mini-lesson):

Coloring effects

- **Tint**—A simple way to apply an overall color cast to a clip.
- **Change Color**—Like Tint but with more control, and you can change a wider range of colors.
- **Ramp**—Creates a linear or radial color gradient that blends with the original image colors.
- **4 Color Gradient**—Like the Titler's eponymous feature. But this has more options and you can keyframe the parameters for some wild results.
- **Paint Bucket**—Paint areas of a scene with a solid color.
- **Brush Strokes**—Apply a painted look to a clip.
- **Channel Blur**—Creates a glow by blurring red, green or blue channels separately and in user-specified directions.

Color removing or replacing

- **Color Pass****—Converts an entire clip to grayscale with the exception of a user-specified color.

- **Color Replace****—Changes a user-selected color in a scene to a different user-specified color.

- **Leave Color**—Similar to Color Pass with much more control.

- **Change to Color**—Like Color Replace but with more options and control.

Color correction

- **Color Balance, Color Balance (HLS), and Color Balance (RGB)**—Color Balance offers the most control over red, green and blue values in midtones, shadows and highlights. HLS and RGB control only overall hue, saturation and luminance or red, green, and blue colors.

- **Auto Color**—A quick, simple generic color balance.

- **RGB Color Corrector and RGB Curves**—Offer even more control than Color Balance, including controls over the tonal range of shadows and highlights, and controls for midtones values (*gamma*), brightness (*pedestal*), and contrast (*gain*).

- **Luma Color and Luma Curve**—Adjust brightness and contrast in the highlights, midtones and shadows of a clip. Also correct hue, saturation and luma in a selected color range.

- **Color Match****—A useful but difficult-to-master tool that lets you take scenes with different color lighting and have their overall color schemes match. In this way you can color match scenes shot under fluorescent lights (blue-green) with scenes shot with tungsten lights (orange).

- **Fast Color Corrector****—This is a tool you will likely use frequently. It lets you make instant color changes that you can preview in a split-screen view within the Program Monitor.

- **Three-Way Color Corrector**—Gives you the ability to make more subtle corrections by letting you adjust hue, saturation, and luminance for highlights, midtones, and shadows.

Technical color effects

- **Broadcast Colors**—Conforms video to display properly on TV sets. Corrects problems created by overly bright colors and geometric patterns due to some effects or added graphics.

- **Video Limiter**—Like Broadcast Colors but gives you much more precise control to preserve much of the original video quality while conforming to broadcast TV standards.

Adjusting and enhancing color: Lesson 14-1

In this mini-lesson you will work with four color-oriented effects: Color Replace, Color Pass, Color Match, and Fast Color Corrector. I'll briefly touch on a few others.

1   View the Lesson 14 Intro video.

2   Open Lesson 14 to the Lesson 14 Practice sequence.

3   Drag Video 13 to the Video 1 track.

This is the clip you applied the Green Screen Key to in Lesson 13.

4   Apply the Color Pass effect to that clip.

5   Click its Setup button to open the Color Pass Settings window shown in the next figure.

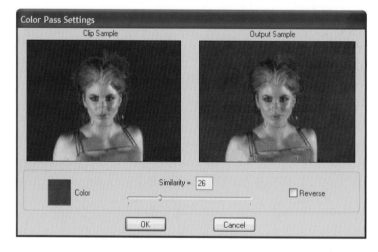

6   Move your cursor into the Clip Sample screen on the left and click the Eyedropper tool on the model's purple hair.

That selects the color you want to retain. All other colors in the clip will switch to grayscale.

7   Adjust the Similarity slider to retain as much of the purple as possible while removing as much of the other colors as you can.

A setting of about 26 should do the trick.

8   Click OK.

Note: Feel free to delete Color Pass from the Effect Controls panel and apply Leave Color. It is the same type of effect but its extra level of control might lead to better results.

9   Drag Video 14a to the Video 1 track after the clip you just worked on.

Apply Color Replace to that clip.

10   Click its Setup button to open the Color Replace Settings window shown in the next figure.

11   Move your cursor into the Clip Sample screen on the left and click on the back wall.

The goal is to find a gray color with average lighting—not too dark or light. That will be the color you'll replace.

12   Click the Replace Color swatch and select a color from the Color Picker.

I selected bright purple to make the change more obvious. The color you select will retain the shadows, midtones and highlights of the scene it's replacing, so if that scene is generally dark, the color in the scene will look darker than the color you select.

13   Adjust Similarity. A value of 28 should work well.

14   Click OK.

Note: Feel free to delete Color Replace and try Change to Color. As with Leave Color, it has more options and will probably lead to better results.

Color Match

Color Match can be a very effective way to take scenes shot under two different lighting conditions and make them look much more similar to each other. It's a tricky effect to master and usually takes some trial and error to get satisfactory results.

The two scenes you will use were carefully shot under the same lighting conditions. I used the Fast Color Corrector on Video 14c to give it a warmer look. You will do the same to Video 14b later in this mini-lesson, but first I want you to try the Color Match effect. Your goal here is to make Video 14b have the same color appearance as Video 14c.

1   Drag Video 14b to the Video 1 track past the clips you just worked on.

2   Double-click Video 14c to display it in the Source Monitor.

You will select *target* colors from the clip in the Source Monitor and assign those colors to *sample* areas in the clip on the Program Monitor that you want to change.

Note: I find the use of the words target and sample in the Color Match effect to be confusing. You'd think you'd sample a color from the clip with the colors you like and place those samples in appropriate target areas in the clip you want to change. However, the reverse is the case.

3   Apply Color Match to Video 14b and open its disclosure triangles in the Effect Controls panel.

4   Change the Method to RGB (red, green, blue).

It's more forgiving than HSL (hue, saturation, and luminance) or Curves.

5   Twirl down the Match disclosure triangle to reveal the Match button.

6   Click the Shadow *Target* Eyedropper tool and Ctrl+click (to create a 5x5 subsample color) on a shadow in the clip in the Source Monitor (see next figure for a suggested location).

Note: When you hover the Eyedropper over the Source Monitor screen and press Ctrl, the Eyedropper gets fatter, indicating it's going to sample more than a single pixel.

7   Click the Shadow *Sample* Eyedropper tool and Ctrl+click in the dancer's shadow in the Program Monitor to apply the target color to that sample color. Nothing will happen. You need to do one more step.

Note: You are applying both the color and brightness (luminance) values of the Target pixels to the Sample pixels.

Select a Shadow Target Sample from the Source Monitor (left) and apply that color to a Shadow Sample in the Program Monitor (right).

8   Click the Match button.

That applies the Target color and luminance information to the Sample color.

Note: If the shift in color does not look good (frequently it'll be too bright or the color will be skewed), press Ctrl+Z two or three times to undo your selections. You can see the color swatch next to each Sample or Target change back to the default black value as you undo each selection.

9   Follow the same steps for Highlights (spots of bright light—I suggest the dancers' hands) and Midtones (look for areas of average brightness on both walls).

Here are those steps: Click the appropriate Target Eyedropper, Ctrl+click in the Source Monitor, click the respective Source Eyedropper and Ctrl+click in the Program Monitor. Then click Match.

10   You can also try a Master Target and Sample, but that might only throw things out of whack.

To check your work, you can add the clip in the Source Monitor to the sequence and play the clips side by side. I put the before and after I came up with in the next figure.

Before applying Color Match (left) and after (right).

Color correction

Depending on how you define *color correction*, there are at least nine color correction effects. They run the gamut from basic color balance (like an auto white balance on a camcorder) to the richly detailed and complex Three-Way Color Corrector (new to Premiere Pro 2.0). This mini-lesson will focus on the middle ground: Fast Color Corrector.

The Fast Color Corrector and the Three-Way Color Corrector effects offer what are called Hue Balance and Angle color wheels, something new to Premiere Pro 2.0. You use them to balance the red, green, and blue colors to produce the desired white and neutral grays in the image.

Note: The Three-Way Color Corrector effect lets you make separate adjustments using individual wheels, to adjust tonal ranges for shadows, midtones, and highlights.

Depending on the desired effect, you might not want the color balance in a clip to be completely neutral. That's where color enhancement comes in. For example, you can give your videos a warm orange or a cool blue color.

Before tackling the Fast Color Corrector, I'll briefly show you two other color correction effects.

1   Drag Video 14e to the Lesson 14 Practice sequence.

2   Apply Color Balance (RGB) to that clip.

This is probably the most intuitive color correction effect. It has a settings window where you can manually adjust the red, green and blue levels. The starting point for all clips is 100 no matter what the actual color levels in the clip are.

3   Change the RGB settings to give this overly gray scene some warmth.
Try Red—110%, Green—95%, and Blue—80%.

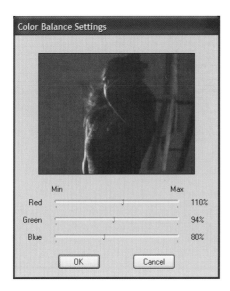

4   Delete Color Balance (RGB) and replace it with Auto Color.

This effect analyzes frames based on your parameters.

5   Try out some parameters.

Temporal Smoothing looks at several frames at once and averages their values to smooth any color balance differences. Higher Black and White Clip values increase contrast.

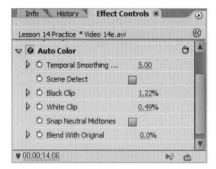

6   Delete Auto Color, replace it with Fast Color Corrector and take a look at its parameters in the Effect Controls panel.

This very detailed effect signals a tidal shift in editing possibilities. It is loaded with options including a color wheel—an intuitive means to adjust hue and saturation. You'll find three color wheels in the Three-Way Color Corrector to individually adjust hue and saturation in shadows, midtones and highlights.

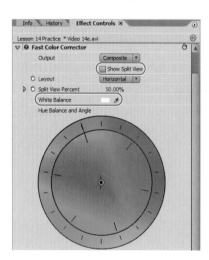
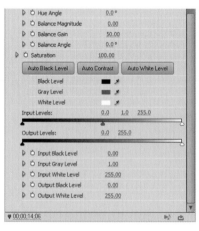

7 Drag the White Balance Eyedropper tool (highlighted in the previous figure) into the Program Monitor and click on an area that has a neutral color (to the right of the dancer on the wall is a good spot).

You don't have to have a white area to do a white balance. A neutral, medium gray area will work well. Setting a new white balance is only a supporting role for the Fast Color Corrector. The purpose here is to change the look of the clip.

8 Click the Reset button to undo the white balance.

9 Click the Show Split View checkbox (highlighted in the previous figure) and set the Layout to Vertical (the left side will show any changes you apply).

You can adjust the relative sizes of the two split screens.

10 Take a look at the color wheel. Here are its parameters (refer to the next figure):

• **Hue Angle**—Moving the outer ring clockwise shifts the overall color toward red, counterclockwise shifts toward green.

• **Balance Magnitude**—The intensity of the color introduced into the video. Moving the circle out from the center increases the magnitude (intensity).

• **Balance Angle**—Shifts the video color towards a target color.

• **Balance Gain**—Sets the relative coarseness or fineness of the Balance Magnitude and Balance Angle adjustment. Moving the handle towards the outer ring makes the adjustment very obvious. Keeping the perpendicular handle of this control close to the center of the wheel makes the adjustment very subtle.

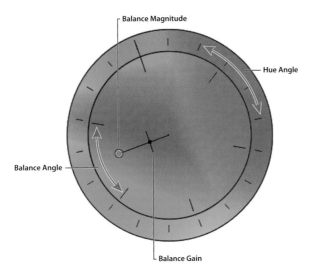

11 Make some adjustments to the Color Wheel (you can use the sliders below it as well):

• Drag Balance Magnitude to about 60 to increase the color intensity.

• Drag Balance Gain (the small perpendicular line) to about 10. That will let you fine-tune your adjustments.

• Change the Balance Angle to about -140 (if the Color Wheel were a clock, that would be about 10:30) to shift the color to orange.

• Change the Saturation parameter (below the Color Wheel) to about 115 to make the colors richer.

12 Click the Auto Contrast button (below Saturation).

That applies both the Auto Black Level and Auto White Level simultaneously, which makes the highlights appear darker and shadows appear lighter. You'll fine-tune this in a moment.

13 Select the Black Level Eyedropper tool and Ctrl+click on the darkest area in the scene.

14 Select the White Level Eyedropper tool and Ctrl+click on the brightest area in the scene.

15 Take this fine-tuning one step further and adjust the Input Black Level (I suggest 40) and the Input White Level (try 185). Input Gray Level should remain at its default level of 1.

16 Uncheck the Show Split View and play the clip.

17 Select Window > Workspace > Color Correction.

Note that you have a third video screen: a Reference Monitor.

18 Click the Reference Monitor Fly-out Menu and select All Scopes.

These are three Waveform monitors and a Vectorscope (in the upper right corner). For decades broadcast TV station engineers have used these to ensure TV signals meet standards (do not get too bright or have too much contrast).

As you ramp up your color enhancing skills, you might want to use them for that reason as well as to adjust color. To learn more about them, check Premiere Pro Help > Applying Effects > Vectorscope and Waveform Monitors.

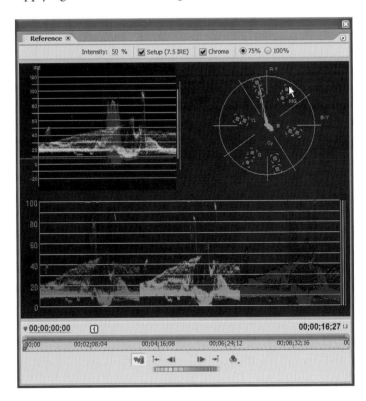

Using nested sequences: Lesson 14-2

Nested sequences first appeared in Premiere Pro 1.0 and replaced something called virtual clips. Nested sequences are a huge improvement. I won't explain virtual clips; I'll only say that things could easily go wrong with them and they were confusing. Nested sequences are much easier to work with and are more effective.

A nested sequence is a sequence-in-a-sequence. You can break your project up into more manageable chunks by creating a project segment in one sequence and dragging that sequence—with all its clips, graphics, layers, multiple audio/video tracks and effects—into another sequence. There it will look and behave like a single audio/video clip.

A prime use is to apply color correction to a long sequence with multiple edits. Instead of applying that effect to each clip in turn, you simply place—nest—that sequence in another sequence and apply a single instance of that effect to it.

And if you want to change the effect parameters, you can do it in on one nested sequence clip rather than changing each individual clip within that original sequence.

Multiple uses for nested sequences

Nested sequences have other uses:

• Apply an effect or effects to a group of layered clips such as the Cross Dissolve you used on a nested sequence in Lesson 2-6. That saves having to apply effects to each layer, one at a time.

• Simplify editing by creating complex sequences separately. This helps you avoid running into conflicts and inadvertently shifting clips on a track that is far from your current work area.

• Reuse sequences, or use the same sequence but give it a different look each time.

• Organize your work, in the same way you might create sub-folders in the Project panel or in Windows Explorer. It avoids confusion and shortens editing time.

• Apply the Motion or other effects to un-Enabled clips or to effects switched off by the Echo effect. You'll do both in this lesson.

• Apply more than one transition between clips. You'll do that in this lesson.

• Build multiple picture-in-picture effects.

Enhancing three video effects using a nested sequence

In this section, I explain workarounds for three Premiere Pro video effects. All have issues that a nested sequence can address:

• **Echo video effect**—This effect disables all effects applied above it (before it) in the Effect Controls panel. Frequently you want to apply some other effects before using Echo. For instance, you might want to use a key effect to remove a background and then apply Echo. But adding Echo switches off the key. A nested sequence resolves the problem.

• **Texturize and Blend video effects**—You've already seen that these two effects work with another clip on a higher track in a sequence. You have to un-Enable the clip on the higher track to keep it from covering the clips below it. But switching off Enable means you can't put the textured or blended clip in motion or use other effects with it. A nested sequence fixes that.

Seeing how Echo behaves

Before you use a nested sequence, go through this mini-lesson to see why you need to use one. The purpose is to show you that when you run into roadblocks in Premiere Pro, there's usually a detour somewhere that will get you to your destination. And nested sequences frequently set you back on the correct road.

1   Open the Lesson 14 Practice sequence.

2   Either marquee select the clips in the sequence and delete them, or add the clips for this exercise after those in the sequence.

3   Drag Background 14 to Video 1 and Video 14d to Video 2 above Background 14.

4   Apply the Green Screen Key to Video 14d.

5   Use Mask Only to find the best parameters.

I suggest Threshold—41% and Cutoff —30%. Uncheck Mask Only when you're satisfied with your settings.

6   Apply Echo to the clip on Video 2. That switches off the Green Screen.

Echo turns off all effects applied before it (that appear above it in the Effect Controls panel). You will remedy this with a nested sequence.

7   Delete Echo from the Effect Controls panel.

Note: You've already seen that the un-Enabled clips used with Texturize and Blend cannot have effects applied to them, so I won't have you go through the same kind of exercise to see that.

Using a Single Nested Sequence Clip for Three Effects

In this mini-lesson you will use only one nested sequence, adding clips to it as you work through the steps. The purpose is to show you that you can cut a nested sequence clip to use only a part of it.

1   Right-click on the clip on Video 2—Video 14d—and select Cut (you'll Paste it, with the Green Screen key you applied to it, into a new sequence in a moment).

2   Select File > New > Sequence. Type in a name—I suggest *Lesson 14 Nested Sequence*—and click OK.

That new sequence should open with the CTI at the beginning and with the Video 1 track selected.

3   Press Ctrl+V to Paste Video 14d—the clip with the Green Screen Key—at the beginning of the Video 1 track.

4   Place two other clips directly after it: Texture 14 and Video 14b.

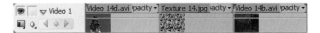

5   Apply Wave Warp to the second clip—Texture 14.

6   Select parameters that you think give it the smoothest waves (a reminder: Wave Warp has built-in animation). I suggest changing Wave Type to Circle and Direction to 45°.

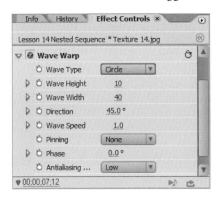
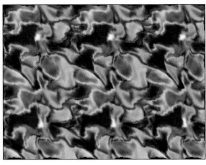

7 Apply Horizontal Flip to the third clip—Video 14b.

This effect has no parameters. It simply creates a mirrored version of the clip. The purpose here is to blend this dancer (now flipped to the left side of the screen) with a tighter shot of her dancing on the right side of the screen. She moves from right to left in that second shot so you'll make the nested sequence clip move from left to right.

8 Adjust the Motion parameters and keyframes for the third clip: Scale from 100% – 200% from the beginning to the end and Position starting centered (360, 240) and moving to the right side of the screen by the end of the clip (about 720, 460).

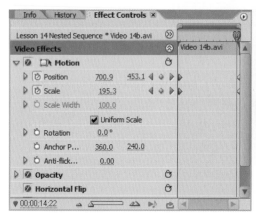 

9 Open the Lesson 14 Practice sequence.

10 Drag Lesson 14 Nested Sequence from the Project panel onto the beginning of the Video 2 track.

11 Cut that nested sequence clip in two places at 5:00 and 10:00.

12 Spread the second and third clips out a bit along the Video 2 track to create some space between the clips.

13 Apply Echo to the first nested sequence clip (the one on the Video 2 track—the DJ with the Green Screen Key).

Echo offers all sorts of possibilities. I suggest you set these parameters: Echo Time—.25, Number of Echoes—3, and Starting Intensity—.5.

Note: Depending on the Echo Operator (in this case Add), as you add echoes the clip can get brighter. My rule of thumb to keep the clip at its original overall brightness is to subtract one from the Number of Echoes and divide that into one (creating its reciprocal) to come up with a Starting Intensity. In this case 3-1=2 and 1÷2=.5 If you had 5 echoes the Starting Intensity would be .25.

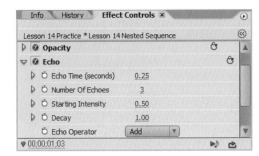 

14 Play that clip.

Without a nested sequence, this cool effect would not be possible.

15 Drag two instances of Video 14e to the Video 1 track, putting them under the two nested sequence clips on Video 2.

Your Timeline should look like the next figure.

Note: The audio clips on the Audio 2 track are there by default. When you nest a sequence into another sequence, that nested sequence clip shows up as a linked A/V clip even if its original sequence has no audio.

16 Right-click and uncheck Enable on both the second and third nested sequence clips in the Video 2 track.

Note: You can drag an effect to an un-Enabled clip and it'll show up in the Effect Controls panel, but the effect will not work.

17 Apply the Texturize video effect to the second clip—Video 14e—on the Video 1 track, set the Texture Layer to Video 2 and adjust the other parameters to your liking.

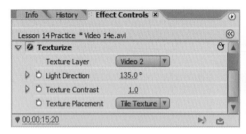 

18 Play that clip.

The Wave Warp effect animation will show up clearly. The only way to apply an animated texture to the Texturize effect is via a nested sequence.

19 Apply Blend to the third clip—Video 14e—on the Video 1 track, set the Blend With Layer to Video 2 and move the Blend With Original slider somewhere toward the middle.

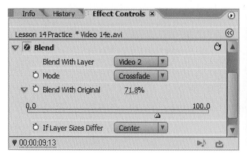 

20 Play that clip.

Without the nested sequence, you could not have used the Horizontal Flip and Motion parameters on the un-Enabled clip on Video 2.

Applying more than one transition at the same place

You cannot apply more than one transition to an edit point between two clips. But you can use a nested sequence to do something like it. I don't know that you'll run into this opportunity very often, but applying two transitions (or more if you want to put a nested sequence in a nested sequence) at the same point is a fun exercise.

1 Open the Lesson 14 Nested Sequence.

2 Drag Video 14e directly after the third clip on the sequence—Video 14b.

3 Trim the out-and in-points respectively of these two clips to give them some tail and head frames for the transition.

4 Apply an obvious transition to them.

I suggest Center Split. For my example, I added an orange border with a Border Width of 20.

5 Open the Lesson 14 Practice sequence and drag the Lesson 14 Nested Sequence to the Video 1 track past the other clips you just worked on.

6 Move the CTI to the center of the transition (after it's opened up a bit), select the Razor tool (C) and cut the clip there.

7   Apply another obvious transition.

I used Center Split again and gave it a bright red border. Play this. Without the nested sequence you could not have done this.

Three quick editing techniques: Lesson 14-3

In this mini-lesson you'll complete these fun and fast tasks:

- Obscure someone's identity.

- Create a real, animated mirror effect.

- Add a white flash transition.

Obscuring someone's identity

This is one use for a traveling matte (a Track Matte Key put in motion). You combine that with an effect like Mosaic or Fast Blur to block out someone's face.

1   Drag two instances of Video 14c to the Lesson 14 Practice sequence and place them one above the other on the Video 1 and Video 2 tracks.

You will use the Track Matte Key to put the dancer's face in an oval and to turn the rest of the clip transparent. Then you will apply Mosaic to that second clip to turn the oval into a collection of moving rectangles. That oval mosaic will play on top of the unaltered clip below it so only the oval portion is in a mosaic.

2 Use the Titler to create an oval (you can use the one I created for this exercise—Oval—in the Project panel).

As a reminder, to make an oval that will work with the Video 14c clip:

- Move the CTI into that clip.

- Press F9 to open the Titler.

- Name the title.

- Select the Ellipse tool (E).

- Alt+click in the center of the dancer's face.

- Drag to form an oval that's a bit larger than her face.

If the default Style is selected (the one highlighted in the next figure), the oval will be solid white. But in this case, any solid color will do.

- Close the Titler.

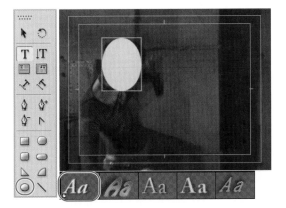

3 Drag the Oval graphic to Video 3 above the two Video 14c clips.

4 Use Motion on that oval to follow the motion of the dancer in the clip below it. You've done this before:

- Select the Oval clip.
- Place the CTI at its beginning.
- Open Motion in the Effect Controls panel.
- Click the Position Toggle Animation stopwatch to turn on keyframes.
- Drag the oval in the Program Monitor to position it over the dancer's face.
- Move the CTI until the dancer's face moves to a new spot, and reposition the Oval.
- Do this as many times as necessary to define a path that follows the dancer's motion.

You'll end up with a fairly convoluted path, something like that shown in the next figure.

5 Apply the Track Matte Key to the clip on Video 2 and select Matte: Video 3 and Composite: Matte Alpha (although Matte Luma will also work).

You will see no change, since the face in the oval and the portion of the scene made transparent matches what's below it in the sequence.

6 Drag Mosaic to the clip on Video 2.

7 Set the Horizontal and Vertical Blocks values to about 25 (a higher number makes the blocks so small they no longer obscure the dancer's face and a lower number looks too blocky).

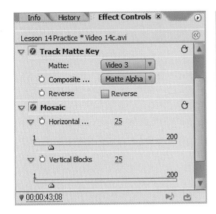

8 Play the clip.

If your Motion Position settings are reasonably accurate, the oval mosaic will follow the dancer's face.

Note: There are several other things you can do instead of or in addition to using Mosaic. You could use a blur effect. In that case, also adding a blur to the oval track matte clip makes the entire effect look better. You can darken the clip used with Mosaic or Blur. And if the dancer had moved toward or away from the camera, you could have used the Motion Scale parameter to adjust the size of the oval accordingly.

💡 A faster and easier alternative

Using Premiere Pro to create a traveling matte and applying motion settings to it can be relatively simple if the motion is easy to follow and generally falls on a straight line. Curved or convoluted paths are a trickier proposition. That's where Adobe After Effects shines. The Professional version of that powerful video production tool has a Motion Tracker that builds a traveling matte path in a matter of moments. You tell it what object to follow and it automatically tracks that motion. I demonstrate that later in the book.

Creating a real, animated mirror effect

Premiere Pro has a Mirror video effect that works like a charm. It divides a clip along a user-defined line and creates a reflection of only that portion of the clip. What it doesn't do is create a reflection of the entire clip or of a user-defined part of a clip.

Here's one quick way to do that.

1 Put two instances of Video 14e, one above the other on the Video 1 and Video 2 tracks of the Lesson 14 Practice sequence.

2 Check out the Mirror effect by dragging it to the clip on top, dragging its Reflection Center crosshair target around the Program Monitor, and changing its Reflection Angle in the Effect Controls panel.

You'll see that it has lots of possibilities but it does have a kaleidoscope look to it, which might not be what you want.

3 Delete the Mirror Effect.

4 Apply Horizontal Flip to the top clip.

That makes that entire clip a mirror image of the clip on Video 1 but for the moment the clip on Video 2 is covering the clip below it on the Timeline.

5 Use Motion on the top clip and change the Scale to 50% and the Position parameters to 540, 240 (that slides it to the right half of the screen).

6 Use Motion on the bottom clip and change the Scale to 50% and the Position parameters to 180, 240 (sliding it to the left half of the screen).

7   Play that clip.

This creates a mirror effect using the entire clip. You can increase the scale and use Crop to mirror a specific part of the clip or enable you to expand it to full-screen size.

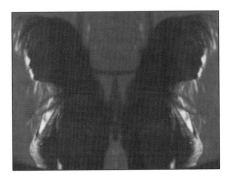

Mirrored graphic animation

You can use this same approach to rotate mirrored graphics.

1   Put two instances of Graphic 9.psd, one above the other on the Video 1 and Video 2 tracks of the Lesson 14 Practice sequence.

2   Apply Mirror to the clip on Video 2 and you'll get an idea that it can do some fun stuff, though there's no way you can rotate the two graphics independently.

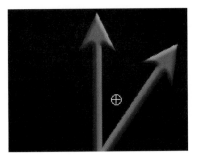

3   Delete the Mirror effect.

4   Right-click on the Video 14c clip on Video 2, select Copy, right-click on the Graphic 9 clip in Video 2 and select Paste Attributes.

That applies the Motion Scale and Position parameters used in the previous mini-lesson (it also applies the Horizontal Flip effect but that doesn't affect this symmetrical clip).

5   Right-click on the Video 14c clip on Video 1, select Copy, right-click on the Graphic 9 clip in Video 1 and select Paste Attributes.

6   Select the Graphic 9 clip on Video 2, move the CTI to its first frame, click the Rotation Toggle Animation stopwatch to turn on keyframes (with a default setting of 0 for Rotation), move the CTI to the end of the clip and put in 10x for the Rotation value.

7   Apply Rotation with keyframes to the other clip but use –10x for its ending value. Play these composited clips.

The arrows will spin side by side, in opposite directions. You could have them spin into the frame from off the screen, start small and grow, spin in opposite corners, or spin side-by-side from one side of the screen to the other. Mirrored animation is a useful editing tool.

Adding a white flash transition

This is a very easy effect that is an eye-catching way to move from one scene to another.

1   Create a white matte.

As a reminder: Click the New Item button at the bottom of the Project panel, select Color Matte, select white, click OK, name the matte, and click OK (or you can use the White Matte in the Project panel).

2   Right-click the newly created matte in the Project panel, select Speed/Duration, set the duration to 6 frames (click on the Duration time, type in 6 and press Enter) and click OK.

3 Open the Lesson 14 Nested Sequence, move the CTI to the edit point between the Video 14b and Video 14e clips at the end of the sequence and press the equal key (=) four times or so to expand the view of that edit point.

4 Delete the transition you put there (click the transition rectangle between the clips and press Delete).

5 Drag the White Matte to that edit point, press S to temporarily turn off the Snap feature, and center that 6-frame (one-fifth of a second) clip over the edit point.

6 Drag the video Cross Dissolve to that White Matte clip and set the Duration to 2 frames (so it'll fade up in only two frames).

7 Drag Cross Dissolve to the right side of the White Matte clip (so it dissolves out) and set its duration to 2 frames.

Your white flash transition should look like the next figure.

8 Play that segment.

There will be a momentary flash between the clips.

Note: This is an effect you can create in a separate sequence and then nest that sequence anywhere. There's no need to create it over and over. Or, you can export it as a video clip and use it in any video project. I explain how to export clips, single frames, sequences, and audio later in the book.

Recommended keyboard shortcuts

Premiere Pro has more than 100 keyboard shortcuts. You won't use all of them. But there are about 25 that should become a part of your repertoire. You can customize them and create additional ones to suit your needs.

To get an idea of just how vast the shortcut opportunities are, select Edit > Keyboard Customization. That opens the window shown in the next figure.

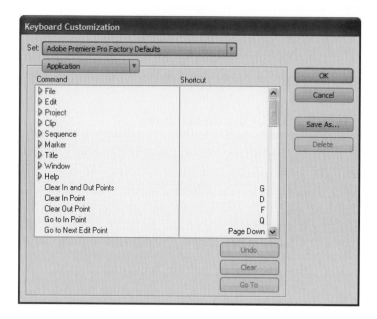

Note that the Adobe Premiere Pro Factory Defaults list uses the Main Menu headings: File, Edit, Project, and so on. You can open each of those lists and find commands that match virtually everything available in the main menu.

Many mimic standard Windows shortcuts:

- Save=Ctrl+S
- Copy=Ctrl+C
- Undo=Ctrl+Z

Some others take far too much effort. For instance, when in the Source Monitor, you frequently want to target a track for an overlay or insert edit. The keyboard "shortcut" to target the audio track that's numerically higher than the current targeted track is Ctrl+Shift+=. It's a heck of lot easier simply to click on the targeted track's header.

Premiere Pro has three sets of keyboard shortcuts: Factory Default, and sets for two competing products: Avid Xpress DV 3.5 and Final Cut Pro 4.0. The latter two are to facilitate migration from those products to Premiere Pro.

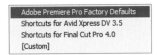

Changing a shortcut

You can create a fourth, custom set of shortcuts. The more you work with Premiere Pro the more you'll want to do that. Here's how:

1   Select Edit > Keyboard Customization.

2   Open the Edit list and click on Redo.

You'll see that the keyboard shortcut to Redo something you've Undone is Ctrl+Shift+Z. That shortcut is in various Adobe products. Your experience with other Windows products might be to use Ctrl+Y.

3   Click on the Redo shortcut to clear it, then press Ctrl+Y.

That puts *[Custom]* in the Set drop-down list. You'll name and save this as a custom set in a moment. But first check out what happens when you try to change a keyboard shortcut to one that's already in use.

4   Click Copy to highlight it in the list, then click its shortcut—Ctrl+C—to clear that entry.

5   Press Ctrl+Y.

That pops up the little warning shown in the next figure that notes you are about to delete an existing shortcut. If you click just about anywhere in the dialog box, you will make that change.

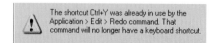

The shortcut Ctrl+Y was already in use by the Application > Edit > Redo command. That command will no longer have a keyboard shortcut.

6   Click Clear to Undo that change.

If you were to click OK, you would close the dialog box and the [Custom] set would have the new shortcut for Redo and would be the currently selected set of keyboard shortcuts. Better to give that [Custom] collection a more descriptive name.

7   Click Save As, give your customized keyboard shortcut collection a name, and click Save.

Name Key Set

Key set name: P Pro 2.0 CIB Custom Set

Save

Cancel

Most frequently used shortcuts

There are about 25 shortcuts I use all the time (including Windows shortcuts like Ctrl+C). In no time at all, the following shortcuts will become second nature to you:

- **Tools**—Each tool has a single-letter keyboard shortcut. To remind yourself of those shortcuts, open Keyboard Customization, click the Application drop-down list and select Tools.

You'll use these frequently. At the very least, Selection (V), Ripple Edit (B), Rolling Edit (N), and Razor (C) should be ingrained in your brain. In case you need reinforcement, roll your cursor over each icon in the Tools panel and Premiere Pro's Tool Tips will pop up, noting each Tool's keyboard shortcut.

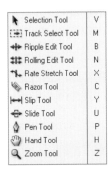

- **Backslash (\)**—Resize the Timeline to display your entire project. It's a great way to get a handle on where you are in the workflow.

- **J and L**—Playback Controls. J is reverse. L is forward. Press two or three times to incrementally increase speed.

- **K**—Multi-function, playback modifier key. Pressing K will stop playback. Holding down the K key while either tapping or holding down the J or L keys changes playback speeds.

- Hold K while tapping J—Play in reverse one frame at a time

- Hold K while tapping L—Play forward one frame at a time

- Hold K and J simultaneously—Play in reverse slowly (8 fps)

- Hold K and L simultaneously—Play forward slowly (8 fps)

- **Plus Sign (+) or Minus Sign (-) and a Number**—To move a clip by a specified number of frames. Select the clip, then type + or - on the numeric keypad (not Shift+= or the hyphen key), followed by the number of frames (you also need to use the numeric keypad). Press Enter to move the clip.

Note: When viewing the Timeline panel in Audio Units, the clip will move by the specified number of audio samples.

- **Home and End**—Moves to the beginning or end of a sequence (if the Timeline is active) or the first or last clip in the Project panel if it's active.

- **Page Up and Page Down**—Moves to the beginning or end of the selected clip in the Timeline or to the top or bottom clip currently displayed in the Project panel.

- **Asterisk (*)**—Add Marker. The asterisk key on the numeric keypad (not Shift+8) adds a marker to the timeline. I'll cover markers in more detail when we discuss exporting your project to a DVD in the final lesson.

- **S**—Snap. Pressing S turns on or turns off the Snap feature (the little two-pronged icon in the upper-left corner of the Timeline window). You can toggle Snap on or off even while dragging or trimming a clip.

Note: The CTI does not snap to items. Items snap to it. The reason: If the CTI did snap to edit points, moving the CTI through the sequence would become a jumpy mess.

- **T**—Match Frame. No matter what panel is active, pressing T will identify whatever clip the Timeline CTI is on (in the currently targeted video or audio track), load that clip in the Source Monitor and place the Source Monitor's CTI on the same frame.

Note: Shift+T will show that match frame in a nested sequence.

- **Alt**—Temporarily Unlink Audio and Video. Pressing the Alt key as you click on the video or audio portion of a linked A/V clip unlinks that portion, enabling you to trim or move that portion of the clip without affecting the other portion.

- **ALT+[and ALT+]**—Set Work Area Bar end points (show in next figure). If you want to render or export a part of your project (I cover exporting later in the book) you need to set the beginning and end of that section. Pressing Alt+[sets the beginning to wherever the CTI edit line is. Alt+] sets the end. You can simply drag the ends of the bar to those points as well. The Work Area Bar end points will snap to clip edit points.

Note: Double-clicking the center of the work area bar sets the bar ends to the visible area of the sequence or to the full length of the sequence if it's visible in its entirety in the Timeline.

- **F1**—Opens Premiere Pro Help.

- **F9**—Opens the Titler.

- **Marquee Select**—Dragging a marquee to select a group of clips in the Timeline or Project panel should be a routine part of your workflow. Marquee selecting clips in the Timeline lets you move a whole group of clips, and marquee selecting clips in the Project panel lets you add all of those clips at once to a sequence.

- **Import Folders**—Instead of importing a file or collection of files, you can import an entire folder. Select Import and click the Import Folder button in the lower right corner of the Import window. That creates a bin in the Project panel with the exact folder name and imports the associated files.

Review

▶ **Review questions**

1   What's the difference between the Color Pass and the Color Replace effects?

2   What's the basic workflow order for Color Match?

3   Why don't you want to use the Mirror video effect to create a split screen with mirrored animated action?

4   What are the basic settings you apply with the Color Wheel in the Fast Color Corrector?

5   Why do you need to use two instances of the same clip when using a Track Matte to obscure someone's identity?

6   What keyboard shortcuts enable you to rewind, stop, and play your project?

▶ **Review answers**

1   Color Pass turns everything in a scene gray with the exception of objects that have a user-selected color. Color Replace replaces a user-specified color with another color.

2   Apply the effect to the clip you want to change. Select a Target color/ luminance in the Source clip (the one with the color you prefer) and apply that to a Sample area in the clip you're changing.

3   Mirror slices a single scene into two connected parts. You can't apply animation to those parts separately. Use Motion to make a mirror effect so you can put an two instances of the same clip on both sides of the screen to create a true full-clip reflection with animation.

4   The Balance Angle (the color added to the clip) and Balance Gain (the intensity of that color). You also can adjust the overall Hue Angle to move all colors in a clip toward a selected color.

5   You apply the track matte to one of those clips to carve out the person's face and apply an effect like Mosaic to that cutout section. The rest of that clip becomes transparent so the clip below it (the second instance of the clip you're altering) shows through unaltered.

6   J, K, and L. Pressing J or L more than once speeds up the reverse and forward speeds. K stops playback.

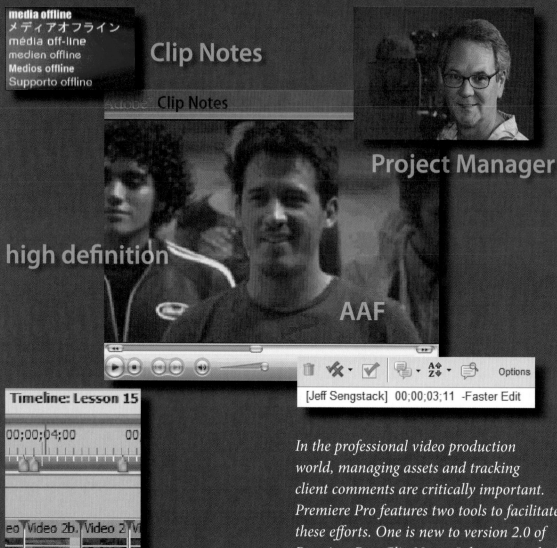

Clip Notes

Project Manager

high definition

AAF

media offline
メディアオフライン
média off-line
medien offline
Medios offline
Supporto offline

Adobe Clip Notes

Timeline: Lesson 15

00;00;04;00   00

eo Video 2b. Video 2 Vi

Options

[Jeff Sengstack] 00;00;03;11 -Faster Edit

In the professional video production world, managing assets and tracking client comments are critically important. Premiere Pro features two tools to facilitate these efforts. One is new to version 2.0 of Premiere Pro: Clip Notes. It lets you embed a project into a PDF file so a client can make written comments tied directly to timecodes. Video production companies are turning more frequently to high-definition video. Premiere Pro fosters that migration. And starting a video production business can be a rough road. I present some tips on how to avoid the potholes.

15 | Project Management

Topics covered in this lesson:

- Project Menu overview.
- Using the Project Manager.
- Conducting a Clip Notes review.
- High definition video features.
- Expert advice on the business of video production.

Getting started

If you are a one-man band, tracking projects is probably a snap for you. However, once you start bringing others into the production mix, you need to find ways to manage your assets. Premiere Pro has a slick project management tool that reduces a project's storage size and consolidates the files associated with a project.

Premiere Pro Clip Notes streamlines a collaborative workflow by facilitating feedback from clients and colleagues. You can embed a rendered sequence either as a video file within a PDF file or store it on a server and put a link to that file in the PDF. In either case, a reviewer can open the PDF file, play the movie, and enter comments directly into the PDF file. Later you can read those comments from within the Timeline.

Premiere Pro lets you capture, edit, and output full-resolution, high-definition (HD) video. If you are venturing into this growing medium, Premiere Pro offers you a number of solutions.

Taking the step into HD goes hand-in-hand with starting a new production company. Making the shift from video shooter/producer to business owner and employer rarely goes smoothly. I call on a friend and former colleague who made that transition (and encountered a few glitches along the way) to present his advice.

Project Menu overview: Lesson 15-1

Project management starts in the Project Menu. It presents several options that let you track projects or reuse assets. In particular, it offers three ways to export your project:

- **Batch List**—A text file of audio/video asset names and timecodes. It contains no information about your project such as edits, transitions or graphics.

- **AAF (Advanced Authoring Format)**—AAF is a widely recognized file exchange standard for video editing that includes clip, sequence, and editing data. It has some strict limitations. Premiere Pro's implementation has been tested only with the Avid Xpress family of products (see Premiere Pro Help—*About AAF* and *About the AAF plug-in*—for more information).

- **Project Manager**—Creates a trimmed version of your project by saving only the portions of the assets you used in your sequences, or consolidates the project by storing all its assets in a single file folder. If you choose to create a trimmed project you can use only offline file names that you later re-capture. Whether you trim or consolidate your project, the Project Manager also stores a copy of your original Premiere Pro project file with all its information on edits, transitions, effects and Titler-created text and graphics. I cover the Project Manager in Lesson 15-2.

> ### Adobe Certified Expert exam objectives
> Given a command from the Project Menu, explain the purpose of the command.

I will briefly run through the Project Menu commands, then focus on its most important feature—Project Management.

1   View the Lesson 15 Intro video.

2   Open Premiere Pro to the Lesson 15 project.

It uses the sequence from Lesson 2.

3   Click in the Project panel to select it but do not select any of the clips (otherwise several options in the Project Menu will be inaccessible).

Note: If you select a clip, that will be the sole entry in the Batch List you will make in step 5.

4 Select Project to open that menu.

The Project Menu has the following options:

- **Project Settings**—You worked with these in Lesson 4.

- **Link Media**—Use this to link offline file names to their actual files or videotapes.

- **Make Offline**—Convert an online file to offline.

- **Automate to Sequence**—Move selected files to a sequence. You worked on this in Lesson 5.

- **Import/Export Batch List**—Create or import a list of file names.

- **Project Manager**—You'll work with this in the next mini-lesson.

- **Remove Unused**—A quick and easy way to clean up your project. Select it to remove any assets from the Project panel that you are not using in your project.

5 Select Export Batch List, accept the default name and location (the current project folder) and click Save.

That creates a comma-delimited—CSV—file that you can read with Windows Notepad. The contents are simply the file names, timecodes and original source tape names (if any). The Batch List stores only audio and video file names, not graphics or images.

6   Select Import Batch List and double-click on Lesson 8 Batch List.

That adds a bin to the project panel.

7   Open the Lesson 8 Batch List bin.

Note that all its files say Offline next to them.

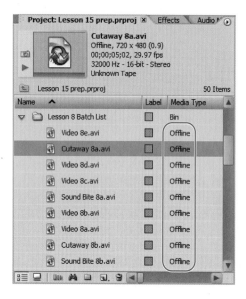

8   Click on Cutaway 8a.avi.

9   Select Project > Link Media (or right-click on Cutaway 8a and select Link Media from the context menu).

Note: The Import Batch List feature has a severe limitation in functionality. It can link to only A/V files. If you attempt to link to audio-only or video-only files, you will get an error message.

10   In the Attach Which Media window, navigate to the Lesson 8 folder and double-click on Cutaway 8a.avi.

Note: If you select more than one offline file, the Attach Which Media dialog box appears in turn for each file you select. Pay attention to the offline file name in the title bar of the dialog box so that you relink the correct source file to each offline file.

11   Click on Video 2f in the Project panel to select it.

12   Choose Project > Make Offline (or right-click on Video 2f and select Make Offline).

13   Select Media Files Remain On Disk.

In that way the file will be offline in the project but remain on the hard drive. Selecting Media Files Are Deleted will take the file offline and remove it from the hard drive. If you select that option and you want to use that file in a project, you'll need to recapture it (or, in this case, copy it from the DVD).

14   Move the CTI to the Video 2f clip in the Timeline and note two things:

•   The clip remains in the project with all its effects applied.

•   The program monitor displays a *Media Offline* placeholder graphic for that clip.

This is useful if you work with massive files and want to speed up editing. The drawback is that you can't see the video if you want to make frame-specific edits.

Note: If you're using the clip in another project, it will still be online there.

15 Select Project > Export Project as AAF, give the file a name and location, click Save, and click OK in the AAF Export Settings dialog box.

An AAF Export Log information window will pop up letting you know what elements of the project were not included in the AAF file. For example, AAF files cannot include single-sided transitions (transitions at the beginning or end of a clip).

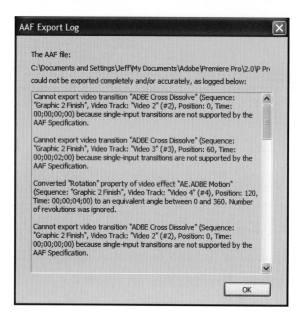

Note: Premiere Pro has one other text-based export option: Edit Decision List (EDL). It's used primarily to take a sequence created in Premiere Pro and perform final editing on production studio, high-end hardware. You access it by selecting File > Export > Export to EDL. I cover EDLs in Lesson 17.

Using the Project Manager: Lesson 15-2

The Project Manager comes into play typically after you complete a project.

You can use it to create a separate file folder that consolidates all the assets used in your sequences into one spot. This is a great way to archive a project and make it easier to access it later. Once consolidated, you can remove all the original assets if you choose.

You can conserve hard drive space by saving only those assets you used in the project and trimming them to the portions you used in your sequences, then saving them (or offline references to them) in a single file folder.

If you originally captured your footage at a low resolution to save hard drive space, you can use the trimmed project, in conjunction with batch capture, to recapture only the footage that you need at the highest possible quality.

To see its options: select Project > Project Manager.

You have two basic choices, each with its own set of options:

- Create New Trimmed Project.
- Collect Files and Copy to New Location.

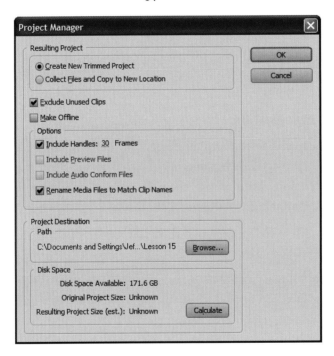

Trimmed project

In the trimmed project, the resulting files (or offline file references) refer only to the portions of the clips you used in the project sequences. You have some options:

- **Exclude Unused Clips**—This almost goes without saying when you are making a trimmed version of your project.

- **Make Offline**—Instead of storing the clips as files, create a list of file data so that you can capture them from videotape (see following Note).

- **Include Handles**—This works the same as video capture in that you retain some extra head and tail frames to allow for smooth transitions or slight editing changes later.

- **Rename Media Files to Match Clip Names**—If you changed the clip names to make them more descriptive, you can use the new names in the trimmed project.

Note: If you select Make Offline, Project Manager checks all the video files to see if they have source tape names associated with them. If not, because they can't be recaptured, it will copy those files into the newly created project rather than just list them as offline.

Collect files and copy to new location

This option will store all the media assets from the current project to a single location. You might use it to prepare a project for sharing or archiving. This selection shares two options with the Trimmed Project selection: Exclude Unused Clips and Rename Media Files to Match Clip Names. And it has two others:

- **Include Preview Files**—These are files created when you render effects. It saves you time later but takes up more disk space.

- **Include Audio Conform Files**—This is only a minor time-saver. Audio conforming goes on in the background when you import files with audio into a project. There generally is no need to include audio conform files.

Final project management steps

Click Calculate (at the bottom of the Project Manager dialog box) and Premiere Pro will determine the size of the files in the current project and the resulting trimmed project's estimated size. You can use this to check what difference it'll make to select Make Offline or include preview files, audio conform files or handles.

Finally, select (or create) a file folder for the trimmed or consolidated project and click OK.

Note: Because the video files in all of this book's lessons do not have source tape names associated with them, clicking Calculate with Make Offline checked or unchecked will yield the same results. By default, even if you select Make Offline, Project Manager copies all video files that don't have source tape names associated with them to the new project to ensure you don't delete them accidentally.

Conducting a Clip Notes review: Lesson 15-3

Anyone who has sought feedback on a project from a client will embrace Clip Notes. It resolves the headaches and miscommunication common to collaboration.

You use Premiere Pro Clip Notes to create an Adobe Acrobat PDF (portable document format) file. PDFs have become the de-facto standard in multi-platform document exchange. Clip Notes PDFs contain either a video of your selected sequence or a link to a video on a server.

A reviewer opens the PDF, plays the video and enters comments into the PDF, which automatically tags them directly to the timecode. You import those comments into Premiere Pro and they appear as markers in the Timeline.

You don't need a copy of Adobe Acrobat to create a Clip Notes PDF, since the engine is built into Premiere Pro 2.0. To make comments you do need Acrobat (Standard or Professional) or the Adobe Reader (available as a free download at http://www.adobe.com/reader).

This is not a Project Menu line item. The purpose is to review a single sequence. So you will find this command in the Sequence Menu.

1   Check that the Lesson 15 Practice sequence is open and selected.

2   Select Sequence > Export for Clip Notes.

You have three Export Settings options:

- **Format**—Windows Media or QuickTime.

- **Range**—Entire Sequence or Work Area Bar.

- **Preset**—High, Medium, or Low Quality video.

- **Video Options**—Embed or Stream. Embedding the video means the PDF will have a larger file size but ensures that all reviewers will be able to play the movie regardless of their network connection. Streaming the video means a smaller PDF file size, but reviewers must have access to the server you're using to post the video file. If you choose to stream the video, enter a URL in the URL field. If you choose to upload the movie to an FTP server, click the FTP Settings tab to access those options.

- **PDF Password**—You have the option to enter a password which would be required for opening the PDF, as well as PDF instructions.

- **Return Comments To**—You have the option to add an email address to which comments will be returned.

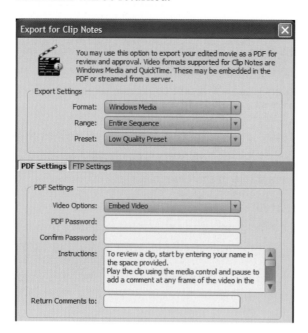

3   Click OK to accept the default settings: Windows Media, Entire Sequence, Low Quality Preset and Embed Video.

4   Navigate to an appropriate file folder, give this Clip Notes PDF a name and click Save. Premiere Pro will display a Rendering information window that shows its progress as it converts the clips and effects into a Windows Media file.

Review your Clip Notes PDF

You can email the PDF file to a client or circulate it in-house. In either case, anyone with access to the file can view its associated rendered sequence and make comments.

1   Minimize Premiere Pro by clicking the dash in the upper right corner.

2   Open Adobe Acrobat or the Adobe Reader, select File > Open, navigate to the newly created PDF and click Open.

Note: I created a PDF for your use, if needed. It's in the Lesson 15 folder.

3   Make a selection that suits you in the Manage Trust for Multimedia Content dialog box.

4   Read the Instructions (you can access them at any time by clicking the button in the reviewing area) and click OK.

5   Enter your name in the Reviewer Name text box.

6   Click the Play button in the movie viewer.

7   Click Pause when you want to enter a comment (clicking Stop will put the CTI back to the beginning of the video).

Premiere Pro automatically enters a timestamp in the comment box.

8   Type in your comment.

9   Click Play to continue reviewing the movie and adding more comments.

10   Click the Go To drop-down list to jump to any of your comments.

11   Click the Comments tab (on the left side of the interface) to open the comments list.

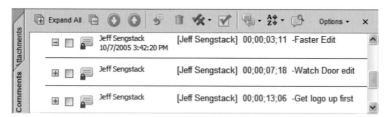

12   When you're done entering comments, click the Export button (in the lower right corner below the screen), give your comments a name (the default is [*original PDF file name*]_data) and file folder location, and click Save.

That creates an XFDF (extensible markup language forms data format) file.

View the Comments in Premiere Pro

1   Close Acrobat and re-open Premiere Pro.

2   Make sure the sequence you sent out for review is open in the Timeline panel.

3   Select Sequence > Import Clip Notes Comments, navigate to that file and click Open. Comments will appear as markers in your sequence.

Note: I created an XFDF file for your use, if needed. It's in the Lesson 15 folder.

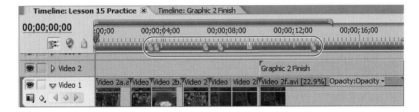

4   Double click a marker to view the comments.

Alternatively, select Marker > Go To Sequence Marker to move from one marker to another.

High definition video and film features

Premiere Pro 2.0 lets you work with any high-definition (HD) format, including HDV (JVC and other companies), HDCAM (Sony), DVCPRO HD (Panasonic), and D5-HD (Panasonic). Premiere Pro supports these formats at any resolution (including 720p, 1080i, 1080p) and frame rate (including 24, 23.98, 30, 60fps).

You can choose from a wide range of capture cards and other hardware to best fit your needs and budget. Premiere Pro 2.0 support extends from low-cost FireWire for DV and HDV editing up to high-performance workstations capturing uncompressed 10-bit 4:4:4 HD. Standard definition (SD) and HD hardware from vendors including AJA, Blackmagic Design, BlueFish444, and Matrox let you handle any video and film format.

To learn more about these various formats, resolutions and products, I suggest you read "Understanding and Using High Definition Video" at www.adobe.com/products/premiere/pdfs/hdprimer.pdf. The Premiere Pro Help file has a short explanation under "About high definition (HD) video." For now, here's a brief overview.

HDV editing

HDV is a compressed high-definition format created by JVC, Canon, Sharp, and Sony. It compresses the video signal, using MPEG-2, and stores it on standard DV cassettes. Premiere Pro can handle HDV natively—that is, with no additional hardware or software. In addition, editing is done on the video in its original MPEG-2 form with no additional compression. To use it, simply select Adobe HDV in the New Project window and choose from one of the three presets.

MPEG video does not edit as cleanly as DV. Since most MPEG video frames only note differences between keyframes, you generally cannot make frame-specific edits. And effects and transitions don't always work smoothly.

HD production with the AJA Xena HS video card

Adobe designed Premiere Pro to handle any kind of video you can throw at it. The only limitation is your hardware's ability to handle the significantly higher data rates inherent with HD.

Several hardware firms have created video cards that can take on the video data processing, freeing up your PC's central processing unit for other functions.

These cards come with plug-ins for Premiere Pro to handle video capture and export as well as some editing functionality. As we went to press, only one hardware manufacturer, AJA Video Systems, had its plug-ins built in to Premiere Pro.

The AJA Xena HS captures and exports HD. The minimum system to handle the throughput necessary to work with HD is substantially more powerful than the standard minimum platform for Premiere Pro. You'll need a PC with at least two processors, 2 GB of RAM, a high-end video processing card, and a RAID (redundant array of independent/inexpensive disks) hard drive system.

Film projects

This is a realm few beginning and intermediate video producers will venture into. If you do want to pursue producing film projects on Premiere Pro you might consider working with video cameras that record in 24P (progressive) and 24PA (advanced) frames per second—the same rate as film. Entry-level 24P camcorders are priced at less than $5,000. As we went to press there were two 24P camcorders in that price range: Panasonic AG-DVX100A and Canon XL2. When you set up your project, use one of the DV-24P presets.

The jump from 24P to film is substantial and goes beyond the scope of this book. At the very least you'll probably need to work with a production studio that specializes in transferring film to video and back. For a brief overview of how to produce projects for output to film, check Premiere Pro Help under "Creating motion picture film" and "About 24P footage."

Sam Prigg, "Head Wabbit," White Rabbit Productions

THE BUSINESS OF VIDEO PRODUCTION

Sam Prigg, the "Head Wabbit" at White Rabbit Productions in Salt Lake City (www.whiterabbitproductions.com), has never taken himself too seriously. I enjoyed working with him when he was a news photographer at KSL-TV in Salt Lake City. His skills landed him numerous weekend freelance assignments from networks and corporations.

He turned that sideline business into what has become one of Utah's most successful video production houses. His clients include Disney, 60 Minutes, Dateline, and other network shows. During the 2002 Winter Olympics, he had eight crews working full-time for folks such as Jay Leno, David Letterman, and MTV. His "statues," as he puts it, include Emmys, ADDYs, Tellys, DuPonts, and "Most Improved" in bowling.

The shift from employee to employer had some rocky moments. Sam learned a few lessons along the way and passes them along here so that others venturing into a video production business might not make the same mistakes:

• **Educate yourself about business**—Insurance, taxes, bonding, business plans, advertising, equipment purchases or leases, office space, phones, faxes, furniture, marketing, pricing, invoicing, bad debts, good demo reels, production schedules, contracts, the IRS, accounting, hiring freelance workers, firing freelance workers, security, and credit. It's no surprise that most small startups fail after a few years.

• **Partner up if you must, but be aware of the ramifications**—Dissolving a partnership can be like getting a divorce. Put your expectations in writing, spell out the roles each partner will take, where the money will go, and be prepared to review the contract frequently.

• **Don't put all your eggs in one basket**—Early on, one client accounted for most of my work. Then the client's company got sold and everything stopped. It took two years of scrambling before I felt comfortable again. The time to do your marketing is when you're busy with the project that you're currently working on.

- **Figure out what kind of video production company you are**—When I started out I planned to produce everything: commercials, documentaries, news, corporate videos, sports, and school plays. It took a long time to discover our niche. Once we figured that out, it was easier to focus our marketing and purchase the right equipment.

- **Create a demo reel**—Your demo reel represents who and what you are. It is your most valuable marketing tool. You need to make a favorable impression in the first 30 seconds. Gear your reel for your target audience and have it quickly demonstrate your core values. Our reel has helped us get lots of jobs.

- **Educate your clients**—Help your clients identify their target audience and the audience members' attitudes about the subject. Then outline the dozen or so steps involved with most productions—concept, writing, storyboarding, casting, location scouting, crew, equipment, production shoot, narration, editing, graphics, and music.

- **Don't burn a client**—If you make a mistake with some clients—bad lighting, poor composition, arriving late, faulty equipment, dead batteries—they might forgive you once. TV networks are less forgiving. One mistake and they won't come back.

- **Adapt to change, because things will change**—Stay up on the newest trends in equipment and technology, such as new recording formats and delivery systems. They can change the way you do business. Subscribe to technology magazines and join an industry organization such as the International Television Association for its conferences and seminars.

- **Decide what to charge**—A two-person crew using Betacam SP cameras, professional audio equipment, extensive lighting, and grip equipment can get about $1,500 for a 10-hour day. You can charge additional fees for the use of a wide-angle lens, matte box with filters, specialized lighting, and other production tools. Beginning photographers can usually charge $350 to $550 a day for a mini-DV camera, a small lighting package, and a selection of microphones.

- **Consider working for someone else**—It's easier and much less expensive to work for the kind of company you would like to become. Perfect your techniques and broaden your knowledge. Once you better understand the market and find your niche, branch off on your own. Our company is always looking for a photographer with a good eye as well as audio techs, gaffers, grips, teleprompter operators, writers, producers, and just about anyone else who can help make us look good.

Review

▶ **Review questions**

1   What are the basic differences between Export Batch List, AAF, and Project Manager trimmed projects?

2   Explain the two principal uses of the Project Manager.

3   Why does selecting Make Offline in the Project Manager have no effect for clips with no source tape name associated with them?

4   How do you access Clip Notes comments from within Premiere Pro?

5   How is HDV different than HD?

▶ **Review answers**

1   Batch Lists are simply text files consisting of audio/video file names, timecodes and their source tape names. AAF adds information about edits and some effects and transitions. Project Manager trimmed projects have full project information plus the trimmed original clips or offline file name references.

2   Either to create a trimmed version of your project or to consolidate the original, untrimmed project files in one folder. In either case you can store all your assets in one, easily accessible spot to simplify collaboration or archiving.

3   Premiere Pro has a built-in failsafe mechanism. If it sees that a video clip has no source tape associated with it, it won't allow Project Manager to make that an offline clip since you might not be able to recapture it.

4   Open your project to the sequence you created the Clip Notes for, select Import Clip Notes Comments, and double-click on any of the markers that suddenly appear along the sequence Time Ruler.

5   HDV is a compressed HD format. It displays at the same screen dimensions as HD but has a much smaller file size because it's stored as an MPEG video.

Adobe® Photoshop® CS2 layers

Adobe® After Effects® 7.0

scene index   Motion Tracker

text animation

Opening ←   Body Tap   Drum Fantasy

Model Fantasy   DJ Fantasy   Swi

filters

Adobe Photoshop CS2 and Adobe After Effects 7.0 can play valuable roles in your video production workflow. You can animate Photoshop's layered graphics in Premiere Pro and use it to create DVD menus for Encore DVD. After Effects features text and graphic animation tools that go far beyond anything you can do in Premiere Pro.

16 | Using Photoshop and After Effects to Enhance Your DV Project

Topics covered in this lesson:

- Introducing Photoshop CS2.
- Demonstrating some Photoshop basics.
- Editing Encore DVD menus in Photoshop.
- Photoshop tips for DV productions.
- Introducing After Effects 7.0.
- Trying out text animation with After Effects.
- Using effects and Motion Tracker.

Getting started

In addition to Premiere Pro 2.0, there are two other products in the Adobe Creative Suite Production Studio Standard: Photoshop CS2 and After Effects 7.0 Standard.

Anyone who does anything with print graphics and photo retouching probably has used Photoshop. It is the workhorse of the graphic design industry. Photoshop is a powerful tool with great depth and versatility and it is becoming an increasingly important part of the video production world.

You've seen how you can import Photoshop graphics into Premiere Pro and animate them on a layer-by-layer basis. It's also the tool used to create DVD menu templates in Premiere Pro, and you'll use it if you want to make custom-built menus for Encore DVD. I introduce you to some of its basic features in this lesson.

After Effects 7.0 is the de facto video production industry, text animation and motion graphics tool. If it moves on your TV set or movie theater screen, there's a good chance someone used After Effects to create it.

After Effects is a huge product with limitless possibilities. Working with it is akin to presenting an artist with every medium imaginable and telling him to "be creative." I'll give you a taste of its features.

Introducing Photoshop CS2

Making the move to Photoshop CS2 means joining forces with just about every image-editing professional on the planet. It's that ubiquitous. Photoshop CS2 is the professional image-editing standard.

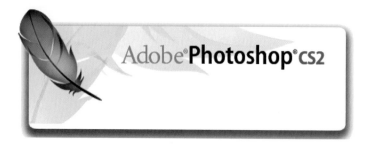

Photoshop CS2 has some strong ties to Premiere Pro and the entire DV production process:

• **Edit in Adobe Photoshop**—Right-click on any Photoshop graphic in Premiere Pro—either on the Timeline or in the Project panel—and select Edit in Adobe Photoshop (or Edit Original). This opens Photoshop and lets you immediately edit the graphic. Once saved within Photoshop, the new version of the graphic shows up in Premiere Pro.

• **Filmstrip export**—This feature is specifically designed to export a sequential collection of video frames for editing in Photoshop. You open the filmstrip in Photoshop and paint directly on the clips—a process called rotoscoping.

• **Create mattes**—Export a video frame to Photoshop to create a matte to mask or highlight certain areas of that clip or other clips.

• **Cut objects out of a scene**—Photoshop has several tools that work like a cookie cutter. You can remove an object and use it as an icon, a button in a DVD menu or animate it over a clip.

Demonstrating some Photoshop CS2 basics: Lesson 16-1

I present a basic introduction to Photoshop CS in this mini-lesson followed by a few tips specifically for DV projects.

At its core, Photoshop CS is an image touch-up tool. You can import images, then burn and dodge, change contrast and brightness levels, repair scratches, remove dust, fix red-eye, and add tinting. Photoshop generally doesn't make these changes directly on the original image. Rather, it places them in layers above the image.

It's sort of like the way cartoon animators work. They build a background image and draw characters on sheets of clear film. Then they layer those sheets one over the other. You can see through the unpainted portions while opaque sections and those elements with reduced opacity completely or partially cover up what's below.

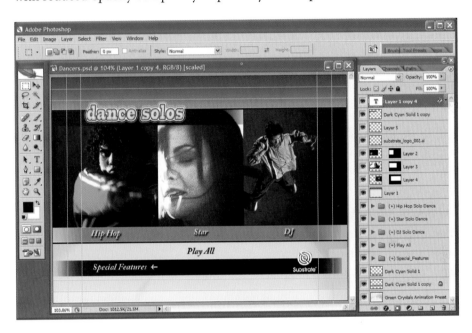

But Photoshop CS goes way beyond image touch-ups. That layering lends itself to graphics creation, editing and effects. Photoshop CS enables you to position graphic elements in those layers, add effects to them individually or collectively, and make adjustments on a layer-by-layer basis.

Taking a tour of Photoshop CS

To see how this works, I'll take you through some standard Photoshop CS image editing and creation tools. Then I'll cover some effects. If you don't have a copy of Photoshop CS2, you can download a trial copy at www.adobe.com.

1   View the Lesson 16 Intro video.

2   Open Photoshop.

3   Select File > Browse (that opens Adobe Bridge), navigate to the Lesson 18 folder (not Lesson 16) and open the Lesson 18 Behind the Scenes folder.

4   Double-click on any image.

That opens the image in its own window. You can drag its corners to expand the view and use menu commands to zoom in or out (View > Zoom In/Out) or keyboard shortcuts (Ctrl+- to zoom out or Ctrl++ to zoom in).

5   Select Image > Adjustments.

That opens a list of tools to fix the overall look of the image. Most will be familiar to you because of your work with Adobe Premiere Pro and with photos in general.

6   Select Photo Filter.

As shown in the next figure, Photoshop offers more than a dozen preset tinting options, including a few that give a warm or cool feel to your photo. You can make a change and click OK or Cancel.

7   Take a look at the Toolbox shown in the next figure.

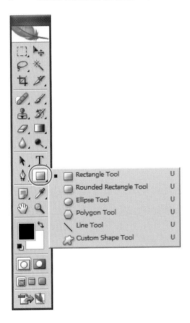

8   Roll your cursor over its buttons, and Photoshop CS tool tips will tell you each button's name.

9   Click on the Rectangle tool (highlighted in the previous figure) and hold down the mouse button. It reveals five other shape tools.

10   Select the Rounded Rectangle tool to open its features in the menu bar at the top of the workspace.

11   Click the small triangle to the right of Style to reveal a default set of Styles associated with shapes.

You can append that default list by clicking the Fly-out Menu, selecting a group from the drop-down list, and when prompted clicking Append.

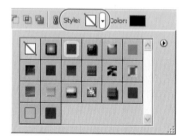

12   Click on a Style.

13   Just as you did in the Premiere Pro Titler, click in the document window and drag to create a rounded-rectangle—something like a DVD menu button.

14   Press Enter to apply it to your image.

A new layer appears in the Layers palette (if the Layers palette is not visible, select Window > Layers). Click the Shape 1 layer disclosure triangle to see all its effects.

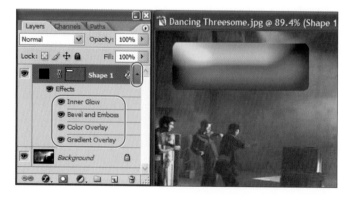

15 Click the Text tool (the large T in the Tools palette), select a font and other text characteristics from the parameters now displayed in the Main Menu bar (or click the Toggle the Character and Paragraph Palettes button), and add text.

16 Click the Commit Any Current Edits checkmark to the right of the text options in the Main Menu bar.

17 Click on the text layer in the Layers palette and select Layer > Layer Style > Drop Shadow.

That opens the Layer Style dialog with Drop Shadow selected.

You can choose from the same styles you find in the Premiere Pro Titler along with a few extras like the three Overlays.

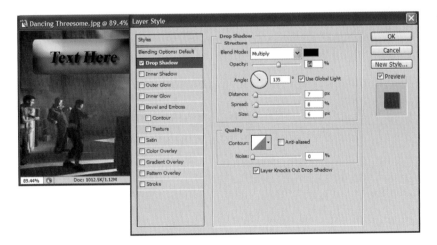

18 Select the Background layer in the Layers palette.

19 Select Filter > Filter Gallery (in Photoshop, effects are called filters).

20 Open any of the Filter groups and select a filter.

As shown in the next figure, that immediately displays how that filter will work with your photo. This is a wonderful and creative tool. Consider using it to create backgrounds for DVD menus or text.

Note: One very slick feature of the Filter Gallery is its layering window. It's in the lower right corner and is highlighted in the next figure. To add more than one effect to the background image, click the New Effect Layer button (bottom right corner next to the trash can), then click on a different Filter.

Photoshop tips for DV productions

Here are a few things to keep in mind when using Photoshop to create or edit graphics for use in a DV project:

• **Keep graphics in layers**—Place each element of your image onto a new and separate layer and don't flatten images when you are done working on them. This allows you to keep your designs editable in case you decide to make changes later.

- **Watch your font sizes**—Font sizes of 24 points or larger work best. Anything smaller may look like dust specks on a TV screen. Avoid thin fonts that may become illegible in an interlaced video signal.

- **Avoid thin lines**—If your Photoshop graphics vibrate when displayed on a TV set, this is likely due to interlacing. This happens when thin horizontal lines, especially bright lines, in your graphic or image fall between the interlaced scan lines of your video signal. Either make horizontal lines thicker or apply the Photoshop Motion Blur filter. Usually applying one to three pixels at 90 degrees will solve the problem.

- **Avoid saturated or bright colors**—These can cause tearing or bleeding—ragged edges around the colors. Blues, yellows, and greens work well. If you use red, tone it down. To make sure your colors will work well on TV, use the Photoshop NTSC Colors filter.

- **Use TV image presets for new projects**—When you create graphics from scratch, it's best to do it in a resolution and aspect ratio that match your video project. Photoshop takes care of that in its New document dialog box. Select File > New to open it, and select a preset from the drop-down list that matches your video project.

Editing Encore DVD menus in Photoshop: Lesson 16-2

I cover Adobe Encore DVD 2.0 in this book's final lesson. One of its most important features is its tight integration with Photoshop. The Photoshop engine is built in to Encore so that when you select the Encore DVD Edit Menu in Photoshop command, any changes you make in Photoshop show up immediately in Encore DVD.

Although Adobe Encore DVD ships with many menu and button templates, you eventually will want to create custom menus or use Photoshop to customize one of the menu templates.

To do that you need to follow Encore DVD menu layer naming conventions. You need to assign certain prefixes to layer names to ensure those elements perform the functions you intend, such as whether video can appear in a button or if you want some text to be a link to the Main Menu.

I won't go through all the layer naming conventions. If you intend to build Encore DVD menus, open its Help file and go to Understanding Layer Name Prefixes for Photoshop Menus. Below is an overview of the ones you will likely use most.

Encore DVD menu editing overview

In Photoshop, select File > Open, navigate to the Lesson 16 folder and double-click DVD Menu 16.psd.

That opens the menu shown in the next figure. I clicked the Opening button's disclosure triangle to reveal its layer set. You'll note that most layer names use the Encore DVD layer naming convention—that is they start with one or more symbols in parentheses. Here are some particulars:

• Each Button is a layer set (a group of layers). A button layer set name must begin with *(+)*.

• All buttons should (but are not required to) have highlights so viewers can tell when they've navigated their remote to a particular button. The highlight layer name must begin with *(=#)*. The number can be one to three (Encore DVD uses three highlight color sets).

• To add a video or still image to a button you need to create a frame layer and name it with this prefix: *(%)*.

• Background images, text, or other graphics do not need special prefixes.

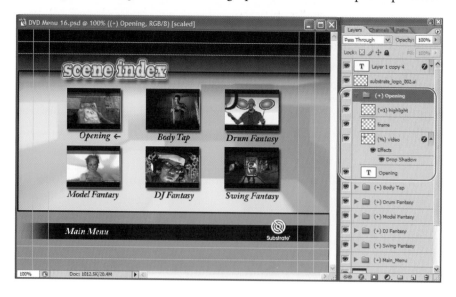

Introducing After Effects 7.0

After Effects 7.0 is the tool of choice for editors who want to produce exciting and innovative motion graphics, visual effects, and animated text for film, video, DVD, and the Web.

After Effects users tend to fall into two distinct camps: Motion Graphics artists and Animated Text artists. Some production houses specialize in one or the other. There is so much that After Effects can do, it's darned hard to wrap your brain around all of it. You will likely use only a sub-set of its creative prospects.

After Effects is available in two editions. After Effects 7.0 Standard provides core 2D and 3D compositing, animation, and visual effects tools. After Effects 7.0 Professional includes all of the features in After Effects Standard plus motion tracking and stabilization, advanced keying and warping tools, more than 30 additional visual effects, and several other high-end tools.

In the following two mini-lessons I introduce you to its powerful toolset including text animation and visual effects. Before tackling those tasks, here's a brief overview.

After Effects features

After Effects has numerous options:

- **Text creation and animation tools**—Create animated text with unprecedented ease. After Effects offers approximately 300 groundbreaking text animation presets. Simply drag them to your text to see them in action. New to After Effects 7.0 is a per-character text blur.

- **Leading-edge visual effects**—More than 150 effects enhance lighting, blur, sharpen, distort, shatter, and more. They go well beyond most effects you've worked with in Premiere Pro. I urge you to check out a sampling of what After Effects has to offer by selecting After Effects Help and opening Effects: Reference > Gallery of Effects.

- **Vector paint tools**—Use built-in vector paint tools based on Photoshop technology to perform touch-up and rotoscoping tasks.

- **Comprehensive masking tools**—Easily design, edit, and work with masks using flexible auto-tracing options.

- **Tight Adobe integration**—Copy/Paste assets, compositions or sequences between Premiere Pro and After Effects. Import Adobe Photoshop and Adobe Illustrator files with layers and other attributes preserved. The new Dynamic Link feature (available only with the Adobe Creative Suite Production Studio Professional) means you no longer need to render an After Effects composition before moving it between After Effects and Premiere Pro or Encore DVD.

- **Motion Tracker**—This option accurately, quickly and automatically maps the motion of an element and lets you add an effect to follow that action (Professional edition only).

A brief look at the After Effects workspace

If you migrate to After Effects, you likely will use it to add special motion effects to Adobe Premiere Pro and Photoshop projects. To see how that works you'll need to open After Effects 7.0 and follow along. If you don't have a copy of After Effects, you can download a trial version at www.adobe.com.

Select Import > File and double-click on a Premiere Pro project or Photoshop file
(I imported the Lesson 2-6 project).

As with Premiere Pro, After Effects has a Project panel, but the icons and terminology are a
bit different. For instance, Premiere Pro Sequences become Compositions in After Effects.

Double-clicking a Composition (highlighted in the previous figure) opens it in the
Timeline. Each numbered line is an asset or effect from the original Premiere Pro
project. Instead of tracks, you work with layers in After Effects.

Edits, effects, motion keyframes, transparencies, nested sequences, crops, and clip speed
changes built in the Premiere Pro project are all maintained when imported into
After Effects.

Look around the workspace and open the Window menu from the Main Menu to see a
listing of all the panels. In particular check out Effects and Presets and Paint. Open the
Paint panel and click on the Brush tool (in the horizontal icon panel at the top of the
workspace) to switch on the Paint panel parameters.

Note: *If you don't see the Paint panel, select Window > Paint. To see the Brush tool's brush
tips options, select Window > Brush Tips.*

Trying out text animation with After Effects: Lesson 16-3

It's a simple matter to add text to an After Effects Composition and then animate it. I'll give you a quick run-through.

1   Open After Effects 7.0.

2   Select Composition > New Composition, select an appropriate video preset, give your composition a name, accept the other defaults, and click OK.

3   Select Composition > Background Color and give your composition a color other than the default black.

4   Select the Text tool, drag a text bounding box in your Composition window and type in some text.

5   Click the Toggle the Character and Paragraph Panels button in the Main Menu bar (highlighted in the next figure) to open those two panels.

You can change the font choice, its size and color, and add strokes. The two color boxes in the upper right corner of the Character panel specify the fill and stroke color as well as whether they're activated (clicking the small box with the red diagonal line will turn off the display of whichever color box is in front). The drop-down list lets you select the type of stroke.

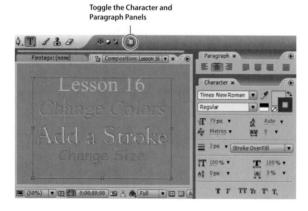

Toggle the Character and
Paragraph Panels

6   Twirl down the text layer's disclosure triangles in the Timeline.

Note: After Effects has the same keyframeable parameters found in the Premiere Pro Motion effect along with some additional options. You can add many, many other parameters to this text layer or to any other object in the Timeline. I offer up a few examples in the upcoming steps.

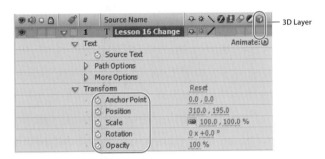

7   Set some keyframes for any of the Transform parameters.

After Effects works just like Premiere Pro. Switch on keyframes by clicking the stopwatch, then move the CTI and change a parameter, and a new keyframe will appear.

8   Press the Play button in the Time Controls panel (or drag the CTI) to see your work.

Working in 3D

1   Click the empty box below the 3D rectangle (highlighted in the previous figure) to switch on 3D animation.

That adds the X/Y/Z icon highlighted in the next figure, as well as X/Y/Z Rotation parameters and Material Options in the Timeline.

2   Twirl down Material Options to see all the very cool options immediately available to you when you work in 3D in After Effects.

3   Place the Selection tool cursor over the end points of the X/Y/Z axis to select one of the three directions and drag the text along the selected axis.

4   Click the Rotation tool (⟳), to the right of the Selection tool, and drag it around on the text in your Composition window. The text will spin all over the place. Any changes you make are keyframeable.

Animating text on a curved line

1   Delete the text layer (select it in the Timeline and press Delete).

2   Add a new text layer by clicking the Text tool, clicking anywhere in the Composition panel screen and typing in a line of text.

3   Click the Pen tool (to the right of the Text tool) and create a curved path using the same techniques you used in Adobe Premiere Pro—click and drag to make one point with handles then click and drag elsewhere to create an additional point with handles. That adds what's called a Mask layer to the Timeline.

4   Twirl down Text > Path Options in the Timeline and select Mask 1 from the Path drop-down list.

That drops the text onto the curved path you created in the Mask 1 layer.

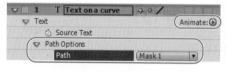 

5   Click the Animate button (highlighted in the previous figure).

Now you can work with all sorts of keyframeable animation parameters. For instance, Tracking adjusts the spacing between characters and First Margin denotes the text's placement on the curve.

Text animation presets

After Effects lets you animate text on a per-character or per-word basis. You can animate text strokes to look like you're writing letters one by one. And you can add animation to text interiors using things like squiggly lines. There are so many text animation and effect possibilities, it would be impractical to go over them here.

One quick way to get an idea of the possibilities is by using a preset. After Effects has about 300 text animation presets. Here's a brief preview.

1   Delete the text on a path layer and add a new text layer by clicking the Text tool, clicking anywhere in the Composition panel screen and typing in a line of text.

2   Check that the CTI is at the beginning of the Timeline.

3   Open the Effects & Presets panel (if you don't see it, select Window > Effects & Presets) and twirl down Animation Presets > Text.

There are more than a dozen Text Animation Preset groups.

4   Open the top set—Animate In—and drag Center Spiral to the text in the Composition panel screen.

5   Press the spacebar to play that animation.

6   Press Ctrl+Z to Undo that effect and try out some others.

This is guaranteed to keep you busy for a long time, as you consider all the ways you can use animated text in your projects. As you work with the presets, take a look at the Timeline and check out all the newly added keyframes. You can customize each of these presets by changing those keyframes.

Using effects and Motion Tracker: Lesson 16-4

After Effects 7.0 has about 200 effects that enable you to correct and enhance your videos. And that's only for starters. The After Effects third-party plug-in business is huge. Scores of effects are available from many developers. Here are a few that come with After Effects:

- **Lens Blur**—Simulates a narrower depth of field by blurring some objects in an image while leaving others in focus.

- **Fractal**—Renders one of two types of fractal images that add a colorful texture to your clips.

- **Turbulent Displace**—Uses fractal noise to create distortions.

- **Warp**—Transforms layers into geometric shapes, arcs, waves, and fish-eye lens views.

- **Liquify**—Distorts clips using 10 brush-based tools.

- **Vegas**—Generates running lights and other path-based pulse animations around an object.

Try out some exciting effects

Working with effects in After Effects is a lot like working with effects in Premiere Pro. Each effect typically has a set of parameters unique to that effect. As you apply effects to a layer, they show up in the Effect Controls panel, and you can adjust parameters globally or with keyframes there. You can also make the same adjustments in the Timeline.

1   Open a new project and a new composition.

2   Double-click in the Project panel, select a video clip, still or graphic (I selected Video 8a), and click Open.

3   Drag that clip to the Timeline and select it to display it in the Composition panel.

4   In the Effects & Presets panel, twirl down the Distort bin disclosure triangle, and drag Warp to the Composition panel.

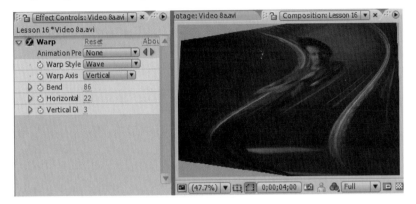

5   Try out the various presets in the Effect Controls panel such as Wave, Flag, and Arc. Move the sliders and grab the bounding box corners in the Composition panel to change the size and orientation of your original clip.

6   Press Ctrl+Z to Undo Warp and drag Liquify (Distort folder) to the Composition panel.

This may be a first for you: icons in the Effect Controls panel. Liquify lets you manually distort portions of an image. To see how that distortion works, you can turn on the effect's Mesh view which shifts and distorts as you drag one of Liquify's 10 tools around the screen.

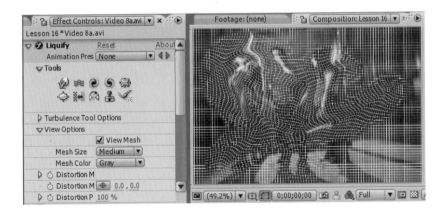

7   Replace Liquify with Colorize-Gold Clip (Animation Presets > Image-Creative folder). Note that it's actually the Solid Composite effect with a preset built-in. Open its two drop-down lists and select a different preset or blending mode.

8   Replace Colorize with Bad TV2-Old (Blur & Sharpen > Box Blur).

This is a preset within an effect that combines five (!) effects: Wave Warp, Box Blur, Color Balance (HLS), Noise, and Venetian Blinds.

Using the Motion Tracker

The After Effects Motion Tracker (available with the Professional version only) enables you to accurately, quickly and painlessly follow motion and then connect effects to those moving objects. You can track any number of moving objects and then link effects directly to those objects.

You can highlight a skier by having a transparent color matte match his every move. Follow a golf swing, leaving an arc that shows the swing's characteristics. Or, in this example, add a lens flare to the DJ's hand movements.

In Lesson 14 you used a manual tracking method in Premiere Pro to obscure someone's identity. Now, with a few simple mouse clicks, the After Effects Motion Tracker does that for you in record time.

1   Import Motion Tracker 16.avi from the Lesson 16 folder.

2   Drag it to the Timeline.

When you track motion, you can apply an effect, text or some other object in the composition to it. In this case you'll add a Lens Flare.

3   Drag the Lens Flare effect (Generate folder) to the Composition panel screen.

4   Click on the Motion Tracker video in the Timeline to select it, then select Animation > Track Motion from the Main Menu.

That opens the Tracker Controls dialog box shown in the next figure.

 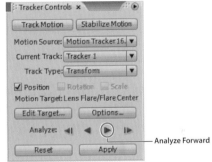

5   Check the Tracker Control settings to make sure the Motion Source is Motion Tracker 16.avi, that the Current Track is Tracker 1, Track Type is Transform, and Position is checked.

6   Click Edit Target, note that Lens Flare/Flare Center is selected and Click OK.

There will be additional possibilities if you have more than one object or effect to choose from.

7   Drag the Track Point 1 double-square/crosshair and center it on the bright highlight on the DJ's forearm (the highlight is easier for Motion Tracker to follow than a dark, non-descript area).

Note: To drag the double-square/crosshair, click somewhere inside the outer box. If you click on its edge, that will expand the box, increasing the area on the screen the program has to examine to track the moving target. As you drag it the box automatically switches to a 400% zoom to help you find the exact pixel to track.

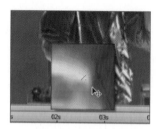

8   Check that the CTI is at the beginning of the video, then click the Analyze Forward button (highlighted in a previous figure) in the Tracker Controls panel.

The video will play and the Track Point 1 box will follow the forearm. Since the highlight changes as the disc jockey rotates his arm, the track might not be exact. If so, click Reset, move the Track Point location and try again.

9   Click Apply, note the default Apply Dimensions setting of X and Y, and click OK.

That adds dozens of keyframes to the Lens Flare Center's line in the Timeline.

10   Play the Timeline and watch the Lens Flare follow the DJ's hand movements.

Review

▶ **Review questions**

1   When you add an effect to a graphic in Photoshop, how does that change the original image?

2   What's an easy and quick way to see how multiple filters will look when applied to an image?

3   Why do you need to use some extra care when creating graphics in Photoshop for display on TV?

4   What happens if you don't use the (+) for an Encore DVD button layer set name?

5   In some ways Premiere Pro and After Effects have similar functionality. Only the terms are different. Give a couple of examples.

6   A strength of After Effects is its easy-to-use 3D animation tool. How do you switch it on and what are its two basic parameters?

▶ **Review answers**

1   It doesn't change the image. It adds a layer above that image. Layers are critical to how Photoshop works and how it's integrated with Premiere Pro.

2   Select that image's layer in the Layers palette and then open the Filter Gallery. Select one filter, click the New Effect Layer button, and then click on another filter. You can add several filters, although more than about three and your image can lose any resemblance to its original appearance.

3   TV sets, NTSC in particular, do not handle bright colors or thin lines well.

4   Encore DVD will consider that layer set to be part of the menu's background, even if the layers within the set have (%) or (=#) prefixes.

5   Premiere Pro has sequences and tracks. After Effects has compositions and layers.

6   Click in the empty square below the box icon in the Timeline to switch on 3D. You can change an object's location in 3D space using the 3D icon's X/Y/Z arrows or rotate it using the Rotation tool.

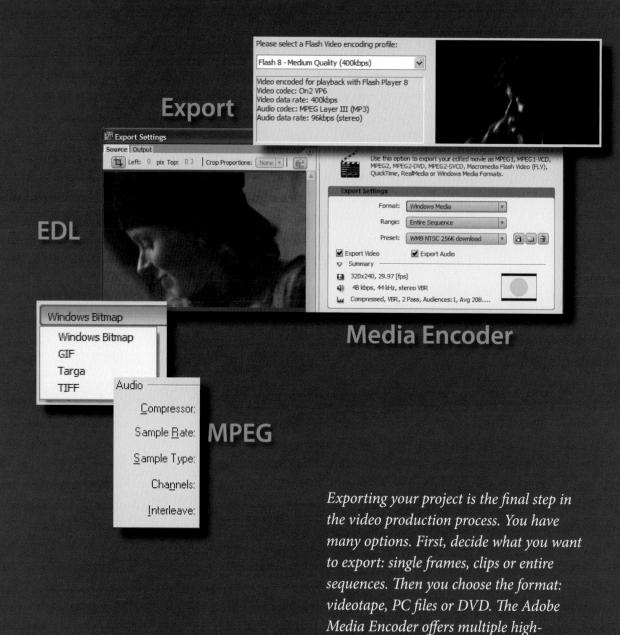

Export

EDL

Please select a Flash Video encoding profile:

Flash 8 - Medium Quality (400kbps)

Video encoded for playback with Flash Player 8
Video codec: On2 VP6
Video data rate: 400kbps
Audio codec: MPEG Layer III (MP3)
Audio data rate: 96kbps (stereo)

Export Settings

Source | Output

Left: 0 pix Top: 0 0 | Crop Proportions: None

Use this option to export your edited movie as MPEG1, MPEG1-VCD, MPEG2, MPEG2-DVD, MPEG2-SVCD, Macromedia Flash Video (FLV), QuickTime, RealMedia or Windows Media Formats.

Export Settings

Format: Windows Media
Range: Entire Sequence
Preset: WM9 NTSC 256K download

☑ Export Video   ☑ Export Audio
▽ Summary
320x240, 29.97 [fps]
48 kbps, 44 kHz, stereo VBR
Compressed, VBR, 2 Pass, Audiences:1, Avg 208....

Media Encoder

Windows Bitmap

Windows Bitmap
GIF
Targa
TIFF

Audio

Compressor:
Sample Rate:
Sample Type:
Channels:
Interleave:

MPEG

Exporting your project is the final step in the video production process. You have many options. First, decide what you want to export: single frames, clips or entire sequences. Then you choose the format: videotape, PC files or DVD. The Adobe Media Encoder offers multiple high-level output formats: Windows Media, QuickTime, RealMedia, Macromedia Flash, and MPEG. Within those formats you have dozens of options. You'll sort through them in this lesson.

17 | Exporting Frames, Clips and Sequences

Topics covered in this lesson:

- Export options.
- Recording to videotape.
- Making single frames.
- Creating standard movie, image sequence and audio files.
- Using the Adobe Media Encoder.
- Working with edit decision lists.
- Exporting to DVD.

Getting started

Premiere Pro offers a full array of export options—methods to record your projects to videotape, convert them into files, or burn them to DVDs.

Recording to videotape is straightforward while file creation has many more options. You can record only the audio portion of your project, convert a video segment or entire project into one of several standard (but somewhat dated) PC file formats, or create still frames, sequences of still frames, or animation files.

Of greater relevance are the higher-level video encoding formats available in the Adobe Media Encoder. You'll use that powerful tool to create projects to post to a Web site, for multimedia CD-ROMs, to create DVD movies and for wide-screen and high-definition videos. In all instances, you can adjust various settings to change quality and adjust the resulting file size, generally as a means to streamline playback.

Export options

When you complete a project you face a number of export choices:

- Select a single frame, a series of frames, a clip, or an entire sequence.

- Choose audio-only, video-only or full audio/video output.

- Export directly to videotape, create a file for viewing on a PC or the Internet, or put your project on a DVD with or without a complete set of menus, buttons and other DVD features.

- Any files you choose to create can be at the same visual quality and data rate as your original media, or they can be compressed.

- Within each of those export formats there are many other choices: frame size, frame rate, data rate, and audio and video compression techniques.

- You can use exported project files for further editing, in presentations, as streaming media for Internet and other networks, or as sequences of images to create animations.

Checking out export options

1   Take a look at the Lesson 17 Intro video.

2   Open Premiere Pro to Lesson 17.

Note: I have included the sequence from Lesson 6. Its primary purpose is to make sure all the appropriate export options are available to you. If you have a project of your own, feel free to export it, but you don't have to actually create any files or export to videotape or a DVD to complete these mini-lessons.

3   Click somewhere in the Timeline to select it and its single sequence (otherwise Premiere Pro will not present Export as an option in the File Menu).

4   Select File > Export.

Premiere Pro offers eight export options (some options might be inactive due to the particulars of the files in your sequence):

- **Movie**—Create Windows AVI or Apple QuickTime desktop video files, or sequences of still images.

- **Frame**—Convert a selected frame into a still image using one of four formats: BMP, GIF, Targa, or TIFF.

- **Audio**—Record an audio-only file in one of three formats: WAV, AVI, or QuickTime.

- **Title**—Since Premiere Pro stores Titler-created objects in the project file, the only way to use the same title in more than one project is to export it as a file. To use this option you need to select a title in the Project panel.

- **Export to Tape**—Transfer your project to videotape.

- **Export to DVD**—Burn your Premiere Pro project directly to a DVD.

- **Export to EDL**—Create an edit decision list to take your project to a production studio for further editing.

- **Adobe Media Encoder**—Transcode your project or a segment into one of four high-end file formats: MPEG, Windows Media, RealMedia, or QuickTime. Use these for Web streaming video or, in the case of MPEG, to play on DVDs.

Movie...	Ctrl+M
Frame...	Ctrl+Shift+M
Audio...	Ctrl+Alt+Shift+M
Title...	
Export to Tape...	
Export to DVD...	
Export to EDL...	
Adobe Media Encoder...	

Recording to videotape: Lesson 17-1

Even with something as straightforward as dubbing your sequence to videotape, Premiere Pro gives you multiple options. All you need is a video recording device—most commonly, the same DV camcorder you used to import the original raw video.

You can use an analog or non-device control videotape recorder, but doing so takes some extra effort. I explain that at the end of this mini-lesson.

1   Connect your DV camcorder to your computer, just as you did when you captured video.

2   Turn it on and set it to VCR or VTR (not Camera as you might expect).

3   Cue the tape to where you want to start recording.

> 💡 **Bars and tone or black video**
>
> *If you're going to have a postproduction studio duplicate your tapes, add 30 seconds of bars and tone to the beginning so the studio can set up its gear. Otherwise, give your project a little breathing room on your DV tape by adding black video to its beginning. To do either one: click on the New Item button at the bottom of the Project panel and select Bars and Tone or Black Video. The default duration is five seconds. Right-click on the clip in the Project panel, select Speed/Duration and change the time to suit your needs. Then drag that clip from the Project panel to the start of your project (hold down the Ctrl key to insert it and slide all other clips to the right).*

4   Select the sequence you want to record.

Note: When using the standard DV device control videotape export method, you can only export an entire sequence, as opposed to a selected segment. To export a segment, follow the analog videotape recording instructions later in this mini-lesson.

5   Select File > Export > Export to Tape.

That opens the dialog box shown in the next figure. Here's a rundown of its options:

- **Activate Recording Device**—When checked, Premiere Pro will control your DV device. Uncheck it if you want to record to a device that you'll control manually.

- **Assemble at Timecode**—Use this to select an in-point on the tape where you want recording to begin. When unchecked, recording will begin at the current tape location.

- **Delay Movie Start**—This is for the few DV recording devices that need a brief period of time between receiving the video signal and recording it. Check your device's manual to see what the manufacturer recommends.

- **Preroll**—Most decks need little or no time to get up to the proper tape recording speed. To be on the safe side, select 150 frames (five seconds) or add black video to the start of your project (see previous "Bars and Tone or Black Video" Tip).

- **Other Options**—These are self-explanatory.

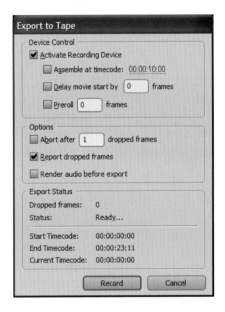

6 Click Record (or Cancel if you don't want to make a recording).

If you haven't rendered your project (by pressing Enter for playback instead of the Spacebar), Premiere Pro will do that now. When rendering is complete, Premiere Pro will start your camcorder and record your project to it.

Analog or non-device control recording

To record to an analog or non-device control machine, set up your camcorder for recording.

1 Render the sequence or portion you want to record by pressing Enter.

2 Play the sequence to make sure that you see it display on your external recording device.

3 Cue your tape to where you want recording to begin, position the Timeline CTI to where you want playback from your sequence to begin, press the Record button on your device, and play the sequence.

4 When the sequence or segment finishes, press the Stop button in the Program screen and then stop the tape on the device.

Making single frames: Lesson 17-2

There are two basic export-to-file processes: standard files and Adobe Media Encoder files. Each uses its own interface. Single frames and frame sequences fall into the standard file category.

1 Move the CTI to the frame you want to export.

2   Select File > Export > Frame.

That opens the Export Frame window. You will see a window like this for all the standard (non-Media Encoder) files. The currently selected file type will appear in the Summary window.

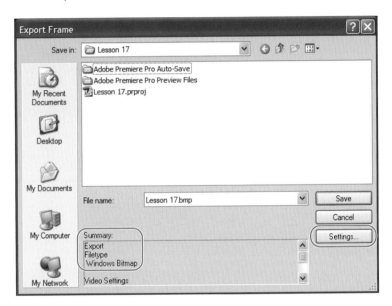

3   Click Settings to change to a different file type.

4   Choose a format for File Type (only GIF has an additional Compile Settings option). You can uncheck Add to Project When Done if you choose.

5   Click OK to close the Export Still Frame Settings dialog box.

6   Specify a hard drive location and file name and then click Save (or Cancel if you don't want to make a file).

Creating standard movie, image sequence and audio files: Lesson 17-3

You can export a clip, an entire sequence or a portion of a sequence as an audio/video, audio-only or video-only file, or as a sequence of still image files. You can use those image sequences in animation programs or apply graphic elements to them (a process called rotoscoping) in programs like Photoshop and Illustrator.

> **Adobe Certified Expert exam objective**
>
> Explain how to use the options available from the Export Movie Settings dialog box when exporting a movie.

- To export an entire sequence, select the sequence in the Timeline or Program Monitor.

- To export a segment of a sequence, place the ends of the Timeline Work Area Bar at the beginning and end of that segment.

- To export a clip, select the clip in the Source Monitor or Project panel and click in the appropriate panel to make it active. To specify a range of frames within the clip to export set an In point and Out point in the Source Monitor.

1   Choose File > Export > Movie.

2   Click Settings.

You have a few additional options than those available when exporting a single frame:

- **File Types**—Check the drop-down list and note that there are six image file types for the image sequence option as well as QuickTime and AVI. Waveform is for audio-only, and is one of the file types you'll find in the Export Audio option.

- **Range**—If you selected a clip in the Source Monitor or Project Panel you have the choice of exporting the Entire Clip or In to Out. If you selected a sequence, your choice is Entire Sequence or Work Area Bar.

- **Export Audio**—Switching this off means you'll create a video-only file.

- **Embedding Options**—Choose whether to include a project link in the exported file. That means you can open and edit the original project from within another Adobe Premiere Pro project or from another application that supports the Edit Original command.

- **Save and Load**—You can save and later quickly load export settings that you use frequently.

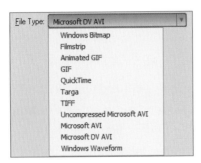

3 Click Video to open that submenu.

Here you can choose a compressor (if one is available for the File Type you selected), as well as color depth, frame size, quality and pixel aspect ratio.

Note: To see most of the compressors available for video files, choose QuickTime as the file type. QuickTime has more than 20 codecs (compression/decompression algorithms) associated with it. Each video and audio compressor has attributes that work best under certain circumstances. For more background on compression, read the DV Compression Primer on this book's companion DVD.

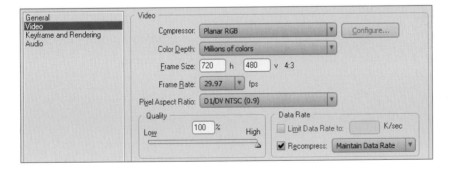

4 Click OK to close the Settings dialog box.

5 Specify a location and file name, and click OK (or Cancel).

Export audio only

You can use the Export Movie settings dialog box to create audio-only files by un-checking Export Video in the Export Movie Settings General Submenu. But it's more intuitive to use the Audio Export command.

1   Select File > Export > Audio.

This gives you access to the three audio file types: WAV, AVI and QuickTime. The latter two formats are primarily intended for audio/video files but they also handle audio-only.

2   Open the Audio submenu.

Here you can set audio quality. You can choose from more than a dozen audio compressors.

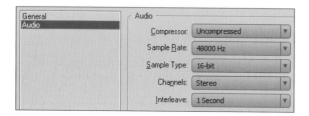

Note: If you want to create a 5.1 Surround Sound file, make that selection in the Audio Submenu > Channels drop-down list. QuickTime does not have a 5.1 option.

3   Click OK to close the Export Audio Settings dialog box.

4   Specify a location and file name, and click OK (or Cancel).

Using the Adobe Media Encoder

The Adobe Media Encoder is an export powerhouse tool that has been completely redesigned for Premiere Pro 2.0. It offers several flavors of MPEG encoding plus Macromedia Flash Video, Windows Media, RealMedia, and QuickTime streaming media (as opposed to the QuickTime MOV files you encountered in Export Audio and Export Movie).

Each of the five encoding engines has so many presets that few editors will need to do any parameter-tweaking. That said, there are customizable options aplenty.

Rather than attempt to explain each encoding engine's unique characteristics, I'll show you how to access them and explain a couple of general concepts. For detailed explanations of all the options for each encoder, open Premiere Pro Help and go to Video Output > Adobe Media Encoder.

Select File > Export > Adobe Media Encoder.

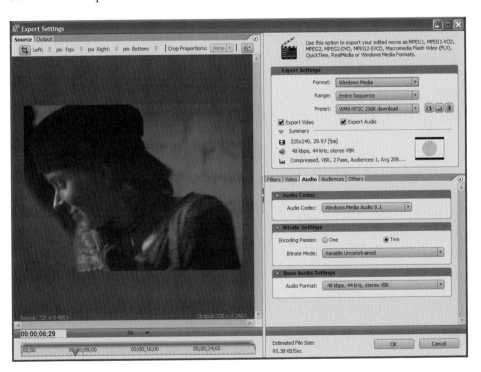

The Adobe Media Encoder consists of a preview display on the left, and tabbed panels containing export settings on the right. In the preview display you can choose to view either your source or output video. The Source tab displays your sequence before any export settings have been applied. The Output tab shows how your video will look once it's exported.

A time ruler lets you scrub through your video. You can crop the source video using the Source display or switch to the Output display and deinterlace.

Note: Use the Deinterlace option if the video in the sequence is interlaced (all standard DV is interlaced) and you are exporting to a non-interlaced medium, such as progressive scan video. Interlaced video displays images in fields of odd-numbered, then even-numbered, horizontal lines. NTSC displays in 29.97 frames (or 59.94 fields) per second.

Export settings

When setting export options, you can choose from a number of presets or create your own custom settings. Custom settings can be saved as presets for future use. As you make changes to your export settings, the Output tab in the preview display updates to reflect your changes.

Adobe Certified Expert exam objective

Given a format, explain how to use the options available from the Export Settings panel when exporting from the Timeline to the Adobe Media Encoder.

Macromedia Flash video

Macromedia Flash Video is based on Flash Player technology so it's ready to play on any PC with a Flash-enabled browser. You don't have to worry about the platform or the format. With Flash Video, when the page loads, the video plays.

1   Select Macromedia Flash Video from the Export Settings > Format drop-down list. Of the five encoders, Flash Video has the fewest options.

2   Click the Video tab (below the Export Settings panel) and click Options.

3   Choose an encoding profile from 150 kbps to 700 kbps. If you click Show Advanced Settings you can adjust the frame rate and frame size as well as a couple of other options.

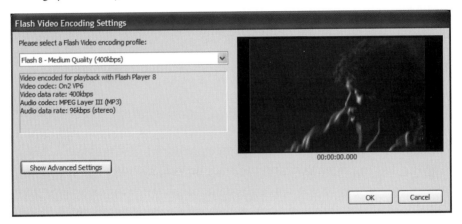

QuickTime

QuickTime offers the most options, but has a limited number of presets—eight each for NTSC and PAL.

1   Select QuickTime in the Format drop-down list.

2   Select QT 256 Streaming NTSC from the Preset drop-down list.

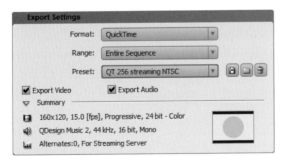

3   Open the Video tab, click the Video Codec drop-down list and note that as with QuickTime's Export Movie option, you can select from a list of more than 20 codecs. Several have additional options.

4   Click the Audio tab and note that the options there are similar to those you encountered in the Export Audio option.

RealMedia

RealMedia takes more of a consumer-friendly, hand-holding approach and offers the fewest user options. Its collection of presets is similar to those in QuickTime with the addition of one for 24P (film frame rate) video.

1   Select RealMedia.

2   Click the Audiences tab.

This is where you can customize the bitrate from the selected preset and choose one- or two-pass encoding. Both RealMedia and Windows Media offer this option. If two-pass encoding is selected, the encoder analyzes the original video project before transcoding it. Encoding will take almost twice as long, but the resulting video will look better than a single-pass version using all the same parameters.

Windows Media

This is the most versatile video format for use in Windows PCs and for playback on the Internet. You can create single files with multiple bandwidth bit-stream rates (as a means to compensate for varying Internet user connection speeds), or you can create high-definition, wide-screen videos with 5.1 surround sound for playback in theaters or on HD TVs.

1   Select Windows Media.

2   Click its Preset drop-down list (the next figure shows fewer than half of the NTSC presets).

```
WM9 HDTV 1080 24p 5.1
WM9 HDTV 1080 60i 5.1
WM9 HDTV 720 24p 5.1
WM9 NTSC 1024K download
WM9 NTSC 128K download
✔ WM9 NTSC 256K download
WM9 NTSC 32K download
WM9 NTSC 512K download
WM9 NTSC 64K download
WM9 NTSC streaming modem
WM9 NTSC streaming
```

MPEG encoding

MPEG (Moving Picture Experts Group) is a working committee of the ISO (International Standardization Organization) and the IEC (International Electrotechnical Commission).

MPEG is in charge of the development of standards for digital audio and video compression. Established in 1988, the group has produced several compression standards, including:

- **MPEG-1**—The standard on which Video CDs and MP3 audio are based. MPEG-1 video is VHS-quality video with CD-quality audio at up to a combined data rate of 1.5 megabits per second. Its resolution is only 352x240 (about 25% of full DV quality).

- **MPEG-2**—DVD and satellite digital video with a data rate for standard definition video from about 3 to 15 Mbits/second (7-9 Mbits/sec is the generally accepted range for high-quality DVD video) and 15-30 Mbits/sec for HD. MPEG-2 also supports multi-channel surround sound audio encoding.

- **MPEG-4**—Multimedia for the fixed and mobile web.

All MPEG standards use similar encoding techniques. They compress video by selecting keyframes or *Intra-frames* (I-frames), then removing a few of the frames between I-frames and replacing them with B-frames (backward frames) and P-frames (predicted frames). The B- and P-frames store only the differences between I-frames.

💡 **Standard DV can't match broadcast-quality or film**

You probably shot your videos using standard DV, also known as DV25, so named because of its 25 Mbits/second video data rate. Combined with audio and error correction data, DV25's actual bitrate is 3.6 MBytes/second. Broadcast quality DV— DV50— has twice that data rate due to extra color information. So when you view DVDs that started as DV25 videos, do not expect them to have the visual quality of broadcast or satellite TV or Hollywood feature films.

1   Click the Export Settings > Format drop-down list and note that there are five MPEG file formats:

- **MPEG1**—1.7 Mbits/second with MPEG-1 audio.

- **MPEG1-VCD (Video CD)**—1.15 Mbits/sec with MPEG-1 audio. This file format is specifically to view about an hour of less-than-VHS-quality video on a CD that will play on most consumer DVD video players and computer DVD and CD drives. You'll need to use stand-alone CD-writing software to create a VCD.

- **MPEG2**—The presets are geared to high-definition and progressive scan videos. If your goal is to create standard DVD content, select MPEG2-DVD. If you want to tweak the MPEG-2 parameters, select MPEG-2.

- **MPEG2-DVD**—Offers the most presets. Select a preset that gives you the best quality while not exceeding the 4.7 GB of space on a DVD. To help you find the right fit, the Media Encoder has an Estimated File Size display that updates each time you change a preset or a customized setting. You'll take a look at that in a moment.

- **MPEG2-SVCD**—Super Video CD. Like a VCD, SVCDs can play on most consumer DVD players. They hold about 35 minutes of low bit rate (2 Mbit/sec) MPEG-2 video.

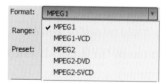

2 Select MPEG1.

Look at the Estimated File Size display in the lower right corner of the Media Encoder. It should read about 7 MB.

Note: The sequence is 30 seconds long. If you were to export it as an AVI file (with its DV25 bitrate of 3.6 MB/sec) it would be about 110 MB—16 times larger than the MPEG-1 file.

3 Select MPEG1-VCD.

Depending on the Preset you select, the Estimated File Size will be about 25% less than MPEG-1.

4 Select MPEG2.

5 Click the Preset drop-down list and select NTSC MPEG-2 Generic.

Check its Estimated File Size and note it's more than twice the size of an MPEG-1 file but still much smaller than the AVI file.

6 Click the Video tab.

7 Click that panel's Fly-out Menu and select Expand Advanced Settings (if the option is to Collapse Advanced Settings, then do nothing).

Note: All the other Formats except Macromedia Flash Video have Advanced Properties. I chose to show you MPEG's because it has the most advanced properties.

8 Scroll down that panel's view and take a look at the Bitrate (the GOP—Group of Pictures—and Advanced Settings go beyond the scope of this book).

• **CBR** (constant bitrate)—This works well for Internet applications because the bitrate does not fluctuate.

• **VBR** (variable bitrate)—Generally gives you better picture quality than CBR at the same bitrate because it increases the bitrate during action scenes. It offers a one- or two-pass option. Two passes take longer but create a higher quality image. Use VBR when creating a video for a DVD.

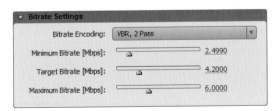

9   Click the Audio tab and change the Audio Format to Dolby Digital.

That gives you a wide range of options including Surround Sound (in the Audio Coding Mode drop-down list shown in the next figure).

Note: Windows Media has a 5.1 option but only for its HD file types.

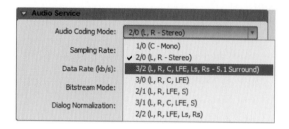

10   Click OK, give your file a name, click Save (or Cancel) and rendering (transcoding) will begin. Depending on the quality level settings and the speed of your PC, this can take about two times the duration of your project.

Working with edit decision lists

An edit decision list (EDL) harkens back to the days when small hard drives limited the size of your video files, and slower processors meant you could not play full resolution video. To remedy this, editors used low-resolution files in an NLE like Premiere Pro, edited their project, exported that to an EDL, then took that text file and their original videotapes down to a production studio. They'd use expensive switching hardware to create the finished, full-resolution product.

These days there isn't that much call for that kind of off-line work. But filmmakers still use EDLs because of the size of the files and other complexities associated with going from film to video and back to film.

The EDL format used in Premiere Pro is more than 30 years old (see following sidebar). AAF (Advanced Authoring Format), discussed in Lesson 15, is a significant step up from EDL. AAF was created to be something along the lines of a "super-EDL." Its purpose is to foster more cross platform interoperability. In the case of the AAF that comes with Premiere Pro, it is compatible with a competing product, the Avid Xpress product line.

CMX is gone but its EDL lives on

There is no standard EDL format. Premiere Pro uses a format compatible with the CMX 3600, a switcher created by CMX Systems, a pioneer of production studio and broadcast-TV computer-controlled video editors. Formed as a joint venture by CBS and Memorex in 1971, CMX owned 90% of the broadcast video editing market by the mid-1980s, It discontinued operations in 1998. But its EDL remains the de facto standard to communicate edit decisions.

If you plan to use an EDL, you need to keep your project within some narrow guidelines:

• EDLs work best with projects that contain no more than one video track, two stereo (or four mono) audio tracks, and no nested sequences.

• Most standard transitions, frame holds, and clip speed changes work well in EDLs.

• Premiere Pro 2.0 now supports a key track for titles or other content. That track has to be immediately above the video track selected for export.

• You must capture and log all the source material with accurate timecodes.

• The capture card must have a device control that uses timecode.

• Videotapes must each have a unique reel number and be formatted with the timecode before you shoot the video to ensure there are no breaks in the timecode.

To view the EDL options, select File > Export > Export to EDL:

• **EDL Title**—Specifies a title to appear in the first line of the EDL file.

Note: The title can be different than the file name. After clicking OK in the EDL Export Settings dialog box, you will have the opportunity to enter a file name.

• **Start Timecode**—Sets the starting timecode value for the first edit in the sequence.

• **Include Video Levels**—Includes video opacity level comments in the EDL.

• **Include Audio Levels**—Includes audio level comments in the EDL.

• **Audio Processing**—Specifies when audio processing should occur. Options are Audio Follows Video, Audio Separately and Audio At End.

• **Tracks to Export**—Specifies which tracks to export. The video track directly above the video track selected for export is designated as the key track.

Exporting to DVD

I devote the final lesson of this book to making DVDs with Premiere Pro and Adobe Encore DVD 2.0. Those DVDs will run the gamut from simple, single-menu DVDs to full-blown DVDs with video menus, music, scene selection menus and animated buttons.

I include the Export to DVD option here because it is part of the Export menu and its implementation is very basic. You use it to create a DVD that will play automatically when inserted into a DVD player. It will have no menus or other DVD features like chapter points.

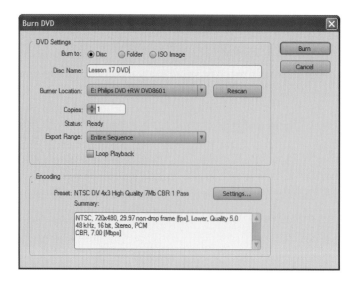

To see the Export to DVD options, select File > Export > Export to DVD. Here is an overview:

- **Burn to Disc**—Use this to create an auto-play DVD.

- **Burn To Folder**—Encodes the files and saves them in a specified folder. You can play that DVD content from your hard drive using DVD player software.

- **Burn To ISO Image**—Encodes to an ISO (International Standardization Organization) image and saves the file in the specified location. You can use just about any DVD burning software to create a DVD from that file.

- **Loop Playback**—The finished DVD will play the video from start to end, and then automatically play the video again.

- **Settings**—This takes you to the Adobe Media Encoder where you can tweak the MPEG-2 settings. As shown in the next figure, MPEG-2 is grayed out, meaning you do not have an option to use any other kind of video encoder.

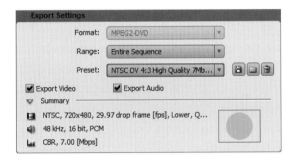

If you want to create a DVD, click Burn. That will transcode your sequence, using the MPEG-2 settings you selected, then burn the DVD. Once completed, you can pop it right into your DVD player and view it on a TV set, or play it on your PC using DVD player software like Windows Media Player.

Review

▶ **Review questions**

1 What's the basic difference between the Export Movie and Export Adobe Media Encoder?

2 Describe two ways to create 5.1 Surround Sound files.

3 When you click Record in the Export to Tape dialog box, your camcorder remains paused. What's going on?

4 What are the three streaming media options in the Adobe Media Encoder?

5 How are MPEG-1 and MPEG-2 different?

6 Why use an EDL versus exporting to an AAF?

▶ **Review answers**

1 Export Movie is geared solely to standard, PC-based files. The Media Encoder offers newer, compression-oriented files. In general, use Export Movie and select AVI to retain the full original quality of your digital video. Use Media Encoder to create files for use on the Internet, CDs, or DVDs.

2 In Export > Audio, select either Windows Waveform or Microsoft AVI, then go to the Audio Submenu and select 5.1 from the Channels drop-down list. Or in the Media Encoder, select the MPEG2 format and Dolby Digital as the audio format, then click the 3/2 option in the Audio Coding Mode drop-down list.

3 Before Premiere Pro can start recording a project to videotape, it has to render it. You can do that in advance by opening a sequence and pressing Enter. Otherwise, when you click the Record button, you'll have to wait a while for Premiere Pro to render the unrendered portions of your sequence.

4 Windows Media, QuickTime and RealMedia. Windows Media offers the most options.

5   MPEG-1 is VHS quality and is intended for use on CDs or PCs. MPEG-2 is much higher quality, has a wider spectrum of quality control possibilities, and is the standard video format for videos and movies on DVDs and digital satellite TV.

6   EDLs are geared primarily for projects that will have additional work done on them in a production studio. AAF is oriented toward moving a project to other NLE editing software, typically between Avid Xpress and Premiere Pro.

Adobe®Encore™DVD 2.0

DVD authoring

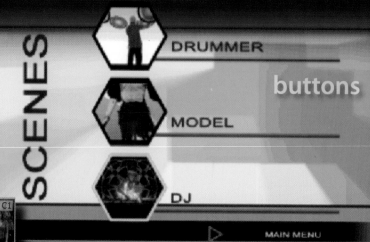

SCENES

DRUMMER

MODEL

DJ

buttons

MAIN MENU

links

MPEG Video 18

arty #13
B1

Play Video
Special Features
Scene Index

Main Menu

Play Video
Special Features
Scene Index

Special Features
B1

Behind the Scer
Dance Solos
Storyboard
Main Menu

Scene Index
B1

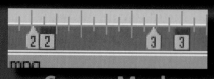

2 2   3   3

Scene Marker

DVDs let you present your productions in their best light. They use high-quality MPEG-2 video compression, can include 5.1 surround sound, and are interactive. Premiere Pro has a DVD authoring module with a wide variety of templates that let you create DVDs complete with menus, scene selection features and video buttons. Encore DVD 2.0, the professional DVD authoring product in the Adobe Creative Suite Production Studio Premium, has even more features.

18 | Authoring DVDs with Premiere Pro and Encore DVD 2.0

Topics covered in this lesson:

- Overview of DVD authoring in Premiere Pro
- Previewing your DVD project.
- Adding DVD markers to the Timeline.
- Creating an auto-play DVD with markers.
- Using DVD menu templates.
- Authoring with Encore DVD 2.0.

Getting started

DVDs are a tremendous media delivery platform. Their images and videos are full-screen (including 16:9 widescreen), the audio quality is top drawer, and they are interactive. Simply click a menu button to jump immediately to a video, a scene, or behind-the-scenes stills.

Creating those interactive DVDs, with all their menus and buttons, used to take a Hollywood feature film budget and expensive hardware. No longer. Now, with Premiere Pro or Encore DVD, you can create professional-looking DVDs on your PC in minutes.

Premiere Pro has a collection of customizable DVD menu templates with backgrounds and buttons—static or animated. If you like, you can use your own images or videos as backgrounds. Each template has two types of menus—main and scene selection. You use the DVD's main menu to access individual videos and the scene selection menus.

Encore DVD 2.0 takes DVD authoring much further. It uses a flowchart to help you map out the elements of your DVD, and lets you create and save customized menus using a full suite of templates and menu elements like graphics, buttons and text editing tools.

It is the only DVD authoring product that creates menus in native Photoshop file format, allowing for instant updates as you edit the menu graphics in Photoshop. Its Chapter List feature enables you to customize the same set of assets to a variety of audiences, its slideshow editor has built-in transitions and pan and zoom capabilities, and it lets you add subtitles and multiple audio tracks for foreign language and director's comments.

Overview of DVD authoring in Premiere Pro

DVD authoring is the process used to create menus, buttons and links to assets and menus. It is also used to describe behaviors such as what the DVD player should do when it gets to the end of a video—does it return to the DVD's main menu, to some other menu, or to another video?

Each DVD authoring product takes a different approach to creating interactive DVDs. Premiere Pro simplifies the authoring process by using menu templates that automatically create buttons and menus depending on the number and types of DVD markers you place in the Timeline.

Premiere Pro lets you create two basic kinds of DVDs:

- **Auto-play DVDs**—These DVDs have no menus. They work best for short movies that you want your viewers to watch from start to finish. You created this type of DVD in Lesson 16 when you used the Export to DVD selection. Before you create an auto-play DVD, you can add DVD markers to the Timeline. Markers let viewers skip forward or back through the movie by using the Next and Previous buttons on their DVD player's remote control.

- **Menu-based DVDs**—These DVDs have one or more menus with buttons that link to separate videos, slideshows, or scene selection submenus. Scene selection submenus let viewers navigate to scenes within the videos.

To create DVDs in Premiere Pro you first place DVD markers in the Timeline. Then you assign a Premiere Pro DVD menu template to your sequence. The Timeline DVD markers automatically create links to the main or any scene selection menus, or tell the DVD player to return to the main menu.

You can replace the menu's background image with another static image or video, move the menu buttons, and change their text.

Once you've edited the menus, you preview your DVD's navigation in the Source Monitor, fix any glitches, then burn the DVD.

Previewing Your DVD project: Lesson 18-1

You will create a DVD with a main menu that links to two videos, a slideshow and two scene selection menus.

A limitation of the Premiere Pro DVD authoring module is that you cannot link to each scene selection menu directly from the main menu. As you add scenes you reach a limit to the number of buttons allowed in the selected menu template. Premiere Pro then automatically creates a second scene selection menu, accessible only from the first scene selection menu.

There's no getting around that, but I will show you something of a work-around that at least lets you have a separate scene selection menu for each video.

1   Play the Lesson 18 Intro video.

2   Open Premiere Pro to Lesson 18.

It has two sequences. You will do your DVD authoring in Lesson 18 Start. But first you'll take a look at how things should look when you're done.

3   Select Window > DVD Layout.

That loads a DVD editing tool into the Source Monitor and a DVD menu text editing tool in the Effect Controls panel. You'll work with both in lesson 18-3.

4 Click the Lesson 18 Finished tab to open that sequence in the Timeline.

That displays a collection of menu thumbnail images in the Source Monitor. This DVD has a main menu and two scene selection menus, as well as three videos.

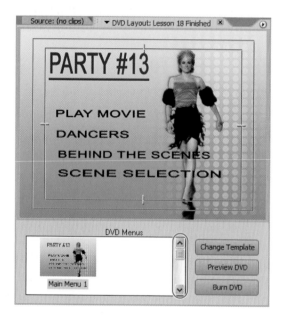

5 Use the scroll bar in the DVD Menus window (highlighted in the previous figure) to display Main Menu 1.

6 Click in the Source Monitor screen to the right of the model to select the menu (not its text).

That displays Menu Background and Audio editing tools in the Effect Controls panel. There you can change the menu background, add audio, and set the duration of button animations (there are no animated buttons in this project's main menu).

7 Click the Preview DVD button.

That simulates how your project will work in a DVD player. Note that the main menu has an audio loop, and that as you move your mouse over its four text lines they highlight in turn, indicating that if you click there you will move to a video or another menu. You also can use the navigation buttons highlighted in the next figure to simulate using a DVD remote.

Note: *Feel free to navigate through this DVD preview in any fashion that suits you. I point out a few highlights in the next steps.*

DVD Preview navigation buttons.

8 Click Scene Selection.

That opens the first of two scene selection menus. Note that the buttons have videos playing in them, there is a link back to the Main Menu, and there is a small triangle that links you to the next scene selection menu.

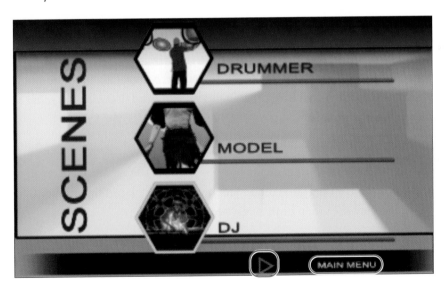

9 Click the triangle.

That takes you to the Scene Selection menu for the second video on this DVD.

10 Click 2nd Dancer and let it play for a few seconds.

11 Click the Next Scene button (highlighted earlier in the DVD Preview navigation figure).

That takes you to the 3rd Dancer scene.

12 Let it play to its end.

When done, it will return you to the Main Menu.

13 Click Behind the Scenes.

That takes you to a slide show—a video of five-second stills. When it ends (it's almost two minutes long, but you can click the Fast Forward button to zip through it), it will return you to the main menu, or you can click the Main Menu button in the navigation bar.

Adding DVD markers to the Timeline: Lesson 18-2

Once you have finished editing a video, you can add DVD markers in the Timeline to denote the beginning point for individual videos, scenes within those videos, and stop points. Premiere Pro creates DVD menus based on the DVD markers. You can move, remove, and add markers at any time in the DVD authoring process.

Note: DVD markers are not clip markers or Timeline markers. Clip markers and Timeline markers help you position and trim clips. Premiere Pro uses DVD markers solely for DVD menu creation and button links.

There are three types of DVD markers:

• **Main Menu Markers**—These create buttons in the DVD's main menu that, when clicked, take viewers to the frame in the video where you placed the marker (usually the beginning) and play the video until it reaches a Stop Marker.

• **Stop Markers**—When the viewer's DVD player reaches a Stop Marker, it jumps to the Main Menu. You generally add Stop Markers only if you've divided your project into separate videos and don't need to play the entire Timeline sequence from beginning to end.

• **Scene Markers**—They create buttons in a scene selection menu. These enable viewers to jump ahead to specific scenes in your videos.

Note: Scene Markers have a behavior that might at first seem counterintuitive but is logical and expected by your viewers. When they go to a scene, the DVD plays that scene then continues on to the next scene as opposed to stopping there and going to a menu. It returns to the DVD's main menu only when it encounters a Stop Marker, or if the viewer uses the remote control to take some other action like Previous or Next.

1   Open the Lesson 18 Start sequence.

It has three videos. The first two are MPEG videos and the third is a collection of behind-the-scenes photos of this music video (see *Assets by Steam* below).

Note: The Source Monitor screen will show "Auto-Play DVD with No Menus." I'll explain that in Lesson 18-3.

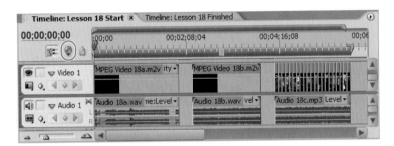

Assets by Steam

Most of the assets you've worked with in this book were created by Steam, a two-man production company based in Los Angeles (www.steamshow.com). Its co-owners, Scott Bryant and Tony Molenda, have degrees in graphic design and cinematography respectively and have worked with ABC TV, Mattel, Aaron Spelling and Sony Pictures.

They shot the video you've been working on using an HD camera recording at 24 frames per second. They used After Effects to convert the 1920x1080 HD video to DV.

2   Move the CTI to the end of the first video (1;58;12 or use Page Down).

3   Click the Set DVD Marker button (highlighted in the previous figure).
That opens the DVD Marker dialog box.

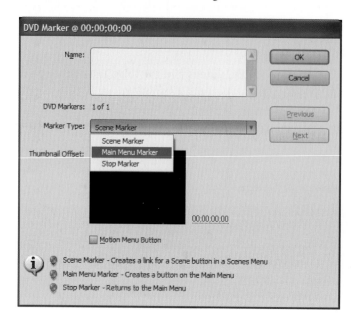

4   Select Stop Marker from the Marker Type drop-down list and click OK to close the dialog box.

Note: Adding a Stop Marker to the first video in a Timeline does two things: It adds a DVD Stop Marker on the Timeline and places a DVD Main Menu Marker above this video's first frame. That's the default behavior. The Play button on all Premiere Pro DVD templates automatically links to the first frame of the first video. If you want to add a Scene Selection point there, you can add that marker later.

5   Move to the first frame of the second video.
Click the Set DVD Marker button, select Main Menu Marker and click OK.

6   Add a Stop Marker for the second clip and a Main Menu Marker and Stop Marker for the third video.

Your Timeline Time Ruler will have six markers: one with a blue triangle for the first Main Menu marker, two with green triangles for subsequent Main Menu Markers, and three with red triangles for Stop Markers.

Before adding Scene Markers you need to move the Main Menu Marker for the second video. This is part of the work-around I mentioned so you can have separate scene selection menus for each video. You need to move it out of the way so you can set a Scene Marker at the beginning of the video (you can't have two markers in the same locale).

7   Move the CTI to about 20 frames before the second video (you'll need to Zoom In the Timeline view to do this).

8   As shown in the next figure, slide the Main Menu marker to the CTI (it will snap to the CTI edit line).

Now you'll add Scene Markers, starting with the first video.

9   Move the CTI to about 46 seconds (where the main dancer is just about to jump through the mirror).

10   Click the Set DVD Marker button (note that the default Marker Type is Scene Marker, which is what you want to set in this case).

11   Type *Drummer* in the Name text box.

12 Check the Motion Menu Button checkbox and change the Thumbnail Offset timecode to 3;02.

That sets the first frame for the Motion Menu Button. The offset time is how far the first frame of the motion menu button is from the DVD marker frame. You'll set the button's motion duration to 5 seconds when you work in the menu template.

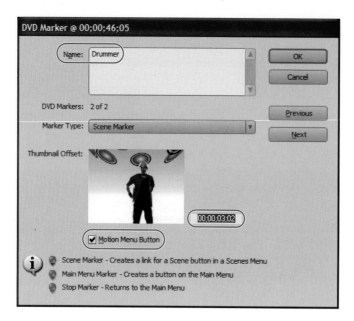

13 Click OK.

Note: *That adds a DVD Marker with a blue triangle to the Timeline Time Ruler.*

14 Add Scene Markers at the following timecodes.

In each case check the Motion Menu Button checkbox and change the Thumbnail Offset timecode:

• 1;02;00—Name this Scene Marker *Model*, set the Thumbnail Offset timecode to 6;00 and check Motion Menu Button.

• 1;22;15—*DJ*, Thumbnail Offset timecode: 1;20.

• 2;17;05—*1ˢᵗ Dancer*, 8;20.

• 2;51;15—*2ⁿᵈ Dancer*, 5;00.

• 3;20;11—*3ʳᵈ Dancer*, 4;00.

> 💡 **Automatically create DVD markers**
>
> *You can automatically add DVD Markers but you're not likely to use this feature because of the limitations I list below. Select Marker > Auto Generate DVD Markers and note you have three options: at each clip, at a specified interval (in minutes), or at an interval determined by the number of markers you specify. This method has several limitations: the clips should be on the Video 1 track, there should be no composited clips, and it does not name Scene Markers.*

15 Double-click on any Scene Marker icon in the Time Ruler and note that this opens the DVD Marker dialog box, letting you change its parameters.

Note: You can delete a marker by right-clicking on a marker and selecting Clear DVD Marker.

Creating an auto-play DVD with markers: Lesson 18-3

An auto-play DVD contains no menus. Instead, it plays automatically when you insert the DVD into a DVD player. You can set DVD markers so that the Next and Previous buttons on the DVD remote control jump to specific points in the movie. Here's a quick run-through.

1 Click the Preview DVD button in the Source Monitor.

That opens a blank Preview screen.

2 Click the Play button.

The first video on the sequence plays.

3 Click the Next Scene button and the DVD jumps to that Scene Marker and plays that scene.

4 Repeat that for the next two scenes.

5 Use the Fast Forward button to wrap this process up.

When it gets to the end of the first video, play stops. It does not go on to the next video because of the Stop Marker.

Note: If you remove the first and second Stop Markers, the Preview will play all three videos and the Next Scene buttons will let you jump to all six scenes in the first two videos.

Using DVD menu templates: Lesson 18-4

Premiere Pro DVD menu templates offer enough variety to suit your purposes.

Each template includes a main menu and a scene selection submenu. As I mentioned earlier, you're going to do a work-around that enables you to have scene selection menus for each video. To accomplish that, you will work with a menu template that has a scene selection menu with only three buttons—just enough for the three scenes in the each of the first and second videos. If you select a template with more than three buttons in the scene selection menu, then scenes from the second video will show up with scenes from the first video in the first scene selection menu.

You can continue where you left off or open Lesson 18 Finished and use it to complete this mini-lesson.

1   Click the Change Template button.

That opens the DVD Templates window.

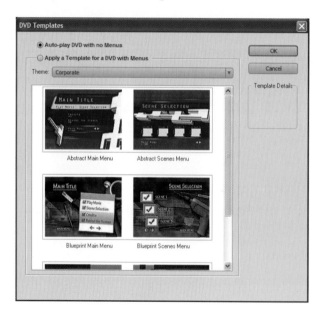

2   Use the DVD Templates Theme drop-down list to take a look at the various templates. Make note of a few things:

- Scene selection menu buttons sometimes have frames in which a thumbnail image or video of the selected scene will display.

- Button labels can be on either side, above or below the thumbnail. For this exercise you'll select a template that has all of its labels on the same side so it'll look good with the custom images you'll use for menu backgrounds.

- The number of scene selection buttons in the templates varies from three to six. If you have fewer scenes than buttons, your project's scene selection menu will display only that number of buttons. If you have more scenes than buttons, a Next button will appear on the scene selection menu linking to another scene selection menu to handle those additional scenes. This can go on, with several linked scene selection menus to handle a large number of scenes.

- All the main menus have four buttons with the same text from menu to menu. The number of buttons that actually shows up in the menu for a particular project depends on the number of videos and whether there is a scene selection menu. If there are more than four things to link to, a Next button will show up in the main menu linking to a sub-main menu that has those additional links.

- You can change the text (including button labels) and alter font, size and color. You can change the size and aspect ratio of the buttons.

> ### Editing templates in Photoshop
>
> *Each DVD template is a Photoshop file. You can find them in the main Premiere Pro 2.0 file folder. Each template has eight files: 4:3 and 16:9 aspect ratios for both main and scene selection menus with versions for NTSC and PAL. You can edit them in Photoshop, but you should do so carefully. They use special layer-naming conventions with characters in parentheses like (+>) to designate certain functions. Not disturbing the existing layers and always working with a copy are important safety measures.*

3   Select the Corporate > Numbers menu template.

I chose it for three reasons:

- It has three scene selection buttons to match the number of scenes in the first video.

- Its scene button names all fall to the right of the buttons.

- The hexagon button thumbnail placeholders demonstrate that you don't have to limit yourself to rectangles for video buttons.

4   Click on the Main Menu thumbnail in the Source Monitor DVD Menus screen.

5   Click on the larger version of that menu in the Source Monitor to select it (don't click on the text just yet).

Note: *Once selected, the Menu Background parameters show up in the Effect Controls panel.*

6   Drag Lesson 18 Menu-1.psd from the Project panel to the Video or Still, Drag Media Here box in the Effect Controls panel.

That replaces the default background.

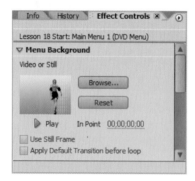

7   Drag Audio 18b to the Drag Media Here screen in the Audio section of the Menu Background parameters.

8 Click on the Scenes Menu 1 thumbnail in the Source Monitor and drag Lesson 18 Menu-2 and Audio 18b to its Drag Media Here boxes in the Effect Controls panel.

9 Scroll down the Effect Controls panel and change the Motion Menu Buttons Duration to 5;00.

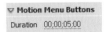

10 Repeat steps 8 and 9 for the Scenes Menu 2.

11 Select the Main Menu in the Source Monitor and drag its four text links to the left.

Note: Each text string has a blue highlight box. These should not overlap. As shown in the next figure, if they do overlap, red lines appear. You need to fix this for your DVD to play properly.

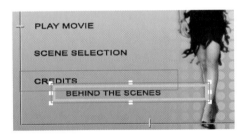

12 Click on any of the four text buttons to select it and change its size using the text tool in the Effect Controls panel (I recommend 18 pt).

13 Change the other three text buttons to match.

14 Double-click Credits and type *Dancers* in the Name text box.

Note: Double-clicking button link text opens the DVD Marker dialog box. As you'll see in the next step, double-clicking unlinked text opens a simple Change Text box.

15 Double-click Main Title, change the text to *Party #13*, and click OK.

Note: To delete text from a menu template, double-click to open the Change Text or DVD Marker dialog box. In the Change Text box, delete the text and click OK. In the DVD Marker dialog box, click Delete. That will also remove the Marker from the Timeline.

16 Change its color to something more suitable for the background by clicking the Color Picker swatch in the Effect Controls panel.

17 Rearrange the text button boxes in the order shown in the next figure.

18 Change the color of the text in the two Scene Selection menus.

19 Adjust the location and size of the word *Scenes* to fit between the two horizontal black bars (just as the word *Dancers* is aligned in the following figure).

20 In the second scene selection menu change *Scenes* to *Dancers*.

21 Click Preview DVD.

Test your DVD. Go through all the main menu choices. Use the Next and Previous buttons to jump to different scenes. Make sure that when the videos end you automatically return to the main menu. Look at the buttons to see that all were set to Motion Menu Buttons and see if the thumbnail offsets need changing.

22 To see how a video menu background works, drag MPEG Video 18c to the Video or Still screen in the Effect Controls panel and then click Preview DVD.

You can use that video or go back to the still image by dragging Lesson 18 Menu-1.psd back to the Video or Still screen in the Effect Controls panel.

Burning your DVD

You burn your DVD using the same menu you used in Lesson 16. To access that menu click Burn DVD in the Source Monitor. As you did previously, you can click Settings to access the Adobe Media Encoder where you can select the DVD transcoding of your preference.

Even though this project uses MPEG videos, Premiere Pro will re-transcode them. That can lead to some quality loss. So, in general, wait until you are ready to burn a DVD before converting your files to MPEG. I used MPEG here to save space on the book's DVD while retaining most of the original quality of the video.

Authoring with Encore DVD 2.0

Adobe Encore DVD 2.0 is designed to simplify DVD production while providing complete control over your work. You can design and map DVD navigation quickly and with confidence using a new visual flowchart view, jumpstart menu design with templates and royalty-free artwork, and easily create dramatic slideshow presentations.

Here are some Encore DVD 2.0 features:

- It's the only DVD authoring application that creates menus in native Photoshop file format.

- You can change menu element characteristics like location, color, size, font and styles with ease.

- You can use grid lines in its menu layout panel for convenient and precise object positioning control.

- It allows you to enhance slideshows with audio, transitions, and pan and zoom effects.

- You can add director's comments and foreign language tracks to videos, as well as subtitles.

- It's easy to create links to timeline markers using a *pick whip* or simple drag-and-drop methods.

- Chapter playlists help you to avoid creating duplicate content on discs, thus saving space and allowing for improved MPEG compression and video quality.

Previewing an Encore DVD 2.0 project

As with the other products in the Adobe Creative Suite Production Studio Premium that you've worked with in this book, this mini-lesson's purpose is to give you a feel for what Encore DVD can do for you and how it works. This will be more a demonstration than step-by-step instruction. If you have a copy of Encore DVD 2.0, I urge you to try to follow along. You can also download a trial copy at www.adobe.com.

1   Open Encore DVD 2.0, click Open Project, navigate to the Lesson 18 folder and double-click Lesson 18 Encore DVD Project.ncor.

The interface has the same features—panels, frames, and tabs—that you've worked with in Premiere Pro as well as in After Effects and Audition.

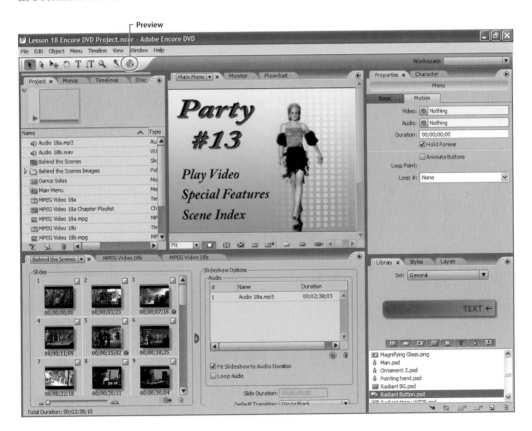

2   Click the Preview button (highlighted in the previous figure) to see how this DVD is different than the one you created in Premiere Pro.

3   In the Preview panel, click Play Video.

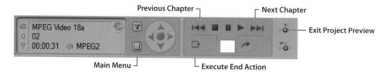

4   Click the Next Chapter button (highlighted in the previous figure) a few times, and then click the Execute End Action button to return to the main menu.

5   Click Scene Index.

Make note that this video now has six scenes (the Dancers video will have three as it did in the Premiere Pro DVD). In Encore DVD you can place any number of links (that you can fit) in a single menu.

Note: These thumbnails display as static images but are motion menu buttons just like those in the Premiere Pro DVD project. Encore DVD displays the preview in higher resolution than Premiere Pro, so to see the video buttons you first need to render the menu. To do that, click the Render Current Motion Menu or Slideshow button on the left side of the Project Preview control panel.

6   Click the Execute End Action button in the DVD control panel to return to the main menu (I disabled the Main Menu text button in the Scene Index Menu so you can create a link from it in the next mini-lesson).

7   Click Special Features.

This takes you to a submenu with links to two slideshows and a scene selection menu. Encore DVD allows you to add a submenu with links to other menus and videos—something Premiere Pro cannot do.

8   Click Storyboard and note that this slideshow uses a Dip to Black transition. You can place any of about a dozen transitions between any two images in a slide show, or apply a single transition between all images in the slideshow.

9   Click the Execute End Action button.

That returns you to the Special Features submenu. Again, Premiere Pro cannot do this. All of its end actions (Stop Markers) take you all the way back to the main menu.

10   Click Behind the Scenes and note that it uses the slideshow Pan and Zoom feature. You can select from 16 panning presets and choose to zoom in or out for any or all images in a slideshow.

11   Click Execute End Action.

12   Click Dance Solos, play one of the three dancers then click Execute End Action. That will take you back to the Special Features menu. You set the end action for each element in the DVD project. It can be to any other asset or menu in the project.

13   Click the Exit Project Preview button.

Taking Encore DVD 2.0 for a test drive

1   Click the Flowchart tab and use the scroll bars to take a look at the layout of this project.

The Flowchart helps you map out the ideal menu navigation scheme for your content. As your projects increase in size and complexity this tool can become invaluable.

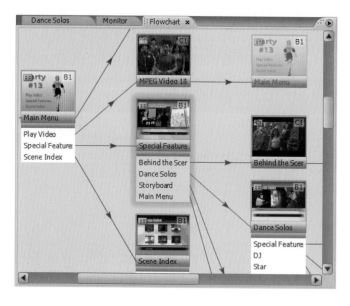

2 Click the Menus tab and double-click Scene Index.

That opens that menu in the Menu panel.

3 Click the Show Guides button (highlighted in the previous figure) and drag the button thumbnails around.

Note how they snap to the guidelines. You can move the guidelines (hover your cursor over one and it'll change to show that you can drag that guideline) and add new guidelines to help arrange buttons and other menu elements.

4 Click the Project tab and double-click on Storyboard.

That displays the Storyboard slideshow. Note that it has an audio file associated with it. You can string together more than one audio file if you choose. I clicked the Fit Slideshow to Audio Duration checkbox. That automatically adjusts the length of each slide.

5   Click on any slide thumbnail and look in the Properties panel (upper right corner of the workspace).

You can click the Transition tab to select from more than a dozen transitions, and click the Effects tab to pan or zoom this image.

6   Click the MPEG Video 18a tab in the Timeline (along the bottom of the workspace).

Note that it has two types of scene markers: one to mark the beginning of a scene and another that marks the thumbnail used in that scene's menu button.

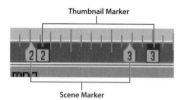

Creating links to buttons is a snap. You can drag a Timeline marker to a menu button, select a link from a drop-down list in the Properties panel or use the Pick Whip tool. Here's how to do the latter:

7   Click the Menus tab and double-click Scene Index.

8   Click on any of the six thumbnail buttons.

9   Click the Layers tab and note that it looks just like the Layers display in Photoshop. You can click on any layer, and it will highlight that element in the Menu panel where you can change its size, location, appearance or text.

Note: *Encore DVD has the Photoshop CS engine built in. While you can make some style changes within Encore DVD, you'll need Photoshop to make significant changes like creating new graphics.*

10 Open the Project panel, and then in the Scene Index menu display, click the Main Menu text button to select it and display it in the Properties panel.

11 In the Properties panel, drag the Link Pick Whip (◉) to the Main Menu link in the Project panel (the Pick Whip is highlighted in the next figure). That creates a link from the Main Menu button to the Main Menu itself.

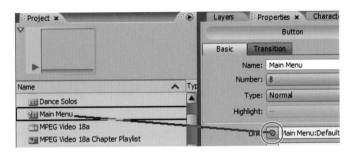

12 Click the Project tab and double-click MPEG Video 18a Chapter Playlist.

This lets you set a specific order to play selected chapters. In this way you can customize a DVD to suit a particular client or audience.

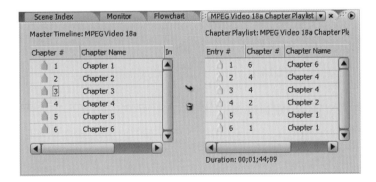

There are many more features, including a direct link to Photoshop to edit any menu or menu item; a huge collection of templates, styles, and graphic elements; extra audio tracks for foreign languages and director comments; a means to add subtitles; and a Check Project feature that looks for things like buttons without links, overlapping buttons, and assets without End Actions.

Encore DVD is the tool you can use to make compelling DVDs.

Review

▶ ## Review questions

1 There are two types of auto-play DVDs. Describe them.

2 How is a Main Menu Marker different than a Scene Marker?

3 If you have more than one video in a Timeline but do not use any Stop buttons, what will happen?

4 You preview your DVD and decide you want to change the starting frame of a motion menu button. How do you do that?

5 You substitute your own menu background for a template's and want to remove the template's text. How do you do that?

6 List three ways to create links in Encore DVD.

7 What the principal difference between how Premiere Pro Stop Markers and Encore DVD End Actions behave?

Review answers

1 An auto-play DVD can have markers or not. Markers let viewers use the Previous and Next buttons on their remotes to quickly navigate through the DVD.

2 A Main Menu Marker creates a button in the main menu and denotes where you want a video to start. A Scene Marker places a button in a scene selection menu and lets viewers jump to a segment within a video.

3 There will be only a single button in the main menu for the entire Timeline. It will play the entire sequence. Viewers will not be able to access the second video directly unless you put a Scene Marker at its beginning.

4 Double-click on that button's Scene Marker in the Timeline to open the DVD Marker dialog box. You can change the Thumbnail Offset there. If you want to change the motion button duration, do that in the Effect Controls panel. The duration is set on a menu-by-menu basis, not by individual buttons.

5   Double-click the text to open the Change Text dialog box, delete the text there and click OK.

6   Drag and drop a Timeline marker to a button, use a drop-down list in the Properties panel, or use the Pick Whip tool.

7   Premiere Pro Stop Markers return viewers to the DVD's main menu. Encore DVD End Actions perform whatever action you assign to them. Usually it's to return to a menu, but it could link to another video or a slideshow.

Index

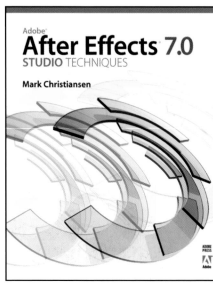